Life *is* Rosi

JESS ROBINSON

Life *is* Rosi

Grandma, me and
our diaries at 23

Mudlark
HarperCollins*Publishers*
1 London Bridge Street
London SE1 9GF

www.harpercollins.co.uk

HarperCollins*Publishers*
Macken House, 39/40 Mayor Street Upper
Dublin 1, D01 C9W8, Ireland

First published by Mudlark 2026

1 3 5 7 9 10 8 6 4 2

Text © Jess Robinson 2026

Jess Robinson asserts the moral right to
be identified as the author of this work

A catalogue record of this book is
available from the British Library

ISBN 978-0-00-872930-1

Printed and bound in the UK using 100%
renewable electricity at CPI Group (UK) Ltd

All rights reserved. No part of this publication may be
reproduced, stored in a retrieval system, or transmitted,
in any form or by any means, electronic, mechanical,
photocopying, recording or otherwise, without the
prior written permission of the publishers.

Without limiting the exclusive rights of any author, contributor
or the publisher of this publication, any unauthorised use of
this publication to train generative artificial intelligence (AI)
technologies is expressly prohibited. HarperCollins also exercise
their rights under Article 4(3) of the Digital Single Market
Directive 2019/790 and expressly reserve this publication
from the text and data mining exception.

For cool bitches everywhere …

Prologue

Diary of Rosi Schul
Sunday, 5 November 1938

While walking in the chaos around me, an idea came to me to do something. The children and I played together, and I told my usual stories to an ever-growing crowd. It made me feel so good to see them happy and interested. Since then I have been back every day. It feels right to fill my time this way.

———

It's 2021, and as the world slowly reopens after the chaos of Covid, I find myself emerging from the haze of deep grief after losing my brilliant, beloved father, Brian Robinson, to lung cancer. I bounce between blind positivity and utter despair as I will myself to stumble forward, wading through treacle, one foot in front of the other, grasping for some sense of normality.

I am 'keeping busy'. I have a checklist and I've been back to tick something off it every day. It feels right to fill my time this way.

I mark '*get up*' and '*leave the house*' as 'done' before blithely firing off an email to the German Embassy (as you do), casually inquiring if I qualify for German citizenship.

Why? Well, take your pick: I want to feel like a proud European again/I selfishly don't want to stand in endless airport queues/deep down, I just need something to focus on. (Delete as appropriate.)

It was actually my agent, Sophie, who suggested I look into getting a German passport to make travelling and working as a 'professional show-off'* easier in Europe. In fact, while I'm at it, I've decided to get passports for the rest of the family, too – my mum, my auntie Stephie, my sister Katy and my niece, Sasha.

So, with a spring in my step, a song in my heart and a glass of rosé in my hand (don't worry, it's past 11 a.m.), I type out the email and hit send.

All aboard the passport train – *toot-toot!*

All the following emails, texts and diary entries throughout this book are <u>real</u>. Some names have been changed … but only because my family made me.

EMAIL TO: German Embassy
SUBJECT: Citizenship
Monday, 23 August 2021, 14:06

Hello there,

My name is Jessica Robinson. I am British and was born and live in England. However, my German Jewish grandmother had to leave Germany during the Nazi regime. I was wondering if I am entitled to dual citizenship, please?

Kind regards,
Jessica Robinson
www.jessrobinson.co.uk

---

* My dad's description of my job, not Sophie's.

Chapter 1

Diary of Rosi Schul – age 23
Thursday, 17 November 1938

How is it possible amid such chaos, that we can still find the strength to sing and dance, to put on shows? We keep going, but what will happen to us? Nobody knows …

———

Here we are. This is where it all begins – with a German passport I hope I'm eligible for, thanks to my grandmother, Rosi Schul.

Grandma Rosi was a formidable lady: table-tennis champion, musician, really dodgy cook and proud (in all senses) German woman who never lost her accent. She was my mum's mum. Mum squared.

I've always known about my Jewish roots, and from as early as I can remember Grandma Rosi would talk lovingly about her early life in Germany. She was very open about her 'big adventure', as she'd refer to it, and in her nineties was interviewed by filmmaker Alan Reich for a documentary, *The Last Boat*, about the children (his father included) who travelled to Britain by Kindertransport. That's how my grandma made it to Britain. Kindertransport does make it sound fun, doesn't it? I've said it before and I'll say it again: Kinder Eggs have a lot to answer for.

If this were a film (and it bloody *will* be one day), this bit of backstory would be acted out by whimsical little puppets. In fact,

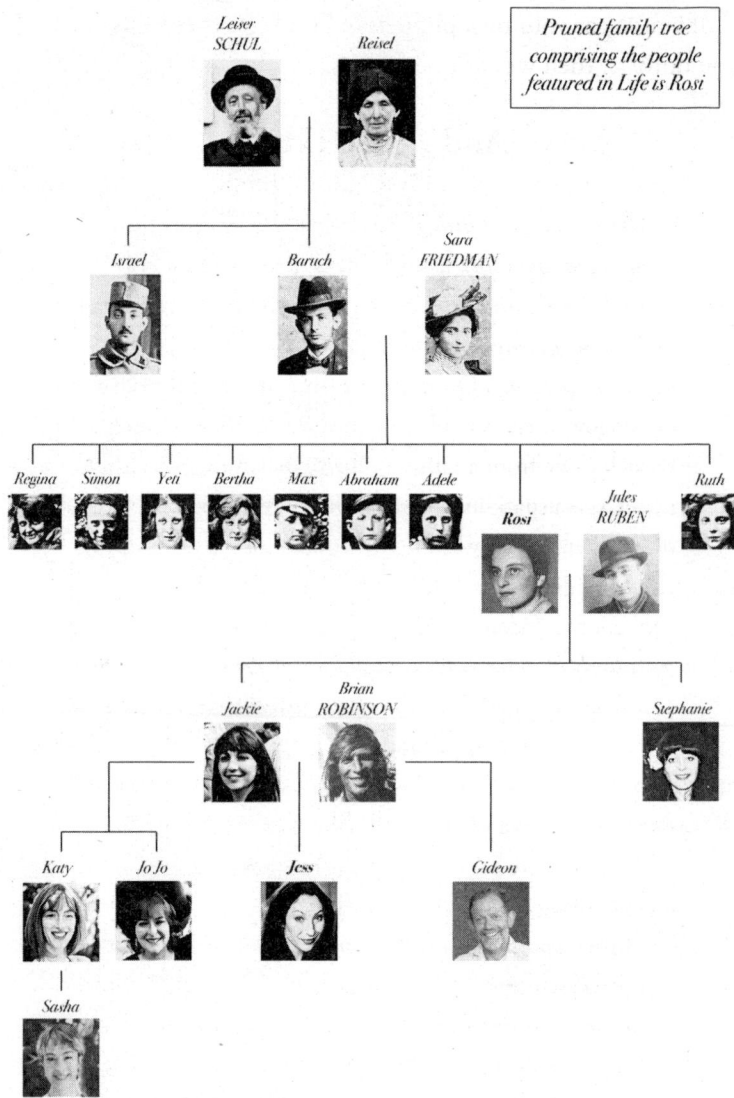

Rosi – in very early-nineteenth-century German behaviour – owned some adorably creepy puppets, which she'd do little shows with, and kindly handed them down to me … so this potted Schul family history will be written like a puppet show. I shall be taking no further questions at this time.

If you've got your own puppets at home, feel free to use them. If you don't … then we can't be friends.

And … ACTION

[EXT.] A quaint little puppet town. The sun rises (on a string, of course) over tiny, wobbly houses, accompanied by a traditional Polish folk melody. The puppets of Baruch and Sara Schul enter, holding hands.

NARRATOR: *(warmly)* Once upon a time, in the tiny Polish town of Głogów, there was a boy named Baruch Schul. Now, Baruch came from a rather industrious family. His father, Leiser, ran a sparkling pearl factory (not a euphemism), and his mother, Reisel, was the town's beloved philanthropist, always finding ways to lend a helping hand (also not a euphemism) through the many charities she supported.

A lively klezmer melody plays. Puppet Reisel appears, carrying a basket of goodies. She hands out loaves of bread to the other puppets. Puppet Leiser, sporting a monocle, examines a large pearl.

NARRATOR: Reisel and Leiser arranged for their son Baruch to marry the lovely Sara Friedmann – a pretty girl from a neighbouring town …

Puppet Sara twirls. Puppet Baruch, with a theatrical flourish, bows deeply and produces a bouquet of flowers. They kiss under the wedding chuppah and Baruch stamps on a tiny glass with his little puppet foot.

NARRATOR: After tying the knot, the newlyweds decided Poland wasn't quite their cup of tea, so off they trotted to Germany.

CUE Bavarian music as the scenery changes from Poland to Germany.

NARRATOR: They settled in their cosy little home on Theodore Strasse in Hannover, with a maid to keep things ticking over, and Baruch, ever the entrepreneur, thought, 'Why not follow in the family footsteps? I will have my *own* factory, but with a twist! Instead of pearls, I fancy myself a shoemaker!'*

Puppet Baruch dons an apron and proudly holds up a tiny puppet shoe. A triumphant little fanfare plays.

NARRATOR: And my word, didn't they go on to have quite the brood! Nine children in total! Let's see now … there was Regina, Simon, Yeti, Bertha, Max, Abraham, Adele and Ruth. Rosi, the hero of our story, was the second youngest, a musical, sporty, headstrong little girl – born in 1915, right in the middle of all the excitement.

Nine children puppets pop up one by one. Rosi is the last to appear and jumps up between Adele and Ruth accompanied by a joyful accordian trill.

---

* Quite the twist, I think. Pearls to shoes in one generation?! What's his son going to make, dog shit?

NARRATOR: There it is, Schul's Schuhwaren (Schul's footwear)*, back in the good days with the family peeping out of the windows above and Sara standing proudly by the door.

NARRATOR: Now, Rosi was a proud little German, through and through! Never mind that her parents were Polish – she had absolutely no interest in learning the language. If Papa Baruch and Mama Sara ever needed to discuss anything in private, they'd switch to Polish, knowing their children wouldn't have the foggiest idea what they were on about!

Puppet Baruch and Puppet Sara have a puppet argument, while the children tilt their puppet heads and shrug.

NARRATOR: Don't worry, children, they're probably just discussing why Baruch leaves tea bags in the sink rather than just throwing them in the bin … Rosi's father, Baruch, was a wise, scholarly type, but it was Sara who really ruled the roost. She was big on education, something she hadn't had much of in Poland. So she made sure her children grew up with great love and respect for German literature and art. And oh, how the Schul household was filled with music! Every child played at least one instrument!† Rosi adored the piano. She just couldn't live without it. When her sister tragically passed away, Mama Sara declared a no-music rule for a whole year and locked the piano tight.

Puppet Sara pulls out a large padlock and chain, which she slaps onto the piano. Puppet Rosi clutches her chest and lowers her head …

NARRATOR: But Rosi wasn't having any of that! She'd sneak off to the neighbours' houses, where she'd play to her heart's

---

* I wonder whether Baruch made extra wide shoes to cater for the bunions that run in the family. It's probably a vape shop now.
† God, imagine having them as neighbours!

content. How did the neighbours feel about this? We do not know, or care; this isn't about them.

Puppet Rosi tiptoes across the stage, looking left and right, accompanied by a sneaky bassoon melody, then bursts into a neighbour's house and starts playing a piano with wild enthusiasm.

NARRATOR: Rosi also learnt the guitar, all thanks to her big sister Regina, who became like a mother to her.

Puppet Regina hands Rosi a guitar, which she strums.

NARRATOR: It was a bit of a do-it-yourself childhood. When their mother was too busy, which was often, the siblings brought each other up – stepping into the role of parents and teachers. Each taught the other all sorts of things – from tying shoelaces to table tennis, chess and bridge. This made Rosi fall in love with the idea of becoming a teacher. By sixteen, Rosi was leading youth groups, and by twenty, she'd become a fully-fledged kindergarten teacher. Then she got the chance to go and work at an orphanage. But oh, it was so far from her home, and convincing her parents to let her go was no easy task!

Puppet Rosi pleads with Puppet Baruch and Puppet Sara, dropping to her wooden knees and clasping her little hands as a melodramatic violin swells. Her parents fold their arms and shake their heads. After much exaggerated crying from Rosi, they finally give in. Rosi leaps up, does a little victory dance and starts packing an oversized suitcase.

NARRATOR: So off she went, leaving Hannover for the first time all by herself, on a seven-hour train journey to the beautiful medieval town of Esslingen, nearly 300 miles away. When Rosi arrived, it was dusk, and there was no one at the station to meet her!

Puppet Rosi steps off a toy train, looking around, only to find an empty stage. She pulls out an enormous map, and starts marching up a steep hill, with the 'hill' being a conveyor belt that takes her upwards.

NARRATOR: But Rosi, ever determined, found her way to the orphanage – a grand, gothic-looking castle with rooms fit for a fairy tale. When she arrived, she was greeted warmly by the teachers and given a little bedroom at the very top. As she set up her gramophone and washed her face, she looked out of the window and saw the picturesque town stretching out below. The headmaster of the orphanage, Herr Rothschild, was a kind soul. He soon became like a second father to Rosi. In fact, everyone at the orphanage – adults and children alike – called him 'Herr Vater', a term of respect and love.

Puppet Herr Rothschild enters, beaming with kindness, and pats Puppet Rosi on the head.

NARRATOR: And so, Rosi settled into an idyllic life in a German haven, filled with music, love and laughter.

The puppets join hands in a wobbly line, bowing together as the curtain falls with a flourish to the sound of joyful German folk music.

Aaaaaand BLACK OUT!

Yep. I think that's quite good. I might recast the puppet who played Rosi. She was a bit wooden. HA! In fact, would you like to see the actual puppets, children?

You would?

WARNING:

If you are reading this before bed, DO NOT TURN OVER THE PAGE …

The actual puppets

Everyone OK? Imagine this lot reading a CBeebies bedtime story. A whole generation, scarred for life. I mean, if you saw these at a car boot sale, you'd pay money to have them burnt.

Grandma Rosi blossomed in Esslingen – a town and time she adored so much that throughout her life she'd compare everything with Esslingen so we'd know whether or not she approved …

The rolling English hills – just like Esslingen.

The people she met – not like in Esslingen.

The food she ate – I'll come to her cooking later.

In general – nothing could ever measure up.

A German Jewish Maria von Trapp in the making, Rosi looked after twelve young boys and girls between the ages of five and eleven. She was in her element, teaching music and needlework, telling stories, playing her guitar and entertaining/traumatising them with her puppets. It was so much more than being a teacher. Grandma used to say she was like a mother and father to the children. They needed love and young Rosi had so much to give, convinced her affection for children came from the tender parenting she was shown by her older brothers and sisters.

Rosi was busy living her best life at the orphanage, where she also took up agricultural training, learning how to work the land and even staying up all night in a stable as she had her first experience of bringing a baby calf into the world.

Headmaster Theodor Rothschild brought culture into the house, arranging private chamber concerts and lectures – which any Jewish teachers could not enjoy in the outside world any more. Each night, after the children had been put to bed, the young teachers would go to each other's rooms to discuss art and literature.*

Many years later, in an interview with documentarian (and now family friend) Alan Reich, my grandma spoke of how safe she felt in Esslingen, recalling that between 1935 and 1937, although she knew about the Nazis and Hitler Youth, she was mostly 'undisturbed' by anti-Semitism. Yes, there had been a few instances in 1933 when the shops were defaced with '*Juder!*' ('*Jews!*') graffitied on the windows, but the only time she felt that something 'wasn't quite right' was when she and her other Jewish friends weren't allowed in the public swimming pool. However, she reported that she didn't feel 'oppressed' by it in any way.

* For context, at this age I was weighing up whether to work for a psychic hotline or a sex phone line. More on that later …

Well, I happen to know that Grandma didn't really like public swimming pools anyway. (As well as bunions, we're prone to verrucas in our family.) Anyway, sometimes it's nice to have an excuse *not* to go swimming, isn't it? Maybe she hadn't had time to go and get a wax. (Sorry, Grandma!)

Rosi's cherished pictures from her time caring for the children in Esslingen.

So, that's Rosi's German heritage, which, now Britain is no longer in the European Union, I am trying to lay claim to …

I wish I could say Grandma Rosi was outraged by Brexit and voted to Remain, but I can't. She was 100 years old at the time of the referendum and, frankly, more interested in what was going on in her own backyard than in Europe. Literally. She adored her garden in the suburbs of Hendon, tending to the flowerbeds, playing ping-pong and hosting tea parties for her family and the few friends she hadn't outlived.

I, on the other hand … also wasn't very politically engaged. When the Brexit vote came around in 2016, I was freshly divorced from someone who I now refer to as 'Practice Husband'. I've actually become so used to this that I often forget what his real name is – which is quite pleasing, really. So, I voted to Remain not out of any real conviction, but because that's what my friends were doing. I didn't have the brain space to think too much about it, because in all tragic seriousness, I was too focused on 'completing' Tinder, surviving on pasta with Philadelphia, trying to find 'Replacement Husband' on *Guardian* Soulmates and writing off my third car from 'divorce exhaustion' to care about what was going on outside my miserable little North Finchley flat.*

The Brexit vote was just another thing to tick off my to-do list as I 'kept busy' … which I am now beginning to realise is my survival tactic when things go tits up.

EMAIL TO: jess_robinsons_grown_up_email_address@aol.com
SUBJECT: RE: Citizenship
Tuesday, 31 August 2021, 16:55

[You have sent a message in English language to the German Federal Office for Administration (Bundesverwaltungsamt). I may kindly ask you to understand that I will respond in German, which is the official language used by the public administration and courts in the Federal Republic of Germany. Thank you for your understanding]

>>TRANSLATE TO ENGLISH? ✅ >>

---

* These days I live in Brighton with Husband 2.0 … (Don't worry, I often *can* remember his name.) Upgrade Husband is just about the kindest man on Earth. (He upgrades to 2.1 with a nice haircut, and 2.2 when he learns a new skill, like putting the toilet seat down. Well done, Steve! Or Marvin, whatever your name is.)

Dear Ms Robinson.

Thank you for your email and for sharing the information and documents available.

Unfortunately, indications are strong that your grandmother was Polish. As I mentioned when you called earlier, being born in Germany at that time was not grounds for citizenship. In fact, many people lived in Germany with Polish citizenship for decades.

I'm sorry that we are not able to help you further at this time.

Best regards,

Matilda Koch

Federal Office of Administration Cologne

Oh. That's a shame. That's it then. No German passport for me. Or my family members. The passport train has been cancelled. Because of Leave(s) on the line. Does that make sense? Because we voted to Leave? Anyway.

I add 'Contact Polish Embassy' to my to-do list, shut my laptop and go off to the kitchen in search of more wine …

Chapter 2

Diary of Rosi Schul
Tuesday, 17 October 1939

I carry such an unbearable sense of loss of my home. What has happened to my beloved Germany?

Group Chat: Cool Bitches

This is my family WhatsApp group. The 'Cool Bitches' in question are: my mum Jackie (seventy-seven), my auntie Stephanie (often referred to as Stephie, or Stemmie) (seventy-one), my big sister Katy (fifty-one) and my niece Sasha (nineteen) – as I say, cool bitches.

Wednesday, 1 September 2021, 12:24

Me: Yo, bitches! Bad news. I just got an email from the Polish Embassy and we're not eligible for Polish citizenship either.

Katy: 💩 💩 💩

Sasha: Why??

Katy: We never even filled in the citizenship forms for 🇬🇧 let alone 🇩🇪. Are you sure??

Me: Yeah 😖 hang on, I'll paste it from the email ...

Me: 'According to the Polish Citizenship Act from 1920 acquiring foreign citizenship by women before 18th January 1951 caused losing Polish citizenship. Since your grandmother acquired foreign citizenship before 1951, she lost Polish citizenship (unless she was married to a Polish citizen) ...'

So basically because she was a WOMAN and she married Grandpa Jules – a British citizen – Poland automatically stripped her of her citizenship, even though she HAD to FLEE in order to SURVIVE! So there we are. Neither country wants her. She's not Polish and she's not German. So that's that. So frustrating and shit. FFS!!!!

Auntie Stephie: She WAS German. She didn't even speak Polish.

Mum: Shame. Never mind. I've got 2 play the organ 4 a christening 😇 And Marywiththeleg* just told me Ken's wife's sister has run off with John the bell ringer!

---

* 'Marywiththeleg' is called such because there's ANOTHER Mary in the traditional English village where I grew up – Marywiththearm – who injured her wrist from slipping on a rogue slice of cheap white bread and jam in the Memorial Hall. Mum still maintains that if it had been seeded sourdough, the slice would have had 'more purchase' and Marywiththearm would have been saved. I know, plot to Midsomer Murders much? Poor Mary had her arm in a sling for ages (even after it healed, according to Mum) – hence the nickname. 'Marywiththeleg' came about just to identify which Mary Mum (and now the village) is referring to. Could she have used surnames? Yes. Did she? No.

Sasha: Poor Ken's wife's sister's husband!

Mum: Derek. He's ever so boring to be fair.

Sasha: Oh that's alright then 😊

Mum: What is FFS?

Katy: For Fucks Sake

Mum: I just asked, no need to be so snappy.

Me: FFS = For Fucks Sake.

Mum: Ah. Sorry Katy xx

Me: So – back to our citizenship. I've heard there might be a new law coming in in the future that'd mean we'd be eligible to apply. But if it does, it won't be for at least another year!

Auntie Stephie: Jew on!* I just fell into the canal.

---

* 'Jew on' is a popular family saying, born out of a misunderstanding I once had during a production of *Hamlet! The Musical* in which I was playing Ophelia. We were opening that night in Northampton, and during the dress rehearsal my drowning scene hadn't gone well. After I'd taken the director's note to make my 'gurgling and thrashing more convincing', I had tripped over one of the floaty blue scarves (it was a very high-end production), which represented the brook, resulting in a head-on collision with a 'water nymph'. The dancer and I were sitting backstage with ice packs on our heads and I burst into tears. She said, 'Ah, you know what my mum always says when I cry? She says, "Due on?"'

But what I heard was – 'Ah, you know what my mum always says when I cry? "Jew on!"' To which I replied, 'Oh my God! Are you Jewish too??' Obviously,

Katy: Oh my god!

Sasha: Are you alright?

Me: Shit!!

Mum: FFSS

Mum: Service is starting. How do I turn my phone to silent again Jessie?

Months have now passed since the disappointing citizenship news, and though I continue to work through my to-do lists (I've re-arranged the living-room furniture, sorted through my underwear drawer *and* won a British Podcast Award), I still can't seem to get past the injustice of it all.

It's not that I can't get a German (or Polish) passport – I'm done with that; it is what it is – but the fact that my proud German grandma Rosi is STILL being rejected by the country that she loved so much in spite of it treating her so appallingly.

It's totally uncharacteristic of me, and those who know me would be aghast at what I'm about to say, but I am so distracted by

---

she meant, 'Are you due on your period?' I thought she meant, 'We got through the Holocaust, we can get through this – Jew on!' ... A Jewish version of 'The show must go on'.

My family adopted it as their mantra. We now use it in every situation that warrants a 'keep going' attitude:

The dishwasher is broken and has flooded the kitchen – Jew on!
I accidentally married a gay guy – Jew on!
Dad only has a few months left to live – Jew on!

It's our version of 'Keep Calm and Carry On'. In fact, I reckon I'll get some tea towels printed for the Cool Bitches. Good Christmas presents.

it that I can't focus on the *Selling Sunset* finale. I know! So, in an unprecedented move, I switch it off *early* (I know!!), deciding instead to delve into the history books … WHAAAAAAAT? (And when I say 'the history books' I of course mean 'Google'.)

Grandma Rosi was twenty-three years old in 1938, when Hitler decided to throw all the Polish Jews out of Germany.

This, I find out, was an event known as the '*Polenaktion*', which I first read (well, the first *three* times actually) as 'Pokémon'. (So sorry, Grandma!) But the *Polenaktion* definitely has *nothing* to do with Pokémon, though it does make sense to me because I also think *Hitler's* catchphrase was 'gotta catch them all' … Too much?

I read an article that tells me the *Polenaktion* – 'Polish Action' – is often described (whenever it's mentioned, which actually isn't very often) as Hitler's 'dress rehearsal' for what was to come. #SpoilerAlert: it was the Holocaust. And to be fair, I, too, learnt the value of a good dress rehearsal at stage school. But '*dress rehearsal*'?! That term feels so reductive for such an enormous and cruel event. It conjures up an image of a sequin-clad Adolf – like something from *The Producers* – feverishly plotting lighting cues rather than mass exterminations.

I stare at the laptop screen wondering why the *Polenaktion* isn't more widely known (it's not just me, is it?). And I still can't wrap my head around the injustice that, based on a technicality – having Polish parents, while other exiled Germans and their descendants are now able to regain German citizenship (hello, Matt Lucas; and apparently, post-Brexit, that number has surged) – Grandma Rosi, who was born in Germany, lived all her life there (until she couldn't) and identified as German (and despite everything, never lost her love for her homeland), isn't 'eligible' to be German. It feels like a dishonour to her life to still deny her recognition, as if the discrimination she faced is being erased.

But something is telling me Rosi's story doesn't end here. I'm as surprised as anyone that a casual email to the German Embassy has sparked a sudden urge to focus on someone other than me for a change. I spend a lot of time thinking I'm stupid. I'm often silly and frivolous, going for the easy laugh, rather than showing anyone apart from my closest people any sort of seriousness.

But feeling I owe it to Grandma, and to myself, to know the whole story, I call up Auntie Stephie. She's delighted that I've shown some interest in her beloved mum's early life, and we arrange a handover of Grandma's important historical photographs and documents, which Stephie has been lovingly preserving. I want to know the young woman Rosi was before she became the grandmother I knew. It's time to piece together the fragments of her past.

That Sunday, the Cool Bitches are all present and correct. On the way to Mum's this morning, I picked up my middle sister Jojo from her care home. (Technically Jojo and Katy are my half sisters.) Jojo has a rare neurological disease – Huntington's (inherited from *her* father) – and although she is a *very* cool bitch, she can no longer cope with a mobile phone, so isn't in the text group. Today she is here for the pastries and 'family time'.

As we cram around the little table in Mum's cottage kitchen with half-drunk cups of her signature laxative-strength coffee, Auntie Stephie hefts the box of paperwork and photos onto the tabletop, and we stand back as she removes the lid. Mum washes up, seemingly disinterested. Stephie hands various pictures and albums to us all, aside from Jojo, who happily sits on the floor stroking Brian – my dog.*

I look at the folder on my lap ... There's Grandma's passport, her birth certificate and the original letter from the Gestapo

---

* Yes, I did name my dog after my dad, and yes, it does cause the neighbours to turn to each other and say, 'Poor Jackie,' whenever my mum calls him in from the garden. It's a lovely joke that keeps on giving and something I know my dad would have appreciated – especially when Mum shouts at him for shitting on the flowerbeds.

ordering her departure – complete with the chilling Nazi stamp. (Then again, I can't imagine there are Nazi stamps that *aren't* chilling.) As I carefully hold the flimsy, yellowing paper in my hands, the weight of history momentarily knocks the breath out of me.

I come across a framed black-and-white photograph of Grandma Rosi in her youth, playing her guitar under a tree – it could have been a still from *The Sound of Music* …

Young Rosi sits beneath a tree strumming her beloved guitar.

I remember this picture from her mantelpiece in Hendon. As I stare at it, my eyes pricking, my mind floods with memories of the Grandma I knew. Of her house. The smells: roses, talcum powder, cinnamon biscuits. The sounds: Wimbledon on the telly, ping-pong in the garden, the piano, the laughter … the arguments.

Der Landrat in Esslingen.
Verfügung vom 28. Oktober 1938.

Die Kindergärtnerin Rosa S c h u l ,
geb. am 24.9.1915 in Dortmund,
wohnhaft in Esslingen, Panoramastr.65
(Israel. Waisenhaus),

wird auf Grund des Erlasses des RFSSuChdDtPol. im RMdJ. und der Geheimen Staatspolizei, Staatspolizeileitstelle Stuttgart vom 27.Oktober 1938, auf Grund § 1 in Verb. mit § 5 Abs.1 a der Ausländerpolizeiverordnung vom 22.8.1938 (Reichsgesetzbl.I S.1053) mit Frist bis 29.Oktober 1938 der Aufenthalt im Deutschen Reich verboten.
    Rosa S c h u l wird zur Vorbereitung des Vollzugs dieses Aufenthaltsverbots mit sofortiger Wirkung in Abschiebungshaft genommen, da ihr weiterer Aufenthalt im Deutschen Reich geeignet ist, wichtige Belange des Reichs und der Volksgemeinschaft zu gefährden. Sie hat daher das deutsche Reichsgebiet unverzüglich bis spätestens 29.Oktober 1938 zu verlassen. Die aufschiebende Wirkung einer etwaigen Beschwerde gegen vorstehende Verfügung ist ausgeschlossen.

Esslingen, den 28.Oktober 1938.
Der Landrat:
I.V.

Gestapo notice ordering Grandma to leave.

Whenever I think about Grandma's house, I'm always transported back to a particular moment in 1993. Ten years old – standing in 'the music room'. My violin under my chin, Mum at the piano. I remember how I wished I could disappear as I looked at Grandma Rosi's expectant face and then back to my Grade 1 Violin book. She made me more nervous than Simon Cowell did …*

It was on one of our typical Sundays. As soon as the church service ended, Mum orchestrated her usual biblical exit – channelling Moses as she swiftly said goodbye to the vicar; parting the good Christian congregation like the Red Sea, as she escaped the sleepy village church.†

Dad and I knew we had to be ready and waiting by the back door with our shoes on, so that as soon as she tooted the horn, we could jump straight into my harassed mum's car, where the air would already be fizzing with tension. I'd be clutching my loathed violin case, while Dad balanced Mum's cheesecake on his lap, keeping it steady with his right hand while he gripped the handle above the car door with his left – white-knuckled, through the winding roads all the way to Hendon.‡ Dad had perfected this 'cheesecake stabilisation' technique over years of enduring Mum's so-called 'Jewish driving' – her term for 'driving assertively', and Dad's definition for 'ploughing through traffic lights and pushing in'. Personally, I loved Mum's driving. More thrills than Alton Towers, and no queues – such value!

---

* Oh, yeah, I was on *Britain's Got Talent* in 2017. Is this the first time Simon Cowell and the Nazis have been mentioned in the same book?
† Where she still dutifully plays the organ every Sunday … even though she's Jewish. I used to think it was because she loved the music so much, but now I think she just doesn't like the idea of something going on in a building without her knowing about it.
‡ I don't think the roads from our village to Hendon are winding – that's just how Mum drives. Terrifying.

LIFE IS ROSI

On this Sunday we'd managed to arrive for lunch at 1 p.m. sharp ... PHEW! Being late was a terrible crime in Grandma's book. You'd be met with a thin-lipped, steely glare that'd make your insides turn to ice, or rather Mum would (it was all hugs and warmth for me and Dad), and no amount of Mum's grovelling would warrant forgiveness until her mother was good and ready to let it go – probably a week or so later, by which time Mum would have made another misstep, like forgetting to pick up Rosi's favourite cottage cheese and pineapple.*

In Grandma's tiny 'morning room', with its Seventies green carpet and white Anaglypta wallpaper, the eight of us (Mum, Dad, Auntie Stephie, my sisters Katy and Jojo, Grandpa Jules, Grandma and me) would cram around the four-seater dining table. I'm no mathematician, but that's not ideal. Grandma would sit in her usual seat – a green plastic garden chair with lots of cushions – while six of us sat on high-backed wooden Ercol Quaker dining chairs and Dad on a piano stool.

A starter of mushroom soup flavoured with an entire jar of Schwartz's Garlic Salt traditionally preceded the even-more-garlic-salted ~~roast~~ *cremated* lamb main. And while urgently gulping down Grandma's 'exotic fruit cocktail drink' (an ancient carton of apple juice mixed with slightly off, now-fizzy orange juice), we'd all refuse second helpings, only to be ignored as Grandma happily spooned more garlicky, salty morsels onto our plates. At least we had definitive proof Grandma Rosi wasn't a vampire.

The meal would traditionally be finished off with one of Grandma's famous trifles – famous, sadly, for all the wrong reasons: layers of ladyfingers soaked in undiluted Ribena, Ambrosia custard, a smattering of grapes, tinned fruit cocktail in some not-quite-set jelly, a couple of surprise Brazil nuts, cottage cheese(!) for texture – all topped off with squirty cream, sometimes

---

* It was very 'in' at the time. The avocado on toast of the Nineties.

miraculously within its use-by date. It was like jazz, but for food.*

As soon as Grandma decided we'd had enough, she'd give the nod, Dad would pick up the piano stool and we'd dutifully traipse into 'the music room' – with its floral armchairs, walls of Grandpa Jules's LPs, signed pictures of the glamorous singers he played with in the Thirties and Forties, bongos, maracas, a melodica,† a shiny black grand piano and that familiar old guitar hanging in its place above the mantelpiece. Grandma would sit regally in her favourite chair, hands clasped, looking at us all expectantly.

The next-door neighbours – who'd evidently forgotten what day it was and ducked down too late when my eagle-eyed Grandma spotted them over the garden fence – had been jostled in, plates of our leftover lunch benevolently thrust into their reluctantly outstretched hands. Grandma had provided us with an 'audience', and backing out or showing even the slightest hint of reluctance to perform for the grand dame and her resigned vassals would have resulted in deep offence – with my mum caught in the crossfire. I lifted my orange 'made in China' violin – I knew nothing could save me now ... We WERE the concert, and we WOULD perform ...

Half an hour has passed. My big sister and niece, now off to Watford shopping centre, hug me goodbye as I still clutch the picture of my young grandma, which transported me so vividly back in time. I sigh as I look back at it; sad that she's gone, relieved to have given up the violin. I never did manage to achieve a classical tone – Vivaldi, Elgar – no matter how hard I tried, I always seemed to play as though I was wearing a headscarf in a rubbish

---

* With all the musicians in the family, it's amazing we didn't appreciate her jazzy trifle (not a euphemism).
† One of those little handheld keyboards that you blow into – weird.

production of *Fiddler on the Roof*. Even the perkiest of Mozart's melodies become mournful, Eastern European folk music in my hands. If anyone wants to play very sad, very bad violin, simply hold the bow in a clenched fist. That's my gift to you – free with the purchase of this book.

We move to the sitting room and Stephie chats away to Jojo and me, as Mum plays from her book of Bach preludes and fugues on her treasured grand piano, oblivious to Brian, clearly visible through the window, happily digging holes in her garden. Slightly shaky from all the coffee and with a knot in my stomach at the sight of Dad's empty chair, I reach for an old diary at the bottom of Grandma's box …

I'm a great diarist; I got it from Grandma. She gave me my first little diary when I was eleven. It was from WHSmith, with a picture of a girl sitting under a tree on the front, and a tiny gold lock and key. Grandma's dog-eared old diary isn't locked, but it is impossible to read. Not only do I *not* speak German, I don't even recognise half of the letters. Grandma's script is a mixture of the normal alphabet and an old form of German handwriting – Sütterlinschrift – that was taught in German schools from 1915 to 1941. However, in 2014, Auntie Stephie had the foresight to sit with Grandma while she translated a few passages for posterity.

Auntie Stephie typed them up – (though, if you ask Mum, not without Stephie putting her own spin on things) – and each of us received a copy of the twelve or so A4 pages.

I sit on the floor at my auntie's feet while she reads some of the pages to Jojo and me – my mum, scoffing at some of her younger sister's retelling, which she clearly thinks is too emotional and dramatic, exclaiming, 'Ach! It didn't happen like that,' and rolling her eyes at the poetic language as she continues to play … (Mum's always been an excellent multitasker).

As I listen, though, I realise that some of Grandma's early diary entries aren't so different from mine at that age …

Diary of Rosi Schul – age 12
17 February 1927

I have a crush on Dr Zimmet, a young Rabbi …

Diary of Jess Robinson – age 12¾
23 September 1996

… I keep having sexy dreams about Pat Sharp from Fun House …

Stephie's voice fades into the background as I fondly remember Pat's bonkers hairstyle and my fantasies of him asking me to brush it after we'd snogged in the balloon tunnel.

But my fantasy hairbrush gets stuck in fantasy Pat's hair and, with a jolt back to reality, I realise the music has stopped and Mum is now sitting beside her younger sister looking grim. I ask Stephie to reread the sentence I just missed:

Diary of Rosi Schul
2 November, 1938

… We spent that night in the filthy, stinking barn, lying on damp straw, everyone squashed together like animals, not human beings … Once we were in, the doors were locked and we couldn't get out till morning.

Chapter 3

Diary of Rosi Schul
Saturday, 24 June 1939

I have been here for a long time. Frozen, while others move forward. All was fine until recently. Now it is as if I have woken up from a dream. I look around me – as if for the first time – and observe how others cope with these experiences, and how they have been affected through these times – the impact.

―――

As I lie in the bath that evening, the laptop on the lowered toilet seat so I can watch a classic episode of *Gilmore Girls* where daughter, mother and grandmother bicker at the dining table in a way that feels comfortingly familiar, I realise that searching for Grandma's story is also a search for my own. I've spent so long shaping myself to fit other people's expectations that I'm not even sure who I am without all the noise. Maybe understanding where I come from, finding the roots that connect me to Grandma and Mum, will help me work out where I stand. Having inherited the gift of multitasking, I bathe, chat to Husband 2.3* through the bathroom door, watch Netflix and try not to drop my phone into the bubbles as I text Mum …

* Upgraded cos he just brought me a glass of wine – thanks, Derek! Or Damian?

Message to: Mum

Sunday, 17 October 2021, 22:05

Me: Thanks for today, Mummy. Are you OK?

Mum: Yes, Poopie. Why wouldn't I be?

Me: Because of Grandma's diary thing. Do you miss her?

Mum: Not really.

Me: Doesn't it make you feel funny?

Mum: No. Stephie's translation is very dramatic, darling. She can be so hysterical ...

Me: Hmmm ... well, I was wondering ... do you think we can translate Grandma's diaries properly then? With your friend Bruni? She can read that handwriting, can't she? Would you be up for it? Please?

Mum: What are you looking for?

Me: I don't know. I want to know her story – properly. I know you didn't like Grandma.

Mum: She could be very cold.

Me: Well, I want to know about that too.

Mum: OK

Me: So, will you ask Bruni?

Mum: Yes, OK, tomorrow … Naked Attraction is on Channel 4 now. Are you watching?

Me: No, I'm in the bath watching Gilmore Girls.

Mum: Such dreadful willies!!! I can't bear it!!!!!

Me: Change the channel then.

Mum: No, I want to see who she picks now. Night night, sweetie heart. Speak tomorrow.

Me: Love you x

Mum: Love you too, Dollydumps xxx*

I put the phone on the bathmat …

I've always known that my relationship with Grandma Rosi is different from Mum's. To me, Grandma was warm and affectionate, a cuddly, soft-around-the-edges dodgy chef who dyed her hair copper brown until she let it go a sweet fluffy white in her last couple of years. To Mum, she was proud, cold and demanding. The contrast is stark.

I want to dig deeper into Grandma's life, to understand who she was before she became a mother or grandmother. What shaped Rosi? What burdens did she carry? And how did that shape Mum and me?

---

* Just to reiterate, these texts are *all* real. If you don't believe me then come round my house and spend a night with Mummy and Dollydumps. Not like that.

I'm not sure where this journey will lead or what I'll find, but I'm going to be forty soon and it's freaking me out. Maybe this is a little midlife, pre-forty, what-the-hell-am-I-doing-with-my-life crisis, but I really hope that as I uncover Grandma's experiences, it might somehow give me the strength to live authentically, just as Grandma did in her own extraordinary way.

A week later a box arrives …

Message to: Auntie Stephie

Friday, 22 October 2021, 15:58

Me: Hi Stemmie. I just received the diaries 😺 Thank you so much for sending them! I'm just sitting on the floor scanning some pages to send to Mum and Bruni to translate. You already translated some parts of these with grandma, right?

Stephie: Yeah, that's right, but I don't know which bits. Some of it mummy paraphrased to me.

Me: What made you decide to translate those bits with grandma back then?

Stephie: Well, we all knew Mummy had all these diaries on her bookshelf, completely unreadable. She could read them. But nobody else. And people were starting to ask about her story. So I said, 'Read them to me, Mummy.' So then whenever I'd go there, she read them out and I'd write, and then I'd go home and type it.

Me: I'm so glad you did!

Stephie: And I'm so gassed you're carrying it on, man! I do love you so for this!

Me: 🙈 xxx

A few days later, I check in with Mum …

Message to: Mum

Thursday, 28 October 2021, 16:15

Me: Hi mum, how are you and Bruni getting on with translating the diaries? Have you done any?

Mum: Yes Poopiepoo. I'm here with Bruni now. She can read Grandma's writing. It's a mixture of old-fashioned handwriting and modern. It's ever so complicated!! She reads it out and then I write it down in proper English.

Me: Oh amazing!!

Mum: I do wish you wouldn't say everything is 'amazing'. The orange one isn't a diary actually, it's letters she must have written out 'in rough' before writing them properly. And in the front there's a little register of the children she must have looked after.

Me: Oh cool! Stephie sent me 3 more today. She found a teeny tiny one that she's never seen before too. I'll scan them all for you.

Mum: Gosh Dollydumps!! Really??? It's never-ending!!!!! I do have a life you know. I've got 2 play 4 the golf club choir later and Marywiththeleg is coming round so she can practise her solo. She sings SO out of tune it gives me the giggles.

Me: 😁 I'll buy your Waitrose shopping …

Mum: Alright then … and promise to wipe my bottom when I'm too old.

Me: Promise.

Mum: And promise to NEVER sit me in front of the football.

Me: Promise. Only A Place in the Sun and 'dreadful willies' on Naked Attraction.

Mum: No! Just play me some Bach.

Mum: And I do like A Place in the Sun.

Me: OK! Thank you mum. Have fun with Marywiththeleg. Speak later XXXXXX

When the first batch of handwritten pages arrive from Mum, I call to thank her. I'm surprised when she tells me that while her pal Bruni is very interested in Grandma's writing, she herself really, *really* isn't enjoying the enormous task of translating her mother's diaries. Thinking that many daughters would find it a precious and moving task, I feel troubled knowing she's putting in such time and effort for … well … I don't know what yet. But I wonder if I can somehow help Mum 'forgive' and 'forget' and find the sort of love for Grandma that Auntie Stephie carries.

I sit down on the sofa and Brian, tail wagging, jumps up and settles himself on my lap. As I idly stroke his fluffy head, I leaf through the translations, impressed at the pages and pages of A4 written in slanting pencil, enjoying the look of Mum's familiar loopy handwriting.

Rosi's story picks up when she is just twenty-three. Living, working and looking for love at the orphanage in Esslingen … I am amazed and delighted to discover my young grandma is living quite a showbizzy life that seems to echo my own at that age …

Diary of Rosi Schul
Wednesday, 19 October 1938

Dear God! How good life can feel. My work is lovely, my room is gorgeous. How lucky can I be? Everyone gets on well together. The children's performance tonight was a brilliant success. My Chinese children's band had applause as seldom before. People complimented me. The acts were really

Rosi accompanying her 'Chinese children's band' on the piano. Please note the moustaches. #ItWasADifferentTime.

successful. The costumes were excellent. Black tunics and yellow belts with little hats. The dancing was sweet. The band, with accordion, saxophone, triangle and tambourine, was very effective. It was really astonishing. I accompanied them on my piano. Then there were gymnastics with the bigger girls. Isla Hertz was a bit dreamy at first, but otherwise everything was very nice. The boys' acrobatics were also amazing. Of course, everyone has congratulated me. A glowing experience. Really, it was Samuel and me who organised the thing.

I haven't got any further with Samuel. He recognises my ability and my knowledge. We make a good pair and work fantastically together. I just wish he liked me in the way that I like him. I wish I could let go of my longing for his affection.

Rosi's crush – Fritz Samuel. Funny how she (and I think everyone at the time) referred to guys by their last name. To be fair, he is quite cute. Nice eyes.

Diary of Rosi Schul
Saturday, 22 October 1938

Is it really possible?? My greatest wish! Yes, it has finally come true with regards to Samuel! How long have I loved him for? Since I first saw him. I have longed for him to love me too.

Last night there was music and dancing & that's when it happened. We kissed! My heart could burst!

Diary of Rosi Schul
Monday, 24 October 1938

Now I must be tough – it's hardly bearable! On Saturday evening Samuel had shown how much he liked me but now I know there's really nothing with him. I have a terrible feeling in the pit of my stomach. Yesterday after his unusually reserved behaviour we had a confrontation – he said he couldn't imagine being married to me. I told him this is a ridiculous argument! I'm not necessarily interested in marriage. Who does he think he is to break up our relationship?

It is my own fault. I am a bad person. I'm punished for being so superficial. I encouraged Fritz, and Walter, and Julian while I waited for Samuel to like me. I let them dangle to pass the time, so I didn't feel lonely or undesirable. I am nothing more than a simple prick tease.*

I am disgusted with myself. It had to come to this with Samuel. When one behaves like I have, one must take the consequences. My stomach is in knots and I'm so sorry about everything. God! I wonder if I'll get over this. I see Samuel everyday & my emotions are so stirred up.

---

* OMG, GRANDMA!

At breakfast I had to sit opposite him. He looked gorgeous – such a chiselled jaw. I pretended to just look at the sky. I was seemingly light-hearted. It's uncanny how well I can control myself. It's so painful. At the same time I've got my visitor* and am desperately tired and miserable. Oh sweet darling Samuel. How you hurt me.

Diary of Rosi Schul
Tuesday, 25 October 1938

This heartbreak is so painful. Samuel is in love with Jenna. She is a classroom assistant here and only 18 years old. It is impossible not to admire her. She is very beautiful. Her legs and hips are unbelievable. Again and again I catch myself looking at her. For example, on Friday in the bath, I waited to see her beautiful figure. It's a fantasy image. She has a perfect body. If Samual saw that body, wow! She's excellent in her clothing but so beautiful when she's naked. On top of that, her face is indescribable. How she must catch men's eyes. I cannot compete. I'm an ancient twenty-three-year-old cow!

I must get Samuel out of my head. It will never be.

I feel such compassion and empathy for Rosi, her heartbreak, desperation and that familiar self-loathing I still regularly have to give myself a talking-to about … It's as if I could have written it. Though I'm certain my diaries contain a good deal more swearing … I just want to take young Rosi out for a bottle of Sauvignon Blanc and reassure her that her feelings are valid and she IS beautiful, and then maybe later, when we've had a Chinese (takeaway – not band), tell her that her experiences, no matter how small or

---

* 'My visitor' = her period – Jew on, Grandma!

insignificant they might have seemed to her later in life, were important and worthy of being remembered!

Her story, in all its parts, is a reminder that our histories are made up of the small, intimate moments just as much as the grand, historical events.

Diary of Rosi Schul
Wednesday, 26 October 1938

I have really gained some self-respect. How fantastically I've put things right. I have spoken to Samuel. We have a glowing friendship and camaraderie now. This good situation will continue forever now. Even though I feel more inside, it would have been unbearable to be angry while living in the same building. It is all OK now. Thank God. I have just read him my diaries. He was speechless.

GRANDMA, NOOOOOOOOOOOO!!!!!!!! Don't read your diaries to your crush! Nooooooooooo! This desperate display of oversharing makes me both feel closer to the young Rosi and wonder at how she turned into the woman I knew as 'Grandma' …

I never witnessed my grandma being so starry-eyed, insecure or vulnerable. It's hard to reconcile that girl with the tough, no-nonsense woman I knew … When did it change? Was it a conscious choice to build that armour – for self-preservation, or because life demanded it – or did it slowly form over the years?

I have always felt different from Mum and Grandma. They're so strong. I'm a muddle of sensitivities, always worrying what people think … It is only now at thirty-eight* that I no longer choose to

---

* Though I maintain that when acting I *can* play eighteen, and I MUST play eighteen.

hang out with people I don't actually like just to avoid being alone. I'm just beginning to discover the sort of funny, emotionally intelligent women who understand me, who don't mind if I'm 'too much', or laugh too loudly ... or the fact that whenever I compliment a stranger, for some reason I get a lump in my throat and want to cry. Why is that? Getting choked up when I say to someone, 'Oh, your hat looks beautiful.' Why does that make me emotional? Answer me!

I keep reading about women 'stepping into their power'. I don't think I can do that until I find *my* voice and have the confidence to use it unapologetically ...

You know, as much fun as I have working as an impressionist, being other people for a living has its downsides. For years, I have hidden behind it. Yeah, I can do other people's voices and get a laugh, and I can sing as an array of musical artists, but ... I can't seem to decide what my *own* voice should sound like.

Will I ever have the courage to simply say, 'No, I'm not coming to your party because I'd rather stay in and watch *The Real Housewives of Beverly Hills*,' instead of making up a far-fetched excuse? And if you know me and I've flaked on your party, those excuses weren't for *your* event. I really was tied up. Tied up by a burglar in my own home.

I wish I could grow a pair.*

Mum is always so outspoken, so fearless about doing her own thing. Meanwhile, I've perfected people-pleasing to an Olympic level. The only place where I have always been totally honest, is my diary ... In fact, I'm now starting to wonder what I might learn if

---

* And by 'a pair', I mean a pair of flaps. Not balls. Balls are useless and can't even stand the cold. Fannies go through all sorts! So, the term I like for being brave is 'flapsy'. Verb – to be flapsy. (And speaking of flaps, why did I wait so long to get laser hair removal? Honestly, dealing with ingrown hairs is like dealing with social events – uncomfortable and entirely avoidable.)

I looked back at my *own* diaries. How will a young Jess measure up to Rosi at the same age, on the same-ish date? This is probably a suicide mission, which'll result in more self-loathing, but what if I find glimpses of that same strength, and where it might have disappeared to? Maybe I can pinpoint a moment and put it right? What if, as I uncover Grandma's experiences and look back at my own, I can learn to live on my own terms, just as Grandma did …

OK – here we go. Oh, God! I'm going to do it. Oh, Lord! I feel a bit like I'm showing you my bumhole and asking for approval.

Diary of Jess Robinson – age 23
Thursday, 26 October 2006

I feel sick. Just eaten a very creamy savoury crepe. I'm in Ealing Broadway. It's gorgeous round here. Nice shops, leafy and green. I'm going to look at a flat. Rachel and I have plans to live together. I can't think of anyone I'd rather live with. I trust her completely and I think it'd be such fun!

Mum pisses me off SO MUCH. I've got to leave home. I fucking HATE her. Bloody smug cow. She makes me so angry I want to kill her. She's so negative.* She doesn't know anything. I want to die. I want to die. I want to die.† I don't actually want to die and I don't actually hate her. I really do love mum. But she speaks so loudly in the kitchen so I can hear her complaining to dad about me. I know she does it on purpose. But it winds me up. We SCREAMED at each other yesterday. Literally SCREAMED. I got a sore throat and she cried and then shouted at dad because he went to have a fag in the back garden. She says he never gets involved.

---

* Unlike you, Jess, who sounds an absolute delight. Such a carefree young woman.
† Ironically, reading this makes me want to die.

How am I going to do it? Leave home I mean?* I really hope there's a way. I'm going to say sorry to mum for putting the phone down on her. But how unhelpful of her to say 'Dream On'. I could honestly kill her for that. Sometimes she's like the bloody Gestapo.†

I have big moments of darkness. Of utter black – like that guy on The Fast Show. I just want to leave home and live with Rachel and be an actress and get a boyfriend.

Dream on.‡

Love Jess xxx§,¶

———

Oh, Gawd! I just want to take young Jess out for a drink and, over a bottle of Sauvignon Blanc, tell her that her feelings are RIDICULOUS, and then maybe later, when we've had a Chinese (takeaway – not band), tell her that her experiences, no matter how small or insignificant, must *never be shared*.

I've known my friend Rachel since I was fifteen. At my small-town, middle-class school in the Home Counties, I was so excited to meet another Jewish person that we immediately connected. I called her Rachel Rabbi, and she called me Jessie Jew. Those delightful nicknames have now been shortened to 'Rabbi' and … 'Jess'.

In all future diary entries, Rachel is referred to as 'Rabbi'. She's even saved in my phone as 'Rabbi'. I was once in a meeting when *'Rabbi is Calling'* popped up on my screen, and my agent, Sophie, looked shocked and said: 'Oh! do you need to take that?' – just in case it was a BIG JEWISH EMERGENCY!

---

* Glad I clarified and it wasn't the start of a plan to kill Mum.
† I don't think I knew what they were.
‡ 'Jew on' hadn't been invented yet.
§ I always signed off like this – in a big, flourishing autograph.
¶ I think I'm regretting this now.

Chapter 4

Diary of Rosi Schul
Friday, 28 October 1938

I am writing this in a dark cell, with bars on the windows. Unbelievable. I have to pinch myself that I am here!

There is so much to explain ...

The Thursday-evening reading group embodied the most wonderful time of living and working at the orphanage in Esslingen. I have had so many totally new and beautiful experiences there. Theodor Rothschild, his wife, Aunt Adele, Samuel, Jonas and I were sitting together and chatting. On this particular evening we were focusing on our possible destinies. I was pondering emigrating to America. We moved on to talk about the present political situation and then suddenly – like a bad dream – it all became too real!

I jumped as the doorbell rang. Ten-thirty at night! Then a shout – 'Is Herr Rothschild there? Police!' I was chilled to the core. My heart missed a beat. We nervously looked around at each other. We knew police arriving at this hour of the night certainly meant only one thing – arrest and interrogation for unfounded or fictitious reasons.

Herr Vater calmly took the 'gentlemen' into his office and before we could even adopt a cheerful or ironic attitude as to what it could mean and whom they were seeking, he returned white-faced and called me out. Samuel looked pale, but I was just surprised rather than scared, as at that point, what lay ahead for me was completely unimaginable.

The Gestapo man, a cold and unsympathetic fellow, spoke in a factual, expressionless voice. 'Fraulein Schul, please get dressed and come with me to the police station. Tomorrow you are travelling to Poland.'

I did not answer, nor did I ask anything. I felt a certain calmness come over me – serene and numb. In the face of such relentless, harsh, terrible power as Germany's there is no point in responding with upset, indignation or entreaty. This was happening to me and in the moment, my only thought was, 'You must just let it happen, for whatever will be, will be.'

The significance of being separated from the work and the people whom I love did not even occur to me. Funny. For days, no, weeks beforehand I had had a feeling that this indescribably happy time could not last. A press on my heart – a whisper in the back of my mind told me it was all 'too good to be true'.

As I fetched my keys from the living room I ignored Samuel and Jonas's alarming questions. I shut out what was happening. I did not – I could not discuss it, nor ask any questions, nor express regret. Fraulein Leib, Herr Vater and Frau Rothschild had already gone upstairs to the dormitories to collect the three boys who had also been summoned – Vitus Mandelbaum, Heinz Alter and little Theo Sperber.

Despite being heavily guarded, I was allowed to go up to my room to dress, and I did this quite calmly.

Somehow my mind was clear, and I just knew at that moment that cold, hunger and work awaited me, and so I dressed accordingly. I pulled on a pair of thick knee socks over my silk stockings, wore my heavy lace-up shoes, a thick woollen jumper and jacket under my coat.

A very upset Fraulein Leib rushed in and asked me, 'How can I help you, dear child?' She helped me gather my night clothes, some underwear, an extra sweater, stockings and toiletries. In the meantime Jonas had come upstairs and watched this scene silently from the doorway. When he heard I needed a suitcase he brought his own new suitcase. I refused it but he insisted I should take it. He could buy himself another one. His behaviour was that of a true and loyal friend and it touched me.

Time was pressing on and the 'delightful' Gestapo man was getting impatient. In the hallway, Herr Vater, who was upset and shaken, asked me what else he could do. Give me money? Send news to my home?

Then – perhaps for the last time, I went back to my room – my wonderful, beautiful room – and from my little locked cupboard, I retrieved as many diaries and letters as I could fit in my suitcase.

I walked along the corridor and down the stairs into the hall – trying to drink it all in. When would I return? The three little boys were already downstairs waiting for me. We said goodbye to everyone and I took little Theo's hand. Pretending to be my easy-going, happy self, I told the boys to be cheerful. Herr Vater pointed out that at least we Esslingers could be together. It felt so selfish to feel comforted that I had some of my children with me. But I was glad I could focus on them. The other staff were all very serious while I acted casually. Jonas could do nothing except nod. The goodbye from Samuel made my stomach turn over.

Saying 'goodbye' to these dear fellows was the hardest thing for me.

Then for the last time down the back stairs – those stairs which I had rushed up and down so many times. To leave, to leave forever. (I just know it is forever.) Then outside into the wonderful courtyard for the last time, down the long flight of steps and out into the cold moonlit autumn evening and along the footpath.

Being in complete control of myself, I found myself calmly chatting with the officials and going along with the childish remarks made by the boys while inwardly everything inside me was crumbling. As the shock began to wear off, I let myself wonder what was to come …

All Jewish Poles are to be deported from Germany and must go to Poland immediately! When I think back to yesterday it was another world – in my reality, it feels like a distant beam of light, which is getting more distant and more hopeless. Fading. Fading. Fading.

Diary of Jess Robinson
Friday, 27 October 2006

I have nothing to wear. None of my clothes fit. Just ate ½ jar of Nutella.

Too depressed to write.

Bye.

Christ. Who in the world thought it was a good idea to compare Rosi's diary entries to mine? Me. It was me.

The twenty-three-year-old me and the twenty-three-year-old Rosi are worlds apart. She's so composed, articulate and dignified. Was this one of the first times Grandma learned not to show any vulnerability? Is this where it started? (After she practises at the breakfast table with Samuel.) She was just living her life and it got ripped up … No wonder she couldn't give a shit about learning to make a good trifle. She had quite a lot to deal with.

I can't imagine back then, or even now, that if I'm ever suddenly plucked from my privileged life in Brighton and taken away from everything I love and value by the Gestapo (definitely *not* meaning Mum), I'd write with such eloquence and show such stoicism.

Was Rosi's sense of self-preservation and self-assurance inherent from childhood? Did it come from having so many siblings and having to sort of bring herself up?

I'm an only child ... well, apart from my brother and two sisters. These half-siblings – who in all seriousness I love very much – were fourteen or fifteen when I was born out of Mum and Dad's second marriage, and they'd already left home by the time I was a 'proper person',* so I got all the attention I wanted. The majority of kids at my 'performing arts' school were very well-off, most of them boarding. I longed to be a boarder, and I begged my parents, but we only lived five minutes down the road, so that was a hard no. Our family wasn't wealthy by any stretch. Dad (God, I miss him) was an artist, and Mum is still earning a little from being a piano teacher, church organist, accompanying the 'golf club choir' and playing for the local am-dram revue. Even though she's SEVENTY-SEVEN.

At £3,000 a term, my school attracted the sons and daughters of diplomats, A-listers, bankers and rock stars.† I got a partial scholarship due to my singing voice.‡ In order for me to go to my dream school, Mum took a job there, teaching piano and recorder, and managed to get more money off the fees by playing the piano for ballet lessons AND running the second-hand uniform shop. It only strikes me now just how financially stretched my parents made themselves so I didn't have to go to a 'normal' school, and suffer the indignity of having to participate in sports – a skill I definitely *didn't* inherit from my sporty table-tennis-champion Grandma Rosi – and most likely having my head flushed down the toilet like in *Grange Hill*. It backfired, though, because I soon

---

* I think I've established I'm still not a proper person.
† Claim to fame: I squeezed an Osbourne sibling's first pimple.
‡ I reckon it would've been a full scholarship if they hadn't heard me play the violin and deducted points.

discovered that ballet, which was compulsory, was worse than any PE lesson I'd ever previously experienced at my little village primary school. I hated it. And it hated me.

I was such a dickhead that if I had to be in school earlier than my mum did, when Dad dropped me off on his way into work, I'd make him park around the corner so nobody saw me getting out of his 'bird-shit green' Skoda. I was so ashamed. I wouldn't even wave back before grumpily walking up the long tree lined drive to my school – a beautiful Rothschild mansion. They get around, those Rothschilds (Rothschildren?), don't they? I wonder if Grandma's headmaster, Herr Rothschild, ever visited my school – y'know, when it was just a mansion and not full of rich kids thinking they were going to be famous/just there to get out of PE.

What I'm saying is, I was an ungrateful little shit, and I bet my grandma wasn't. She was amazing during that total upheaval of everything she knew, because she was a better person. This is going to be a theme, isn't it? A cruel juxtaposition between Rosi and me. I am Scrooge and she is the ghost of ~~Christmas~~ Hanukkah past.

Chapter 5

Diary of Rosi Schul
Saturday, 29 October 1938

At the police station we were inspected by the police and officials. A few were apologetic, but most were disdainful. Our personal details were registered and money was inquired about. 'Into which cell should they go?' asked an official. We were taken along a passageway across a courtyard, up a staircase and through a large barred gate into a corridor where I was led into a cell. I was surprised to see that Frau Gold was there – lying on an iron bed against the wall crying – and my friend Ruth, her sister and her father sat there looking puzzled and uncomprehending. I tried to comfort her but Frau Gold only cried in distress, 'Gentlemen, please send me a doctor. My heart is failing.' But the officials ignored everything.

One night in this small cell with four people and this possibly sick woman with her wailing would only succeed in dispelling my cool calm and cause me to be weak and vulnerable. I could not lose myself. Self-preservation became the most important thing; I needed enough sleep and peace. I thought it over very carefully and then allowed myself to be led to a single cell. An iron bed, a little table, a seat in the corner, a cold radiator and a pail with a cover sitting on a large stone slab and above it attached to the wall, a lavatory seat.

I could only discern everything in the cell by the light shining from the corridor. Then the door slammed. Some bolts slid in place and I heard the sound of the key being turned several times. Yet another door was closed and darkness surrounded me. For a while I just stood, not knowing what to do with myself. Frozen there, holding my little case. Then I lay down. I took off my coat and wrapped myself up in a linen sheet. Amazingly I experienced neither fear nor disgust as I lay down without any kind of sheet on the straw mattress on which many a common criminal had lain before me. Thanks to my layers, I was warm enough. I lay there silently. I had plenty of time to reflect on all that had happened as I listened to the sound of a male choir nearby, tunelessly singing the same melody over and over again, as if there was nothing else of concern in the world.

I was not at all surprised at everything that had happened. It was now clear to me that this unbelievably lovely time – this happy and fulfilling phase of my life – had ended. So many things went through my head. In particular, memories of people that I loved. What about my family? I would not be seeing all my friends again. Away with my plans for Hanukkah. What would become of my beautiful room? My books, my records, my pictures and the diaries I left behind? What would Herr Vater and Aunt Adele be saying? What would become of Samuel?

And all the time the sound of the men singing without a care and the clinking of the prison warder's keys. An awful sound.

I could not sleep however hard I tried. The hours went by and suddenly there was loud banging on a cell door and the sound of someone calling. Ruth Gold was making her presence known. The sound of her knocking in the silence was quite eerie. It was a long time before a warder appeared. Despite my calm state, I flinched at every bang of the door. Then a heavy-footed officer arrived and called out angrily, 'What's up?' without even opening the door.

Ruth said, 'My mother is not well.' But the man turned away without saying a word and I heard him sneering to his fellow warders, 'And nor am I.' Then the door was closed and he was gone. A deep sense of abandonment and helplessness overcame me as I experienced total powerlessness. I must have fallen asleep very late and I must have woken up very early the next morning because I was freezing. A torch light was shining full in my face. It was a warder to check whether any cell inmate might have hanged himself in the night because he was having such fun.

No, I did not feel like hanging myself. In spite of the pain of all that I had lost, my mood was determined. I decided I would think of this as a new adventure. I would have an optimistic outlook on life. Now I wanted to play the real prisoner. I got up and inspected my bedroom. I tried out my elegant toilet arrangements, I combed my hair, I changed my stockings, and I listened to a dispute between the Golds and the prison warder concerning breakfast. The Golds rudely rejected their breakfast, but I happily accepted my clay jug with washing-up water and a dry crust of bread. I ate and drank with absolute disdain, for that was part of being a real prisoner.

No w I am recording t his historic mome nt i n m y diar y un til m y i n k r u n s o ut. I … … …

[Scribbles to nothing but faint scratches.]

Diary of Jess Robinson
Sunday, 29 October 2006

Hello,

I'm writing this in bed. Last night I finally had my 'late birthday' party with my friends. Stupid since I'm closer to my next birthday in February now, but Kelly convinced me. I was up for 'letting off steam' after my annoying conversation with mum. Plus the flat Rabbi and I saw was miserable and smelled of damp and I think I saw a mouse.

My friends sang happy birthday when we arrived at Jewel Bar in Piccadilly. So stupid. But also nice.

Then we went to this club in Kings Cross called The Cross.

Omar gave me my first pill!!!! I wanted to impress him because I quite fancy him. Kelly said she'd be my wing woman. I was hoping he might kiss me. I was quite nervous about taking the 'E' because I've never done it before and I didn't want to die.* But Kelly promised she'd look after me. So I took it. It was just starting to kick in and I was having an amazing time. I was dancing loads. Well, more like jogging on the spot. But Rabbi didn't have one and wanted me to come with her and this girl Tracey to get one. Kelly was dancing with Omar and gave me a £5 note to get her an orange juice from the bar on the way. Anyway, Tracey found a guy who gave her a pill and she handed it to Rabbi who waved it about like a prat. Suddenly a big bouncer lurched over and grabbed Rabbi's hand trying to prise it open. Finally she let it go and he took the pill from her. Then he looked at me and saw my clenched fist. I opened it easily cos I just wanted to show him I didn't have a pill, just a fiver for the orange juice. But he roughly took my arm and led me through the crowds of people in the club

---

* Contrary to earlier diary entries.

quite violently and out into the open air outside the club in the freezing cold.

I was so confused and disorientated and by this time I was breathless and whizzing, and I kept trying to explain that I didn't have the pill in my hand – all I had was money. And these big bouncers were laughing at me and told me to fuck off.

I was only wearing my black dress and heels and I told them my bag and coat with my keys and phone were inside. So they got this big woman bouncer to take me inside to find my stuff. But I didn't have my ticket for the cloakroom. Then Kelly appeared. I was falling over and feeling ill. She got me some orange juice and made me drink it all down while I was trying to stand up in this concrete corridor. I kept seeing white fuzz and the room was tipping and I threw up in a toilet.

They found my bag and the woman took me outside again. Kelly gave me all the money she had, but said she was going to stay in the club. I don't know where Rabbi got to. The bouncer led me up to a taxi and shoved me in by my head like they do on The Bill* when they put people in police cars and the taxi took me by myself all the way to Kelly's flat in Greenwich.

I got the key in the door and just got into her bed and lay there on my own while all my friends were still in the club. For a minute I thought about changing my clothes and trying to get back in as a different person. But then I got a bit panicky because my breathing was all uneven and gaspy and my heart was beating so fast. When I woke up Kelly wasn't there. I bet she stayed out at Omar's house. They probably shagged.

Today I was really ill. I kept needing to throw up in the train toilets, but all I had in my stomach was yellow foam.

---

* A British police drama, which I'm sorry to say I never got an audition for.

I was so pleased to get home, back to mum's. She thought I had too much to drink, and I said I was really sorry for putting the phone down on her yesterday. She was kind and made me macaroni cheese and we watched telly. Dad told me off for drinking too much, but he gave me a hug.

I'm up in bed now and I feel really sad for some reason. I feel disappointed that nobody looked after me. Kelly can't be trusted. I'm not sure she's very nice actually. I don't think I'll do an 'E' again. It was an awful experience. Apart from the fun jogging on the spot bit at the beginning.

Rabbi just called to see how I was. She said she was being sick when all the drama was happening and couldn't find me. She just told me that Kelly said she knew I wouldn't be able to handle a pill – what a stupid bitch. I'm tempted to do it again now and show her I can. But I won't. I hate her. She <u>DID</u> go back with Omar. So that's that. He's not Mr Right. And she is Mrs Cowbag.

Oh, AND Rabbi said the fiver in my hand looked like I was the <u>DRUG PUSHER</u> and Rabbi had just bought a pill off me!!!!!!!!!!!!!!!!!!!!!!!!!!!!!!!!

We laughed our heads off at me being a criminal. Rabbi said she was really sorry it all went wrong and we agreed that I'm too good for Omar and Kelly is a total arsehole. I hope she gets an STD.

I think I'll listen to my old Winnie the Pooh cassette tape.

Night Night.

Love Jess xxx

P.s. I've got an audition for Cinderella tomorrow at 5pm. I have to sing an up-tempo and a ballad, so I'm going to sing A Moment Like This by Leona Lewis and Is This the Way to Amarillo by Peter Kay. I'll just stand and look into the middle distance for Leona, but think I could sing Amarillo sort of posh like a princess and I'll imagine I'm in the woods and I'm asking the animals the way to Amarillo.*

I hate myself.

As the months pass, every now and then more handwritten translations arrive from Mum and Bruni. I savour the moment each one arrives, gently unfolding each piece of paper, feeling as though I'm stepping into a portal to Grandma's world. Young Rosi, and even young me to an extent, become like my pen pals. I only allow myself to read the next entry in my own diary when the Grandma pages arrive. I say 'allow myself' – one or two pages at a time is all I can stomach.

But still, our respective diary entries are like postcards sent across decades – hers from somewhere classy, mine from a Club 18–30 package holiday in Benidorm. Two twenty-three-year-old women: one dealing with a dodgy night out, and the other facing actual life-and-death drama.

Listen, I know I was a knob, but I'm determined to come away with more than that.

I can see that our writing styles have similarities. We were both very honest – no sugar-coating. Grandma (and my mum) carried that into the rest of her life, never shying away from sharing her truth, even if it was hurtful … I very much went the other way, never being honest if I thought it would cause pain – even kidding myself into marrying Practice Husband when deep down I knew it was doomed from the start.

---

* This is what I did for many panto auditions over the years. What a KNOB. Sometimes I'd skip (better than jogging on the spot) and pretend I was parting bushes (not a euphemism) and look up into the branches to 'ask the animals'. In the last verse I would always imagine a blue bird perching on my finger and flying off to show me the way, and then I'd run off at the end.

If either of us are suffering (and suffering is relative here), we don't hold back on saying it. We're both so open about our emotions, whether it's me ranting about Kelly, or Rosi describing the grim state of her prison cell – again, I'm not unaware of the chasm between our situations.

Even though we're both open, we do it differently. Rosi is more formal, showing such dignity, even when everything's going pear-shaped. Whereas I was just haphazardly throwing my feelings onto the page, like I'd spilled a can of emotional beans with a bit of self-pity thrown in for good measure.

If I'm being kind, then at least I can admit that young me was sort of resilient. Even if I *was* a bit of a mess, I didn't just give up. I might've been scrambling around, but I got through it, didn't I? Just …

And young Rosi? Well, she was getting through the fear and uncertainty by turning her crumbling world into a kind of game – 'playing the prisoner'.

I can't say I like my twenty-three-year-old self, but I'm falling in love with my twenty-three-year-old grandma …

Chapter 6

Diary of Rosi Schul
Saturday, 29 October 1938

At last! More ink!

... I could not stop thinking about all my lovely children back at the house. Who was getting them all up? Who would be caring for them? Gradually I became more ill at ease in my cell. If I had had to talk to anyone I would have burst into tears. I hummed several of my beautiful children's songs and paced back and forth in my cell like a caged animal. Time passed very slowly – I could hear sounds from the street and the clinking of the warder's keys but my cell door remained firmly locked. Now I have some idea at least of how it feels to be a criminal – whether guilty or not* – awaiting trial and interrogation for days or weeks. It must be terrible. After about an hour there was a rattling at my door. A warder opened it and told me I was allowed to go and wash. I walked along the corridor, through an iron door, and arrived in a tiny open room. Beside a table with writing things and old beer bottles on it, there was a dirty sink. While I washed, my fellow prisoners appeared. The three boys from the school were very jolly and talked about ghosts in their cell – for them it was an adventure, like one of the stories I used to tell them. It lifted me to listen to their excitable chatter.

---

* Just like me and my suspected 'drug pushing'! Wow, so similar.

Mrs Gold was very depressed while my friend Ruth, quite groomed, somewhat loudly described how she had been 'collected' from Esslingen station. I was determined to give the impression of being cool and casual – just as Ruth was trying to be in her own way – but in view of the situation, her behaviour was at odds with reality and felt forced. I was very aware of this because dammit – inwardly I felt so sad.

We didn't use the prisoners' hand towel. I'm glad I had my wash things with me. The Golds had no toiletries of their own.

Afterwards, I agreed to be locked in the same cell as the Golds. Suddenly I was overcome by the sheer hopelessness of the situation, and although I tried to control myself, the tears just ran down my face. Oh, God, how little one can do against it. I wanted just to weep and weep. But suddenly the door rattled and opened. The three little boys rushed into me, and behind them, Herr Vater and Samuel. For a moment, they both just stood there in shock. They had brought food, clothing and cases – for the boys and me. No words can describe the scene. With great self-control I managed to talk to them. Rothschild was deadly white and Samuel looked dreadful. We didn't say much. In one stroke everything that had gone before was torn apart. We said our goodbyes. I felt utterly empty and dead inside and I am ashamed to say that as the door closed, I burst into tears. It all hit me. I suddenly realised everything I was leaving behind. My wonderful life, my friends, all of my beautiful children. The poor little boys couldn't understand what had happened to their ever-smiling, ever-singing Rosi. Seeing their shocked little faces made me pull myself together. I told them that I felt much better and hugged them. They looked relieved.

The Esslingers had packed a lot for me. Sadly not my childhood diaries or precious letters. But there was a new large suitcase for me, a blanket, clothing and my beloved guitar! That was such a ray of light for me and I took it out straight away and began to play. For a little while we were distracted from our circumstances and through the music, our spirits were raised by singing out, truly singing out.

Now sleep.

Diary of Jess Robinson
Monday, 30 October 2006

I'm too depressed to live* and I need to do some plastic surgery research.

I had the shittest day and crappiest night.

I've just got home from half a shift at Stocks Hotel. There was a big wedding. It was all fine (though I still can't do silver service and I had to use a spatula for the salmon), until one of the guests, a really drunk bloke, grabbed me from behind and wouldn't let go. All his mates were laughing. I only managed to twist round so I was facing him but I couldn't get out of his grip and the hot fag ash from his cigarette dropped down my cleavage and burnt a hole in my shirt (it was the one from Tammy Girl in Hemel which has closed now). Then he pretended to try and brush it off, but he groped my boob. I was so embarrassed. There were so many people there and nobody helped for ages.

They just watched. Why didn't anyone do anything?? The people on his table were laughing or shaking their heads – women too. As I got free of him, he smacked my bum – I didn't say anything. I just went to get another tray and my stupid twat manager told me to hurry up and clear drinks.

A woman came up to me a bit later and told me she runs a restaurant and if anyone did that to one of her girls, she'd expect

---

* Clearly, I don't know the meaning of depression. Had I read Rosi's previous entry before writing this, I might have chosen my words more carefully.

them to slap the guy. I couldn't though. I feel so stupid. I just smiled. She said I should tell my manager which I did, but my stupid twat manager just said, 'yes I saw' and I didn't know what to say so I carried on working till dessert was served and then I said I had a headache and came home. I didn't even ask – and I don't even care if they sack me.

Mum is really cross. With the hotel, not with me. I begged her not to call them. But I bet she will in the morning. Then she shouted at dad for 'being silent'. He's gone back into the garden now ... I just feel pathetic. I'm eating leftover mashed potato with melted cheese on it in bed. Bugger I just dropped some. One minute.

Shit, it's left an oil stain. Mum's going to kill me.

I did the audition for Cinderella. I wore my flat New Look ballerina shoes, black tights, Miss Selfridge checked skirt, and my lucky pink Jane Norman top (the one that's ribbed with the square neck). I put my hair half up half down, with cherry earrings and my bangles from Accessorize and I wore a little bow in my hair too so I looked more princessy. Mum said my eyebrows were too thin when she dropped me off at the station. That really PISSED ME OFF! Thanks for the confidence boost. BITCHHHHH. But she did lend me her No.7 lipstick.

On the way home, I bought her and dad a dark chocolate bounty to share because I slammed the door and didn't say thank you for dropping me off after the eyebrows comment. Why does she have to comment though? ARGHHH. I actually bought them a bounty each, but I ate one on the way to Stocks cos I didn't have time for dinner and I was late because of the audition.

Anyway when I went into the audition room at Pineapple Studios, I shook their hands and I was smiley and confident. I think I should have ironed my skirt like mum said. It looked really creased in the mirror. But I sang really well. They saw a bit of Amarillo which I had really practised this morning. I was a bit annoyed that they didn't let me get to the end because the bluebird bit is good and when they stopped me after the first chorus, I sort of kept skipping on the spot for a bit even though the pianist wasn't playing and I wasn't singing anymore.

I don't think they noticed. I hope they didn't. I hate myself. I don't. I do a bit. Then they asked for a chorus of When You Wish Upon a Star, which I hadn't prepared but luckily I knew. The director (who was sooooo queeny), told me just to stand still and sing it – I did sound really good actually and then he said – 'thank you that was beautiful'.

Then we did a scene – it's where Cinderella talks to the fairy godmother before she does 'Bibbidi Bobbidi Boo'. But because it's a pantomime near High Wycombe, and not the Disney version, they're not legally allowed to do that song apparently. So they're doing a kind of soundalike song called 'Magic Foodle Dee Dum'.

But for some reason I really struggled with it.

The end of the script went:

Fairy Godmother: All you need is a little 'magic foodle dee dum'.

Cinders: 'Magic foodle dee dum?'

Fairy Godmother: Yes! 'Magic foodle dee dum!'

And then she waves her wand and the song starts.

But whenever we got to it, I couldn't say 'Magic Foodle De Dum'. I don't know why! I can say it now. But in the audition it kept coming out as Maj-el foo-<u>dick</u> dee dum. Maj-el foo – <u>DICK</u> dee dum. And the queeny director rolled his eyes. And the casting director and the pianist were laughing. Then at the end they said thanks, that's all we need to see. Do you have any questions?

And I said, 'When would I expect to hear by?'

And the casting director looked at the director and they whispered and then he said:

'Well we can tell you now, you've got a lovely voice Jessica, but I'm afraid it's a no thank you. You just look ... too Jewish.'

So I said 'Oh OK. Well, thank you for having me'.

And then I left. Well I actually had to leave twice because I had to run back in for my music which was embarrassing. And then I left properly. And I went to Starbucks and I had a caramel macchiato which made me late for work, and I cried. Then I called Annika* to tell her the bad news. I thought she'd shout at me – she didn't, but she did suggest I should maybe dye my hair blonde.

Anyway I just feel so angry and sad, but I don't know why.†

So now I'm at home. I feel stupid and ugly and stupid. Mum and dad asked how it went and I just said I didn't look right for the part. And dad gave me a pat on the back and went into the garden.

I'm going to look up nose jobs on the internet. I don't think mum will pay for one though, I wonder if grandma might lend me the money.

---

* Annika was my agent at the time. She was a very well-spoken ex-headmistress who smoked a pipe, was sister to a 'lady-in-waiting' and had a badly behaved dog at whom she'd shout, 'PICKLES, GET DOWN!' during meetings, negotiations and phone calls with clients, producers and casting directors alike. I was pretty scared of her. And I was scared of Pickles too. That dog would NOT get down.

† Don't know why??? OK, so everything is relative, isn't it, and I actually feel very sorry for my younger self here. In fact, as I write this I am drinking a bottle of Sauvignon Blanc and having a Chinese (takeaway – not band). I've gone over this moment many times in my head over the years and fantasised about what I should have said, ranging from:

Anger: 'FUCK YOU, I don't want your stupid job "near High Wycombe" anyway.'

To outrage: 'You can't say that! It's anti-Semitic. I'm reporting you to Equity and going to the papers.'

To indignation: 'Too Jewish?? ... Too Jewish to be a PRINCESS?!?! Oi veh!'

To desperation: returning to get my music from the audition room but wearing a dress made of bacon like Lady Gaga, even though she didn't do that till about four years later. Trail blazer? Or magilfooDICKdeedum?

Shall I go blonde? I might like being blonde. I need some more fun.

I might go to the Party shop in Berko tomorrow and get a blonde wig and see how it looks.

We're visiting Grandma for lunch on Sunday. I expect she'll want me to sing something. Maybe I'll do Amarillo and Mum can accompany me on the piano. But I won't skip. Maybe Mum and I can go to Boots and get some hair dye and do it at Grandma's.

I will not let this conquer me. I should be nicer to mum.

I am a good person.

I am a good person.

I am a good person.

Love Jess xxx

In frustration, I throw my stupid diary across the room, startling Brian, my ever-faithful diary-reading companion. As I cuddle him, I replay the audition in my head and brood over why I *still* can't come up with an articulately kickass reply that makes me into the hero. I'm still stupid and impotent. I'm too worried that if I say that something is anti-Semitic, then I'll be expected to discuss politics, and I don't know anything because I'm stupid. It's all tangled up.

Miriam Margolyes would have said something brilliant.

My mum would have said something brilliant.

My grandma wouldn't have stood for it. She would have bitten back something so acerbic they would have been at her feet begging her for forgiveness. But I nodded and smiled and was totally pleasant because I hoped they would cast me another day. I wanted to be an actress so badly – I was like Oliver Twist holding out my bowl. Bowing and scraping. Pathetic. Gratefully accepting my old agent's advice to go blonde. That's how it was and that's very much how it still is in the industry – even if that sort of thing isn't said out loud so much any more. I've been like this all my life: fearful of confrontation – like my dad disappearing into the garden.

Unless I'm absolutely certain that standing up for myself won't result in total rejection and ruin, I don't do it – which basically means confrontation is reserved solely for Dollydumps and Mummy. You know what's worse, though? I cringe far more when I think back to the magilfoodickdeedum incident than I do about the 'too Jewish' remark.

WHAT IS WRONG WITH MY BRAIN? WHERE IS MY SPINE?

This lack of standing up for myself has meant I've betrayed myself over and over and over again. In the past it has shown up as 'being pleasant to work with' and 'being laid-back'. If there's a hair on my plate, I won't send it back. I'll just eat around it or ask for a doggy bag so I can 'enjoy' it later. I'm so fucking agreeable that I would rather nod, smile and then pretend I'm asleep during a taxi ride than *dare* to disagree with the stupid (mostly male) taxi drivers who have lectured me about:

- how I must have children;
- that the earth is flat;
- that the Twin Towers was a hoax and have in fact been moved to Brazil;
- that Saddam bloody Hussein is living a few doors down from him in Stevenage and is actually a really nice guy.

Delete *none* as appropriate. They *all* happened. Five stars and a tip for 'great conversation'.

When people have been VILE to me (boyfriends, friends, colleagues) – people I should absolutely, 100 per cent *cut out of my life* – I have instead done all I could to befriend them and make them like me. WHY? Why didn't I learn to be outspoken like

Mum? She got it from Grandma. It can't just be part of my identity to be passive because 'I got that trait from my dad' …

I'm like a grateful dog that comes back for another kick. WELL, NO MORE!

I wander into the kitchen, followed by a hopeful Brian, wagging in anticipation of a treat or two, and open the fridge in search of something calming to cram into my mouth (wine/chocolate/cheese/all three, probably).

My diary entries are sometimes so confronting they make my heart race. I search for my favourite playlist on my phone, aptly named 'Uplift Me' – an eclectic mix of songs from Stevie Wonder to Kate Bush to Jessie J to Lizzo, and my go-to for times like these: Kirk Franklin and his gospel choir.

I'll tell you now, I've never been sure about God, but if anything were going to make me a believer, it would be gospel music. The harmonies, the voices layered together in perfect, swelling waves – I feel them in my chest, in my core, in my heart. It moves through me like light, lifting something inside me that I can't quite name. The sheer joy of it, the raw, soaring power, takes hold of me every time. My dad felt it too.* Somehow, *gospel music* – so far from my Jewish heritage; so far from Dad's stiff-upper-lip, non-Jewish, white-man-born-and-raised-in-Kent-in-the-1940s background; so rooted in a faith neither of us followed – touched him just as it touches me. And in his last few months, sharing it with him became something precious.

---

* Which is funny, really, because he wasn't a musical man. He was an artist, deeply visual. He did let me teach him to play the tenor recorder when I was nine, sitting patiently through my little lessons as if he were the student and I the master. And yet, he could sing – always perfectly in tune, but only ever in the same octave as the person next to him. If he stood beside a bass, he'd rumble away like he belonged in a barbershop quartet. If he was next to a little girl, he'd suddenly be singing in a high, delicate soprano. It was completely unintentional and completely hilarious. And people wonder why I became an impressionist.

Music moves through my family, each of us feeling it in our own way. For Grandma, that same enthusiasm was reserved for classical music; nothing stirred her soul more than Beethoven and Chopin piano concertos – she would be utterly transported by them. My mum is obsessed with Bach, letting his intricate melodies wrap around her like a language she's always understood. For my sister Katy it's Seventies soul funk. Jojo adores female jazz vocalists. And for Auntie Stephie, it's the Beatles – her devotion as fierce as a teenage fangirl's, as if their songs were written just for her. Maybe that's what music does, I muse, feeling the familiar whoosh of endorphins as I vigorously dance around the kitchen and turn the stereo up when Kirk's choir reaches the chorus of 'Hosanna'.*
Music finds its way to the people who need it, in the form they're meant to receive it, and binds us together in ways we don't always realise.

I think back to my young grandma's latest diary entry, to how music was always her refuge – her guitar a lifeline in the bleakest moments, lifting her spirit and those around her. And I acknowledge that in my own diary, at least I'm singing beautifully, even if I'm not standing up for myself. I love how I mention going to Grandma's, knowing I'll be expected to sing – just as she once played for others to lift their spirits. Music carried Rosi through, and now, without question, it carries me too.

As Brian and I share the last piece of Cheddar, I realise with a jolt that almost a year has passed since I first reached out to the German Embassy. I've just been Jewing on with life, the citizenship quest being a mild frustration, which has popped up in the back of my head every now and then as I get to know young Rosi through her diaries. But today, as I reach for the half-empty bottle of Whispering Angel (well, if it's good enough for the Real Housewives …), some-

---

* An absolute BANGER by the way. If you're about to get married, put that on your wedding playlist.

thing tells me to give it one last punt. It's not the bottle, is it? It's not literally whispering to me? As the great philosopher Justin Timberlake put it, I just have this ... 'feeling inside my bones' (although I wouldn't say it's particularly 'electric wavey'). I feel a 'pull' ... some ... magilfoodickdeedum that is telling me to put the wine down (I know! What witchcraft is this?!) and open my laptop. So, although I've checked off all my tasks for the day, I fire off a quick email to your friend and mine, Matilda Koch ...

EMAIL TO: German Embassy
SUBJECT: RE: Citizenship
Wednesday, 3 August 2022, 15:32

Hello,
    Happy New Year.* I hope you're really well. Do you happen to know if the law has changed/come into fruition yet which would recognise my application for German citizenship?
    Kind regards,
    Jess Robinson†

I stand at the open fridge daydreaming (and cooling myself) for so long it reprimands me with high-pitched beeeeep. I hum a major third above. Another ping chimes in – making a perfect triad. I look down at Brian, then realise – it's my email. As I turn to face the screen my mouth falls open.
MAGIC FOODLE DEE DUM!
Matilda's replied!

---

* Happy New Year?! Well, I suppose it is. We haven't spoken since last August.
† Well done me for not putting a kiss. Treat them mean ...

Chapter 7

Diary of Rosi Schul
Sunday, 30 October 1938

I must be strong. How bravely we all behave. But truly, I could howl like a dog.

The warder generously left the cell door open this morning, so that we could walk up and down the corridor as far as the locked iron gate. To us, that casual gesture gave us hope that things were perhaps not as serious as we'd thought and we might be allowed to go home soon. Our mood became somewhat lighter, although the uncertainty nagged at us and made me nervous.

Then names were called and one by one the prisoners left. To go home? At first we thought we'd got our wish. But I will never forget the way the officers shouted out our names. They would sneer and grimace – 'Lieberwitz!' – as though there was a disgusting taste in their mouths. As the Golds were called they were told that they were to be taken to Stuttgart. Now I was alone and I realised that it was hopeless. I would have to go too.

I broke down and wept.

I was called down last. The Commissar was very kind and let me sign my own deportation papers. Then he shook my hand and said, 'Head up, Fraulein. The three boys are safe and may return to the house … for you as their teacher that should make you very happy.'

I explained the situation to the boys, and they were really pleased. But as I gathered up my belongings I felt no joy.

I was driven along the familiar road to Stuttgart in a very smart car. How many times have I travelled this stretch of road on my bicycle? That lovely journey I made with my friends so many times. As we travelled, I looked out of the window. Silently saying goodbye to all the places I knew. Every corner and street reminded me of something. We travelled quickly through a few more streets in Stuttgart and then into a large courtyard inside the prison there – a huge compound. There seemed to be thousands of people. Jews, Jews, Jews, police, onlookers and helpers from the German Jewish community with baskets of food. As I got out of the car Ilse Herz approached me and cried out in shock, 'You too, Rosi?' She hadn't known about my Polish 'roots'. Well! Why would she? She hugged me tightly and, crying, said, 'Don't worry, everything will be all right soon.' I was losing my composure. Everywhere there were familiar faces, crying women, packages, suitcases, children, Gestapo and civilians.

We were ushered into a huge building where I found out that my suitcase containing all my belongings and my beloved guitar had mistakenly been left in Esslingen! There I stood – frozen again – as I had been in that cell – stuck on the wide staircase not knowing what to do with myself – all around me people milling about and crying. Many miserable wailing people pushed past me. I was buffeted from side to side but still I stood, feeling totally lost, not knowing what to do without my case.

Eventually the Commissar took me downstairs to make a telephone call and we discovered that my belongings were on their way. For a long time we waited in front of a huge gate before we were eventually let through into a long corridor where hundreds of people were waiting inside and outside cells for their deportation arrangements.

It was such a shock to see friends and acquaintances from Stuttgart running backwards and forwards carrying and dragging what they could. And whoever saw me exclaimed, 'You as well, Rosi? Oh, God!'

Eventually I was pushed through the gate. In the passageway there were more people standing around with their belongings, others sitting on cases looking defeated, or urgently talking together in groups. Everyone was tense and worried. I soon saw the Gold family and their youngest, little Inge, who looked as stunned as I felt, and stayed near them.

We had time to observe so much – a mixture of tragi-comedy, especially when one saw how many wanted the doctor to pronounce that they were unfit to travel. Suddenly everyone developed a different illness. But the Aryan doctor merely rejected their pleas and the 'invalids' were continually sent out, despite their pretended symptoms. Some people were squashed thirty or forty into a cell – a cell intended for four. Next to me was a poor old lady – so miserable and fragile-looking. She was breathless and her legs buckled at every step, but despite being such a wreck, the doctor had declared her fit to travel too! She moaned relentlessly. She had no clothes, no suitcase, and no people she knew with her.

And so it was, for hundreds of desperate people there.

Diary of Jess Robinson
Wednesday, 1 November 2006

Hello,

OH MY GOD I HATE ANNIKA. I just got off the phone to see whether the Cinderella people are doing any other pantos and she was too busy to talk to me. She passed me to her assistant Octavia who is always REALLY STROPPY. She makes me feel stupid for asking what they've put me forward for. I have a right to know don't I? I hate Octavia. I'd like to send her a pretend death threat. Then she might be a bit nicer to everyone. What a fucking cow bag bitch mother fucker shit head from hell twat witch minger stroppy bitch crappy twat twat twat fuck fuck fuck fuck fuuuuuuuuuuuuucking BIIIIITCH. WHAT IS HER PROBLEM? I HATE HER! I HATE HER! FUCKER.

Obviously I didn't say any of that to her. I just said OK, thank you so much for all your hard work, all lovely and smiley.

COW!

Phew. I needed that.

I have just eaten half a block of cheddar. Naughty.

Time to go to sleep. Well, after I've taken my dishes and mugs down.

It'll be alright. It'll be alright.

I am grateful for my parents.

I am grateful for my arms and legs.

I am OK.

I am lucky.

~~I hate my cellulite.~~

Goodnight.

Speak soon.

Thank you.

Remember this is going to be a positive month.

Love you.

Kiss kiss.

xxxxxxxxxxxx

EMAIL TO: jess_robinsons_grown_up_email_address@aol.com
SUBJECT: RE: Citizenship
Wednesday, 3 August 2022, 15:55

>>TRANSLATE TO ENGLISH? >>

Dear Mrs Robinson,

Lovely to hear from you, happy new year.

I'm very glad you contacted me and even more delighted to tell you that there has been new legislation 'Section 15' and you can now proceed with an application! Any direct descendants of your grandmother are equally eligible according to this law.

Get in touch with me if you need any assistance,

xx*

Best regards

Matilda Koch

Federal Office of Administration Cologne

I read and reread the email ... I can't believe my eyes because, well, firstly, YES! JUSTICE! YES, YES, YES!!!!!

Secondly: how utterly insane/actually magical is it that I sent that email out of the blue – on a whim – at half past three on a Wednesday in August to see if some GERMAN LEGISLATION had been changed. AND IT HAD. AM I A WITCH?????

I feel high. Shall I start emailing every embassy now? Fire them out like drunken texts. 'Oh, hello, Jamaican Consulate, you up? Can I become a citizen, please? Germany's said yes because I'm a legend (and a witch).'

But back to Grandma ... Justice! Sweet Jamaican – I mean German – Justice!

Grandma Rosi: *so* very proud of Germany's cultural heritage; who forever identified and would describe herself as German *before* Jewish; who never lost her accent – not even after living in England for eighty years; who spent all her days in her beloved Motherland,

---

* Two kisses? Surely that's a fireable offence at the German Embassy? Bit keen too ... Matilda Koch? Matilda Koch-Tease more like. Also, I love that she wished me a happy 'new' year back.

until the Nazis chucked her out; who was deeply and irrevocably heartbroken that she wasn't considered a 'proper German', Grandma Rosi could now finally *apply* to be officially recognised as a German.

SCORE!!!!!!!

Except Grandma died in 2018 …

The End.

(Now, where do I pick up my Pulitzer Prize?)

God, I miss Grandma, and now more than ever I feel frustrated that she was never 'recognised' as German.

Oh, Rosi.

My eyes prick at the memory of Grandma, tiny in her bed, which had been moved down to the living room so she could look out through the French doors at her beautiful garden in her final weeks.

Grandma was a few days shy of 103 years old when she died. She did try her best to wait it out. Although she'd tell me that each morning when she woke up, the first thing she'd think was, 'Oh, shit, am I still here?!' before saying in an uncharacteristically small voice, 'Don't get to this age, Jessie. Everything aches.'

Blinking hard, and feeling a shiver as I wonder if it was really *Grandma* who urged me to get in touch with the Embassy again from beyond the grave (or rather, urn), I text the Cool Bitches.

Group Chat: Cool Bitches

Wednesday, 3 August 2022, 16:01

Me: Coooooool Bitchesssss!!

Mum: Why do we have to be called that Jessie?

Me: GOOD NEWS!! The law's changed and we can apply to get our German passports. Whoop Whoop!!!!

Stephie: Why do we need them?

Me: To avoid the airport queues.

Sasha: And be back in the EU!

Stephie: But I don't go anywhere.

Me: We can all apply together. We just have to fill in the forms and provide proof.

Mum: Of what?

Me: That grandma was living in Germany, before she was deported.

Mum: No, but I DO need pickles and birdseed.

Katy: ??

Sasha: Eh?

Mum: Sorry, that was meant for Marywiththeleg.

Me: OK bitches, so when we have lunch on Sunday please bring:
    Passports (plus grandma's),
    Driving licences,
    Birth certificates (plus grandma's),
    It says adoption documents if applicable … (mum, now would be a good time to tell us)
    ALSO marriage certificates (plus Grandma's).
    Grandma's parents' marriage certificate
    WE ALSO NEED Divorce certificates 'if applicable'

Katy: That's all of us then 😂

Me: Yup 🙀
    ALSO 'certificates of descent, and family registers for all ancestors going back to and including the ancestor who was exposed to National Socialist persecution between 1933 and 1945, and had to leave Germany as a result'

Katy: 😱

Me: I know!
    We also have to supply 'Proof that ordinary residence in Germany was established prior to 30 January 1933 and/or proof that they were excluded from acquiring German citizenship and proof of the reason for persecution and the type of persecution to which you or your ancestor were exposed between 1933 and 1945 AND if possible a document showing the date when your ancestor affected by National Socialist persecution took on a foreign citizenship.'

Katy: Blimey!!

Sasha: So much stuff!

Me: Innit! Fuckinell I've got a headache now. It's a bit overwhelming!! Can everyone please check we have all the docs before we meet?

Mum: Birdseed

Chapter 8

Diary of Rosi Schul
Tuesday, 1 November 1938

To see the children sitting and standing around tore at one's heart. Little Inge sat on her case and watched all the turmoil around her in bewilderment. Although there was a special cell for all the children, little Inge stayed with us, clutching her mother's hand. People were running around with baskets of washing, food and drinking water. More and more people recognised me and a hundred times I heard, 'Rosi, you as well?' We stood there for some hours, until eventually we were called forward with our luggage to retrieve our passports.

Downstairs there were green lorries and cars waiting, which were to take us to the railway station. The officials sneered contemptuously as they pointed to us and called out our names one by one. If anyone didn't respond immediately, they roared fiercely. On and on it went, as each person dragged their luggage out. Every person portrayed a tragic picture. I couldn't believe it, and at the same time of course I could – a familiar image of Jewish fate.

We were the last to leave. As we walked down the staircase which led down to a gateway and into the street, I saw many Jews ahead of me, being herded like farm animals. Cattle would be treated more respectfully. About thirty people were 'loaded' into each lorry. Anyone not moving quickly enough was shoved roughly and their luggage thrown in after them. Children screamed, women cried and the Oberkommissar, a pig of a man, cursed and swore as he forced people forward. German onlookers gaped and stared gleefully.

God! It makes me question everything.

It was rainy and cold and the lorry was open on all sides. I felt a lump in my throat as I looked out, trying so hard to hold back my tears, striving to hang on to every memory of my wonderful times in Stuttgart. As we passed the Königstrasse thousands of memories surfaced. Around the corner we passed my favourite ice cream parlour. I felt so helpless.

Eventually we arrived at the main railway station. As we were pushed into the huge entrance hall we were confronted by crowds who had followed our trucks and who now formed lines on either side of us. These spectators were both hostile Nazis and sympathetic German Jews. We had to pass through this humiliating 'human corridor' and some recognised me and called out my name. Others greedily took photographs of this ordeal.

We finally reached the platform and I half climbed and was half pushed into a train carriage with the Golds and some of my cousins. Three Gestapo men supervised as about twenty-five of us settled down. It was very cramped, but my case was so heavy and I was at least relieved that I could finally put it down. As I looked through the window at the familiar and beautiful Grand Station I thought I would go mad with yearning. And as the train finally began to move, at last I let my tears flow – something I had not allowed myself to do all that day.

It is simply a human need to cry – and the satisfaction of crying gives one an enormous relief. One should always let people cry at such times and not console or stifle them.

Everyone was shocked to see me break down. Jokel Horowitz did not recognise his usually cheerful, fun-loving cousin, but I couldn't hold myself together any longer. Yes, there were a good deal of tears in the carriage.

There was a very old couple sitting opposite me and the woman wailed and cried incessantly, 'They wouldn't even let us take a second shirt with us – we weren't allowed to take anything when they summoned us in the night.' I heard the old man answer her over and over again, 'How can you complain? It is a sin. Haven't we lived in contentment and peace long enough? Just be grateful that we were given it for so long.' Then he looked across at me and spoke in an unbelievably comforting way. This was a poor man who had just lost everything and who probably only owned a silver-plated Shabbat candlestick and a gold watch. He had only been able to bring a shoebox containing a few apples and some bread and butter. Unthinkable! He took out one apple and, cutting it, offered me half. This kindness from one who had so little made me feel so ashamed and I stopped crying.

For a while I played my guitar and we sang, which served as a distraction as much as a comfort. The SS men looked disapproving, but it felt good to rebel! Eventually, though, I couldn't stop my mind from wandering back to Esslingen and racing with questions. What would be going on there now? And where were my mama and papa, and my siblings Regina, Menne, Delli and the others? I hoped and prayed I would see them again in Poland. Where would we really end up and what would happen to us all? My thoughts were interrupted again and again. That poor old woman with the weak legs was sitting all alone with absolutely nothing. 'What shall I do?' she cried. 'Why go on living?' It was the same everywhere.

Everyone had a story to tell about how they had been picked up and what they had been told. Most of them were given absolutely no information about what was to happen to them. Some unscrupulous policeman had told a family they would be back home in an hour – and other such lies. Only later would they realise that their lives were to change forever.

I talked with Ruth Gold as little Inge, now exhausted, slept on her lap, and then with one of the SS men who seemed very decent – but of course it didn't cost him anything. He thought that we would be back in Germany within two or three days. He said that this was only a formality to prevent Polish Jews from becoming 'stateless'. All we had to do, he said, was to get our passports validated and all would be back to normal. He told us that Germany was acting on behalf of Polish Jews so that we could move between the countries more freely. He continued, saying that even though these and many other measures were being taken against the Jews, there were many Germans who disapproved but had to remain silent. His words made me feel quite light-hearted and I could finally breathe easily. We would return to Esslingen, I felt sure of it.

On that journey, I also met a wonderful man who is the owner of a warehouse in Stuttgart. His name is Tanne. He told me he is thirty-six years old and married with four young children. He is very handsome and engaging and the time flew by with interesting conversation. Although he was travelling with other people, he kept returning to continue discussing religion, relationships, music and literature. I looked at him with burning eyes – taking everything in. I wanted to remember his face forever. His wife and children are still in Stuttgart. He is of course very hopeful he will see them again.

In Leipzig we had a longer stop and the German Jewish community brought food parcels to our train. They kindly took our letters to send on to our families. I had written to Herr Rothschild, Samuel and home.

Soon we were travelling again – further and further away from my beloved Esslingen.

Mrs Gold was very kind and we shared our food with one another, agreeing that we should stick together when we arrived in Poland.

We were extremely tired when we arrived at the Polish border Neu-Bentschen. The journey had taken about 20 hours in all. When the train stopped, the SS officers, who had become quite friendly by this point, assured us that the officials just had to sign our papers and then we would be on our way – back to Germany again. For a while the mood lifted. However, things changed when the SS alighted and discussed the situation with German officials waiting on the platform. The attitude of those German officials was despicable towards us. They ordered that all windows were to be closed and threatened and scolded anyone who tried to open them even a little way. Their inspection of us was very superficial and when they checked our passports and suitcases, we realised that we could have taken anything we wanted. However, they were strict about our money. Each of us was allowed no more than ten marks.

After a very long and gruelling wait back in our airless carriage, we are now finally moving across the border into Zbąszyń. Germany lies behind us.

It is best not to wonder what will happen now; if I do, I will not survive the anxiety. I must keep my composure.

Diary of Jess Robinson
Thursday, 2 November 2006

Everything I want to have:

- A flat in a lovely area
- An old pink Beetle VW
- A lovely figure*
- A brilliant career
- A record deal
- A dog
- A boyfriend†
- A circle of friends like Friends or Bridget Jones's Diary where we go out every week.
- Money in the bank and regular performing work
- Piano
- Printer‡
- Smeg fridge and retro toaster

To Do:

- Go blonde
- DIET

I went to see a psychic!!!!!!!!!
    Her name is Betty. It cost £30.00 …
    First I had to make a wish:
    So I wished to get another job

---

* Why am I writing this like a ninety-year-old gay man? 'What a lovely figure!'
† Love that my priorities were Dog >Boyfriend. As it should be.
‡ This tailed off, didn't it? How many other people can say they wished for 'a record deal' and 'a printer' in the same day.

And to have a successful career and play leading roles on tour or something. I know that's two wishes and not as specific as she had recommended, but my agent said we should cast the net wide. Now I'm just worried that the universe will decide to give me another <u>waitressing</u> job and not an <u>acting</u> job. Or maybe it will be confused and not give me <u>anything</u>!

In the main reading the first thing Betty said was that my grandpa is ill.

As I never met grandpa Tom, I think that must definitely be Grandpa Jules. He died in July. ACCURATE!! I mean, you have to be a bit ill to die don't you?!* So she wasn't wrong.

I do miss him a bit. I wish I'd known him better when I was younger. We sort of missed each other in a way. Just as I was getting interested in performing, he had sort of lost interest in everything. He was a nice man. He was very gentle and I liked the way he smelled. Sort of minty and like he'd just had a bubble bath.

Anyway, I recorded the session and I'm copying it out now. Actually it was an hour. So I'll just do notes.

Looking at overall picture:
Stop worrying. Still going to get my dream.

That's good. Which one though? Hopefully I'm not <u>literally</u> going to get my dream, cos I had a really weird one about Pat Sharp last night.

Property:
I'm going to move! I may get a loan. Going to buy an old house one day. There's an older woman in my life. She is a bossy Irish Catholic. She is someone who's in charge of paying me. I bet that's my agent Annika. Although I don't know her religion. She does shout a lot.

---

* That's wisdom right there, kids.

THE DEVIL CARD

I was worried when this came up, but she said 'this isn't such a bad card. It just means a couple of bad things will happen soon', (which has scared me), 'but if you dance and throw yourself into the music it will be good'. I was about to ask her to explain, and ask her what bad things, but she interrupted me and said '<u>You must lose weight!</u>'

The longer I have my hair and the thinner I am, the better fortune I will have.

She said I have a European face and I could be Muslim.*

She said I often wear primary colours. I'm not sure I do, but I don't want to have wasted my money, so I'm now wearing Mum's new red cardigan from Hemel Market. I hope she doesn't mind.

She said Grandma and Grandpa were very close and my grandma crossed water to marry. She said grandma wants me to wear the necklace she gave me for good fortune. I think this must be grandma Rosi, because I never met Dad's mum. Grandma Rosi hasn't given me a necklace yet, but maybe she will if I ask her. I won't say what for though because I don't think she believes in 'good fortune'.

(P.s. Going to hers for tea tomorrow and taking my nail varnish so I can paint her nails. Mum said she won't want me to, but I think she'll like it.)

She said I am going to get my wish on the 7th and I should look forward to the 7th of each month!

My lucky number is 6. SO look forward to the 6th of the month. Also 15th because $1 + 5 = 6$ also 24th because $2 + 4 = 6$. So that's the 6th, 15th, 24th and 7th. I asked 'if my wishes are on the 7th, would they also be on the 25th (because $2 + 5 = 7$)? And the 16th (because $1 + 6 = 7$)?' But she said 'No.'

---

* Makes a change from too Jewish.

So that was the reading. Lots to think about here!!! £30 well spent I think!!

Love Jess xxxx

P.S. because mum complained about the man who groped me at Stocks, they've given all my shifts to someone else!!! She's cross, but I hate it there, so I don't care.

P.P.S. I miss Grandpa Jules now. I bet Grandma does too. I'll give her a call.

———

As I said at the time: £30 well spent ... Honestly! It's amazing what I chose to believe back then, in my utter self-centred desperation to have my idea of a 'perfect' life.

Rosi's diary is full of questions that ping-pong around my mind as I crawl down the M25 on my way to see the Cool Bitches that Sunday. Where were her parents at this point? The uncertainty of whether she'd ever see them again must have been unbearable. And what about her siblings? So many to keep track of! I recite their names aloud – it starts to sound like a bleak version of 'Mambo No. 5' – as I glance at Brian in the rearview mirror – grinning, panting, sniffing the air through the cracked window, proudly settled in his black velvet doggy car seat – a birthday gift from Mum for her *only* grand-dog ...

I roll my eyes, cringing at my old diary entry. I was so consumed with whether the universe would grant me a 'Smeg fridge and a retro toaster' that I didn't stop to think how lucky I was to have a fridge at all. At twenty-three, I was obsessing over my weight and debating whether or not a red cardigan would help manifest my wildly vacuous dreams. At twenty-three, Rosi was being wrenched from her life and praying she'd see her family again. Did they ever get the chance to sit down and write a silly little wish list like I did? It's humbling. And, honestly, it's shameful. I wish I could go back, shake my younger self – tell her to stop worrying about hair dye and start paying attention to the stories that really matter.

And more than anything, I think, as a whiff of something deeply unpleasant hits me from the back seat and I frantically wind the window down, scowling at Brian – who is the picture of innocence – I wish Rosi had grown up in a world where her biggest dilemma was whether or not to get a dog.

The chocolate eclairs and shit-yourself strong coffee sit in the middle of Mum's kitchen table. I'm glad of the sugar and caffeine as I drag my eyes over the intimidating stack of paperwork waiting to be tackled …

For each applicant, a seven-page form needs to be completed in German – a language that Mum and Stephie grew up speaking at home but that my sister Katy and I don't speak, despite downloading Duolingo *four days ago* (I mean, how hard can it be?). Ever since, we've been joyfully exchanging what we deem essential German expressions in a flurry of daily texts. So we are disappointed to discover that one of our most crucially important lines, *Deine Schlange ist sehr gross* ('your snake is very big'), has no place on the citizenship application form. Gutted.

The process is not simple; in fact, as Auntie Stephie puts it, it's 'a bloody ball ache, man!' but we're in high spirits. We soon fall into our usual roles, with Mum as headmistress, my big sister Katy playing 'perfect prefect', my niece, Sasha, doing her own thing and finishing before all of us, Auntie Stephie and I banished to the 'naughty table', and my lovely sister Jojo now dozing on the sofa with Brian (dog – not deceased dad) licking her socks. She only wakes when Mum scolds us for wasting the printer ink as we churn out more forms, having recklessly ditched our pencils and gone straight in with the black biro.

I do feel I show a huge degree of maturity and restraint by not writing '*Ja, bitte!*' next to '*Geschlecht?*' but the fun begins to wear off during the 'Previous Addresses' section – and I have to 'continue on a separate page'. I'm amazed at how many old postcodes are still etched in my brain. Maybe that's why I'm so stupid: there's no room in my head for anything else! Making a mental note to store new postcodes up my arse, I turn to the 'previous names' section and any remaining gaiety (yeah, I said gaiety) fizzles out. The exercise brings back memories of Practice Husband (his actual name still escapes me) and the whole debacle of my eighteen-month marriage.

The alien surname that was once linked to mine makes me want to rip out the page … or at least the precious few remaining hairs on his head. HA! As much as I make fun of it, the echoes are still physically painful in my chest. Shame and heartbreak and self-loathing are all muddled into one knot of hurt. It's such a mad story, you wouldn't believe it if it was a book; a true story of heartbreak, hilarity and shock, and the consequences of being so in love with love that you gaslight yourself into pretending you're happy. In fact, maybe I *will* put it into a book one day … The title? *My Grandmother Fled the Nazis but She Hated You More.*

I hadn't realised how important my 'real' name was until I wasn't allowed to take my old surname back as soon as the marriage ended. Seeing *Mrs Jessica Sophie Practice Husband* on my bank cards and passport was unbearable. It felt like a jibe. A surname I'd once adopted so enthusiastically was now a badge of failure and shame. I had needed my old self back so desperately that I paid to become 'Robinson' again by deed poll, unwilling to wait the two long years it would otherwise have taken to legally reclaim *me* …

Doing today's task sitting around Mum's kitchen table feels so right. This place is a constant in our family's turbulent history of laughter, arguments, sorrow and celebrations. This is where I did my homework, cried my eyes out over a school crush who'd kissed my best friend, applied to reclaim my surname – and now here I am, filling out paperwork for another new identity.

This is also where I told my family I was getting divorced.

People snap pictures of memorable occasions, right? Well, my dad took one of me filling in my divorce petition in 2015. And here's a real coincidence – I swear we didn't plan it, but that day, my sister Katy showed up on the doorstep, all red eyes and quivering lips because she'd just left her husband too. BONKERS.

Left to right: Katy (tearful), Mum (drunk) and me (manic). The photo is blurry, but that's part of its charm; you get to see us exactly as we saw each other: through a haze of tears and brandy. Dad's lack of focus turned out to be spot on. Consider it immersive.

And that's why, in this picture, Mum is *totally* shitfaced. Absolutely blotto. That bottle of brandy? Full five minutes earlier.

I pick up Grandma's old passport and a rush of memories flood my mind. I'm taken back to Grandma's table in Hendon, to a particular afternoon, just a few days after that picture was taken …

We were in the morning room, sunlight streaming in, illuminating dust particles drifting lazily in the air. It was a few days after Grandma's one-hundredth birthday. The shelves were filled with greetings cards and a couple of sagging champagne bottle balloons still valiantly bobbed in the breeze from the open window. In front of us were slices of slightly stale sponge cake, marzipan fruits and Zimtstern, six months past their sell-by date. The air smelled of cinnamon, geraniums and acetone from Grandma's bottle of nail-polish remover.

Our ritual was in full swing.

As was tradition, Grandma showed me the crack on her left thumbnail. We examined it together, and I tried, once again, to fix it with nail glue. We both knew it would never hold. It was just a part of her now, like her *inventive cookery*. That day's lunchtime concoction had been cottage cheese, which she'd mixed with taramasalata and spooned onto bridge rolls – a challenging texture, and the flavour … well, let's just say the cottage cheese could have done without the grated egg.

The family were still basking in the glory of Grandma's birthday party, which had been a huge success. Mum played the piano, and Jojo (who back then was almost unafflicted by her Huntington's), Katy and I performed 'Mr Sandman' in three-part harmony, having changed the lyrics to 'Rosi Ruben' and making the song all about her life. Nieces and nephews from Grandma's long-gone siblings had flown from all over the world to celebrate the centenarian. The only person missing was Practice Husband.

Unbeknownst to Grandma and the wider family, a few days before the party – just hours before the brandy picture – I'd returned early from my *make or break* (it was *break*) holiday with Practice Husband. The days that followed had been busy. As well as helping to arrange Grandma's birthday (to which Practice Husband was no longer invited), I had seen my therapist, visited a divorce lawyer, filled out the paperwork and moved out of our flat – all with Mum's practical help and Auntie Stephie's 'spiritual assistance'; magic spells and white sage smudging included! A little like *not* announcing a pregnancy at a friend's engagement party, the Cool Bitches had kept the break-up secret from Grandma until after her birthday, not wanting to steal her thunder.

But now here we were, sitting at her table, and I knew she knew. *Why had Katy taken Sasha into the garden?*

I gulped.

And she knew I knew she knew.

Where had Mum and Stephie gone?

I held my breath.

I could feel her waiting for me to spill …

Shit.

Where could I even begin? Would she need to know *everything*? Her face morphed from shock to sorrow to disbelief as I told it all – the signs I had ignored. She didn't recognise this version of me, and neither did I. Her disappointment was palpable; Grandma didn't suffer fools. But instead of the reproach I was expecting, she hugged me, her soft arms enveloping me as she kissed my head.

Later, before I left, she held out a cheque in her freshly manicured hand, saying, 'You will always have your egg for breakfast.' It was her way of reassuring me that there were still things in life I could count on.

That moment stayed with me – not just for the shame and pain, but for the love she offered when I felt so lost.

After Grandma died, I noticed a crack on my own thumbnail in the same place as hers. I think I inherited it. No amount of nail glue will allow it to grow back normally, and I don't think it ever will. In fact, I hope it stays forever. It's a daily reminder of her resilience. Her love. A physical mark connecting us across time.

And now, at the risk of sounding stoned, I just want to say: kitchen tables have seen so much, man! 'Fly on the wall' doesn't quite capture it. I think 'crumb on the table' might be better. Mum's and Grandma's tables have been witness to love, loss, laughter, tears, secrets and screaming matches … They hold the story of our family in every grain and scratch. Just as I carry Grandma's crack in my thumbnail, these tables hold imprints of our journey … God, who am I? Pass the sick bucket.

We finally complete our forms in German … well, except for Auntie Stephie, who has so many scribbles and crossings-out on

Grandma receives a card from the Queen on her 100th birthday.

her form that we have to print out a third copy. Mum stands over her and squeaks, 'Write it out in light pencil! No, *don't* press so hard. Right, now go over it in pen. NO! Wait for the ink to dry before you rub it out. Oh, for goodness' sake, Stephie! Now you've made a smudge! Right, give it to me.'

Congratulating everyone on our achievement, I collapse on the sofa, hugging Jojo, who grins and points into the garden where Brian is in a large hole (dog, not deceased dad).* But then Katy

---

* Dad is in a large hole by the church so Mum can visit him every time she plays the organ.

suddenly gasps. I leap up and plant myself in front of the window to block Mum's view, thinking Katy's about to dob me in for letting my dog run wild. At the same moment Stephie and Sasha glance in horror at Mum and then down at the carpet beneath Katy, assuming there must be ink, or spilled brandy – both DREADFUL offences. Either would send Mum into total panic, followed by angry huffing and a lot of frantic rushing back and forth with a damp cloth while scolding us for being clumsy and disrespecting her home in a voice so high-pitched it could summon every dog in the village. Including Brian, who trots into the kitchen proudly holding a tampon applicator in his mouth (deceased Dad, not dog … Joke!)

But it's not the carpet. It's not Brian (dad or dog). Katy's gasp signals something far worse … My sister breaks the news that we haven't finished after all. Not even close. We still have to fill in our police forms to prove we're not criminals before we can go any further in the process. Just as we were starting to relax, it lands like a thud.* Deflated, I heave a sigh and Mum, who has found the form-filling 'irritating and noisy', immediately cracks open the brandy.†

Annoying, but fine … right? Apparently not fine, judging by Auntie Stephie's face as she promptly stands up and stomps into the garden – where she nearly falls down Brian's freshly dug hole.

Twenty-five minutes pass, and Stephie is still puffing on a ciggy by the back door. Why is she still out there? The remaining Cool Bitches remain crammed around the kitchen table, now three-quarters through the bottle of brandy.

---

* I realise I'm describing paperwork with the breathless tension of a political thriller, but to me, filling out a form feels like defusing a bomb … Am I bad at admin or is it cos I went to stage school?

† WARNING: if you ever meet my mum, be sure keep any naked flames away from her or she'll go up like a Christmas pudding! Also, I wonder how many citizenship forms have been completed when totally pissed.

The 'Previous and Pending Criminal Convictions' section is more fun than the title suggests, with Katy and Sasha inventing imaginary crimes we've all committed.

I lean back as I recount one of my favourite memories from when I was twelve: Mum and I were on our way to the supermarket when she was pulled over for not wearing a seatbelt.

The young policeman came up to the car and Mum leant out of the window, smiled flirtatiously and in her *most* seductive voice, by way of an excuse, said to the policeman, 'I'm so sorry, officer, my breasts are very tender.' And the policeman was so flustered, he actually let her off! *Classic Mum.* So flapsy.* So naughty. So pleased with herself. In fact, every time I tell this story, she nods along, grinning, and proudly says, 'Yes, I did!'

What a cool criminal bitch (and dangerous driver) she is. She's always been unapologetically herself; I bet *she* wouldn't have taken an ecstasy pill in her twenties to impress a boy. Her confidence has always been inspiring (and often baffling). It's like she has a shield that makes embarrassment and shame bounce right off her.

A gust of wind catches our attention. Auntie Stephie stands in the doorway, smelling of fresh air and cigarettes. The room falls silent. Then she takes a deep breath and shamefacedly drops the bombshell: 'So listen, man, I'm pulling out of the process. I don't need this. I don't go anywhere, do I? Just the stables and my boat, really, so I don't need a German passport, do I? And anyway, I'm never gonna be accepted as a German citizen cos … well, man … I … I got a criminal conviction.' We all gasp (apart from Jojo, who laughs) and look at each other in shock. Our seventy-year-old auntie stares down at her feet like a little girl.

---

* I'm hoping if I use the word 'flapsy' enough, the youth will adopt it and it'll soon be a new word added to the *Collins English Dictionary*. I'm also not suggesting Mum presented her flapsies to get out of a ticket.

As if possessed by divine justice – or perhaps just the brandy – Mum leaps to her feet, pointing at Stephie, and barks, 'CONFESS!' The force of it makes us jump (apart from Jojo, who laughs again), and causes Mum, who has evidently surprised *herself*, to get the hiccups.

Stephie, not taking her eyes off her size-three red stiletto ankle boots, eventually admits, 'I shoplifted a tin of cat food.'

Is that *it*?? I'm a bit disappointed, honestly. I was at least hoping for lewd graffiti or joyriding, but Mum looks livid and half hiccups, half hisses, 'Wha-t are you *hic* talk-ing *hic* about??' Katy, caught in the crossfire, wipes a fleck of Mum's angry spittle out of her eye. The atmosphere fizzes with anticipation. I can tell Mum is about to launch into a high-pitched lecture about how, at nearly eighty years old, Stephie should know better and when is her little sister finally going to start acting like an adult? But before Mum can unleash her tirade, Stephie admits that this heinous crime, carried out at none other than the Axminster Spar, took place in … the Seventies.

Talk about an anticlimax. Stole a tin of cat food?! It's like a cross between *Les Mis* and *Cats* …*

Mum dissolves into laughter, her hiccups worsening, as we imagine Stephie's daring cat-food caper, and as Katy assures our brilliantly bonkers auntie that it'll probably be OK. We finish our forms and, slightly tipsily – OK, we're hammered now – start choosing our passport-sized photos to include with the application.

---

* Which is quite a good idea for a crossover musical – *Les Chats*. I'll pitch that to my agent later.

COOL CRIMINAL BITCHES MUGSHOTS

Katy: A model citizen with great hair and dungarees, which shows a willingness to get stuck in. What a valuable member of the community – she will plough the fields and milk the cows.

Sasha: Pretty *and* cool? What a bitch.

Jackie 'Tender-tits' Robinson: Do NOT feed this woman brandy.

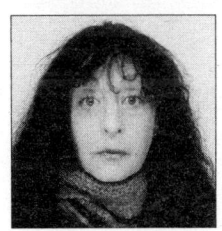

Auntie Stephie: The Axminster Cat (food) Burglar herself! And by the look of the picture she's chosen, this was the *actual* mugshot taken at the time of the offence in the Seventies. What filter is that?!

Dollydumps Robinson: The Cool Bitches Ringleader.

It must be the brandy (and definitely not my ego) that makes me opt for this dead-eyed, highly airbrushed headshot. Such a sinister smile. Am I trying to *make* the police think I'm a drug pusher? I look like a sociopath. This expression says, 'I know where the bodies are hidden, but I want immunity, £100,000,000 and a pink helicopter before I tell you.' Or maybe it's just the face I used to make at Grandma Rosi, while holding her homemade pickled herring, sweetcorn and squirty cream concoction in my mouth, as I nodded and made 'Mmm, delicious' sounds, willing myself to swallow. I think I'd be excellent on *I'm a Celebrity ... Get Me Out of Here* – oh, what's that, Ant and Dec, you want me to eat a buffalo anus? Easy, mate, I grew up on Grandma Rosi's cottage cheese and chopped liver roulade.*

We seal the envelopes, and I can't help but reflect on how, across three generations, we've all had our run-ins with the law: my young grandma locked in a cell, Mum's tender breasted seatbelt evasion, Stephie's cat food heist and my own misadventure as a drug dealer.†

---

* She did not care about mixing meat and milk.
† Oh, and Mum, if you're reading this, I'm REALLY sorry, and I never did it again. Scout's honour.

Chapter 9

Diary of Rosi Schul
Tuesday, 1 November 1938 – Evening

So here we are in Zbąszyń. We are squeezed together like pigs in a pigsty covered in dirt and stinking of body odour. No one was allowed to leave our train for a very long time.

There were other stationary trains on the tracks to our left and right. One from Berlin and one from Karlsruhe. We are able to shout across to each other and have conversations.

We recognised friends, and after a while we dared to get out of the carriages and get some fresh air, walking about on the platforms. Some people fetched water and some even tried to ask for it in Polish. 'Proszę o wodę.'

Handsome Tanne ran to and fro and fetched water for many people. He became the 'leader' of our carriage. He could speak Polish and made himself busy. His mother asked me for some water, so I ran 100 metres in the rainy evening twilight to a pump for her. Tanne bumped into me and then accompanied me to the pump. While walking back together he suddenly said, 'I'm so pleased I met you here. You are such a dear young thing and like a ray of sunshine on the journey.' I was completely taken aback. It lifted me.

Soon orders were given for us all to gather our belongings from the carriages and officially alight from the train, which was to be completely evacuated. Then the trains left. And there we were – standing on the platforms in the pitch black, surrounded by our belongings.

There were crowds on the platforms – thousands – old and young, cases, parcels – everything in chaos. Everywhere people stood in groups talking agitatedly. I remained with the Horowitzes and Golds. We believed that more trains would soon come and we would be returned to Germany. We heard that thousands of people had arrived during the course of the day and they were lodged in barracks, stables and station waiting rooms. On the platform itself there were at least two thousand – standing, sitting or lying down. It was about 8 p.m. and we had not slept for two nights. This would be the third. It was freezing and I felt lucky to have my coat. Many didn't have as much as me. People tried to sleep in any place and any position they could find. It was gruesome to see the children lying there in the wet and cold, wrapped in their parents' coats and blankets and staring incomprehensibly into the chaos of the night. Children, children, children – what went on in their heads? How would these experiences imprint themselves in their psyches? It broke my heart. I sat down next to a few and told them stories.

Every now and then I walked about with Ruth Gold through the huge crowds all waiting … waiting for what?? No one knew anything, but everyone wanted to go back to Germany. What a tragic irony! Hadn't we been repressed and persecuted enough there? No – obviously not.

Somebody discovered a secret route from the platforms into the barracks and waiting rooms, which had been officially closed. One could sneak into them. I heard that there were many who had been deported from Hannover. Thinking maybe Mama, Papa and Ruthi were there, I set out to search for them. But one glance into one of the waiting rooms shook me to the core. There must have been a thousand people in the one room.

It was stiflingly hot and stinking. People slept on top of one another, little children screamed and mothers cried. People kept fainting or becoming hysterical. All night I searched and searched but found only acquaintances from my home town. They told me that there were others from Hannover locked up in the dark stables and barracks. I hope my mother and father are in there, although at the moment it is impossible to get in. The stables will not be unlocked until morning.

I must admit I am struggling to push through this hell of desperation during this night – a night of great misery. Oh yes, how strong one has to be just to bear it all! What will happen to us all? Where is my family?

Diary of Jess Robinson
Monday, 6 November 2006

Hello! Lots to tell and I shouldn't be telling you now – should go to sleep.

OK I will bye.

I CAN'T SLEEP.

It's like psychic Betty said. Everything has changed!!!! Rabbi and I put in an offer today on a house and it has been accepted !!! We went to visit this fantastic house in Finchley Central. Mum was saying we'd never do it but tomorrow I'm going to see a mortgage broker. I can get a 100% mortgage apparently?! WOW!!!!!!!! I just have to take my last pay slip with me and instead of saying it's what I earn per month, I just have to say it's what I earn each week. Mum said I should put on a lot of makeup and wear my Jane Norman low V neck top. She said I should wear my hair down in a side parting so the guy doesn't ask too many questions about my income.*

---

* This worked by the way. Mortgages pre-2008 were absolutely mad.

FLAPS CROSSED!!!!!!!!!!!!!!!!!!!!!!!!!!!!!!!!!!!!!
Also I have an audition coming up, so I need to practise Amarillo tomorrow.
Must sleep.
Love you, bye!

Reading Rosi's diary entry stopped me in my tracks.

I don't think I ever truly understood what Grandma's deportation entailed. Not the filth, the chaos, the children lying on cold, wet platforms. Not the shouting, the waiting, the bone-deep exhaustion. The total desperation. Mum and Auntie Stephie didn't really dwell on this part of her story either. So I never truly realised how bad it was. Not until now. Not until reading it in her own words.

Whenever Grandma Rosi spoke about that time, she recalled events through, what our friend Alan Reich, who spent hours interviewing her, refers to as, 'Rosi-tinted glasses'. I think Grandma genuinely downplayed what she went through, feeling ashamed as she dismissed her experience, comparing it to that of those who didn't survive. She never ended up in a concentration camp, and because of that, she never saw herself as someone who had truly suffered. She framed it all as a strange sort of adventure, and if we ever dug too deeply, she'd reply with a shrug: 'Ach! Life is rosy!' Life is rosy. What stoicism. What bravery. What pride. Conversely, I once updated my Facebook status to say I'd lost my coat on a bus. Oh, Jess, you idiot.

Now, I am struck by the realities she faced. Initially, I imagined her to be stuck in a desolate wasteland, or an enclosed area, like a big open prison ... but I have been completely mis-imagining it. Zbąszyń is a town! I feel stupid and ignorant. I heard Grandma talk about Zbąszyń often when I was younger. Why was I so up my own arse that I didn't look it all up – or enquire, rather than just listen and nod. Arrogant, spoilt idiot. I'm so naive. I went on a political podcast once (I'd say yes to the opening of an envelope), and when I was asked my opinion on the conflict in the Middle East, I said, 'Why can't people just be nice to each other?' HELLO?!!

I now know (because I have looked it up – at the age of thirty-nine (!)) – that Zbąszyń possesses a rich history and dates back to 1231, becoming part of Poland in 1918. In 1938, before the *Polenaktion*, it had a population of about 5,400, including, according to the Holocaust Research Project, around 360 Germans and only 52 Jews.

Perhaps because of Grandma's 'life is rosy' attitude when she spoke about her journey to Poland, I hadn't taken on board the grim reality for so many Jews – believing that because she had made it there relatively unscathed, it would have been as 'civilised' for everyone else. Am I MAD?

On Friday, 28 October 1938, Jews of Polish nationality were rounded up across Germany and forced to cross the Polish border illegally. The arrests were chillingly precise – the majority of which were coordinated simultaneously in cities and towns across the whole of Germany, with the cold, bureaucratic efficiency the Nazis had already become known for.*

The Jewish Museum Berlin indicates that 17,000 Jews were expelled from Germany during this 'operation'. Many were taken at night, given no time to pack, and were forced to leave their homes immediately.

The streets of the towns they passed through were lined with people watching the horrific exodus. Many travelled by train to the Polish border town, but huge groups also arrived on foot, often

---

* Interesting fact: Rosi was one of the 'lucky' few to be arrested the evening before (27 October) and put in a local holding police-station cell overnight to be able to join the others the next morning for the trains leaving for Poland throughout the day.

subjected to beatings as they were forced across the border onto Polish soil. For those on foot, the journey to the border was brutal, with SS men whipping those who lagged behind, shouting at them to run.

So, Zbąszyń was (and still is) not a fenced-off 'area', but a bustling little town, suddenly inundated with thousands of desperate people needing food, shelter and medical care. This led, as documented in Rosi's diary, to utter chaos for both the refugees and the local community.

Despite their own struggles, though, many of the Polish population did their best to offer what they could to these uninvited guests.*

On top of this, the Polish government wasn't exactly rolling out the red carpet for these Jewish outcasts. The political landscape was fraught. On the one hand, there was a sense of solidarity and sympathy among many Poles for the plight of the Jews, and on the other, there were many who saw them as a burden or even a threat … Hmmm, sounds familiar, doesn't it?

In spite of all this, Jewish organisations and local authorities in Zbąszyń worked tirelessly – setting up makeshift shelters and handing out food.

I can't help but draw parallels to the current refugee crisis unfolding across the world. Just like the Jewish refugees, who were abruptly expelled from Germany and found themselves in Zbąszyń, so many people today are fleeing war and persecution, arriving in towns and cities that are often unprepared for them. And the locals are thrust into situations where they have to decide how to respond to these sudden and overwhelming needs.

In Zbąszyń, it seems that the Polish people did their best. I wish we heard more stories in the media of the acts of kindness that take

---

* And 'uninvited guests' isn't another of Grandma's euphemisms for her period, by the way.

place. It might inspire more of us to do the same ... But there I go again. Reductive. Naive. Childish. 'Aww, let's just be nice to each other.'

And what was I doing at twenty-three, while Rosi was sleeping on train platforms and scouring overcrowded barracks for her parents? While she was being uprooted, displaced and cast out of her country, I was just beginning to put down roots – to find my footing in the world.

And now here we are, three generations later, waiting to see if we're of good enough character to gain citizenship from the country that so brutally chucked 'our kind' out.

Group Chat: Cool Bitches

Saturday, 13 August 2022, 14:16

Mum: Jessiepoops, any news on our criminal approvals?

Stephie: Am I going to prison maaaan?

Me: I got an email yesterday saying they'll take 20 working days to process the applications.

Sasha: We sent them first class on Monday, so they should be with them by now.

Mum: SPF! So slow!

Me: It's FFS.

Mum: Sorry SFS

Mum: F

Me: That'll do mum, we get the gist.

Katy: So shall we book the Embassy visit so we can hand it all in together? It's in Belgravia.

Me: Yes!! Shall we make a day of it? We could meet before for a coffee?

Katy: and then go for lunch after?

Me: Yay!

Katy: Yay!

Sasha: Yay!

Mum: Oh no! I don't want to drive all that way.

Katy: Get the train?

Stephie: I haven't been on the train for years man.

Mum: There aren't any humans at the ticket office in Tring.

Sasha: You can buy tickets online.

Me: Stop being such old ladies!!

Mum: We ARE old ladies.

Me: Well you're not allowed to be.

Katy: Come on it'll be fun!

Me: 🙈 🙈

Stephie: Who are they then?

Mum: Us.

Katy: I'll call you tomorrow and we can get the tickets sorted OK?

Mum: Achhhh!

Mum: Yes. Keep Fit tomorrow at 10am and then pub?

Stephie: Eh what, guv'nor??

Mum: Oops sorry.

Mum: Yes. Keep Fit tomorrow at 10am and then pub?

Katy: 🙈

Me: Wrong group mum!

Mum: Yes. Keep Fit tomorrow at 10am and then pub?

Mum: Oh SS

Stephie: What's happening???

Mum: Yes, but I strained my wrist last time.

Stephie: Ooh err, Missus!

Sasha: 💀

Me: Ignore mum. LET'S SORT DATES FOR THE EMBASSY!!

Our group chats are *always* like this ... And don't get me started on voice notes. Sometimes I think it's easier to drive the two hours to my mum's house to ask a quick question than it is to do it over text.

Chapter 10

Diary of Rosi Schul
Tuesday, 2 November 1938

At last this morning the stable doors were unlocked. I rushed in excited and hopeful to find my family. A terrible smell hit me! But as I searched among the huge crowd, I finally saw Papa and Grandma, along with all the Schul uncles and cousins.

Outside the stables a soup kitchen was opened, and hundreds of us milled around it.

Refugees queue at the soup kitchen in Zbąszyń, October 1938.

We spent that night in the filthy, stinking barn, lying on damp straw, everyone squashed together like animals, not human beings ... Once we were in, the doors were locked and we couldn't get out till morning. Large sheets of material had been hung from the rafters to divide the space for 'privacy'. My eighty-eight-year-old grandmother was so proud and dignified, she refused to lie down on the straw, instead opting to sit upright on her small suitcase all night! I looked around me at the desperate situation. There was so much sorrow; weeping and wailing in the foul-smelling, stifling barn, it was difficult to breathe. In the night two people died of heart attacks! Horrific. I felt so frightened. The reality of our situation hit me over and over again. A night from hell.

This morning when we were let out, we had some watery soup and then spent the whole day walking among six to eight thousand Jews. They filled the overcrowded waiting rooms and corridors. Like human sardines. Horrible! Six-month-old children and very old, sick people crammed together, some more dead in the barracks. It is shocking, but it is not surprising.

My father took the money from my grandmother and me and while we wandered through the streets in Zbąszyń, he went to every house in this little town to ask for accommodation.

Now I'm writing this in our small room. It has a little table and just two beds for Grandma, Papa and me – but it's warm. Washing facilities are communal, in a dingy corridor, where there is also only one toilet for all the other people living in the building. We have the use of a tiny kitchen, let to us by a poor postman and his wife – they have a small baby, and they all sleep on the kitchen floor ... they are very grateful for the extra money. Tonight my father cooked potatoes and boiled herring for everyone to say thank you.

Father received word that the rest of my family are now in Belgium. My mother is sending money so we can stay here.

Soon I will have my first proper sleep for days. The first night was in prison in Esslingen, the second night on the train, the third on a platform and the fourth in a horse stable, and now in a proper bed – well, in the middle of the two beds on the wooden frame, in between my papa and grandmother.

Unbelievable!

I'll write in more detail soon but now, I must sleeeeeeeeeeeeeeeeeep.

Diary of Jess Robinson
Wednesday, 15 November 2006

I've been soooooooo busy. I'M ALL OVER THE PLACE!!!!!!!!!!!!!!!!!!!!!!!!!!!!!!!!!!!!!!! I've got loads to write. The house is moving really fast because Mr Parks (that's the owner) has to leave. There's no chain and my mortgage got approved really quickly (mum said she was amazed). I'm SOOOOOOO excited. I can't believe it. I know it's not the first time I've left home, but I thought I'd be back here again forever and I felt like such a loser. And now I'm a mover and a shaker ... or is it shaper?

I'm staying with Rabbi in Acton til the house goes through.

I have a day job. It's for The Parliamentary Yearbook. It's mainly a load of out of work actors there. They let us go for auditions. (I'll tell you about them later!) We're selling advertising space. There are scripts pasted all over the walls. You have to call up different businesses and try to speak to the boss. The company is run by this woman from Bulgaria called Talia who looks and sounds like The Count from Sesame Street, and her husband Marvin who has really sour breath and always has this white crud in the corners of his mouth (yoghurt?) and DEFINITELY wears a wig. He points at which page you have to read. And he listens in. He's quite funny. He marches round the office and shouts 'Don't pitch the secretary'. Also sometimes he makes you do a phone call when you're bursting for the loo. He literally stops you going to the toilet because he says it gives your performance more urgency. And it is a performance. We call ourselves different names because then when the person on the end of the phone says no or hangs up, it doesn't affect you. I decided to call myself 'Camilla DeLeighton Brooke with an E.' I speak in a very loud, posh voice – I actually sound just like Annika my agent haha. I don't really understand what I'm talking to them about. The firms I'm calling have something to do with pensions and actuaries. You have to tell them that they will be in this year's book which goes to all the MPs in parliament and they pay to be listed in it. A page in the year book is £1000. If you get a deal, you fax them a form and then they send it back to you, signed. A few people have done it. When the fax machine starts whirring everyone stands round it and does a rain dance. It's quite exciting. Percy, who is a bit of a gossip and works on the front desk, told me a couple of days before I started, there was a really posh man in a tweed suit banging on the door and saying the year book doesn't exist and he wanted his money back!!! I don't believe him though. Anyway, it's £120 a week plus commission and I <u>really</u> hope I make some deals because I've already spent it all and it's only Wednesday …

———

It's hard to believe we were both twenty-three when we wrote these entries.

Rosi had just found her father and grandmother after days of fear and displacement, and I was dreaming about getting a set of keys to call my own.

She was holding on to what little family and dignity she had left. I was holding on to a fax machine and a fake name.

Different kinds of survival. Different kinds of grit. But maybe the same instinct – to keep going, to find some solid ground.

Group Chat: Cool Bitches

Thursday, 18 August 2022, 13:26

Mum: I took a break from translating mum's diaries and today I have renewed Dad's plaque at Hoop Lane Crematorium for the next 10 years, girls – it says 'Jules Ruben virtuoso jazz pianist' – we must remember his everlasting joy in playing and making music and his gentle kindness xxx

Stephie: Oh! Look up, look up … there's our darling daddy, amongst all the other entertainers! Just what he wanted, and deserved! Xx

Katy: Lovely 🫣

Me: Awww 🖤🖤🖤🖤🖤

The picture Mum sends takes me back in time …

I remember – a few weeks before he died – sitting on my grandpa's bed. Grandpa Jules was drifting in and out of sleep. He had been spending more and more time in bed. 'He eats like a bird!'

Grandma had exclaimed when Mum brought down his cold cup of tea and sandwich, barely touched – only two small bites taken out of it.

Earlier that day, my *We Will Rock You* audition for the West End show had gone *terribly*. In a misguided attempt to look confident, I stood on the stage of the Dominion Theatre in a fishnet top I'd found in TK Maxx and sang 'Only the Good Die Young' with my legs so awkwardly far apart I could barely stay upright. My inner thighs were aching from trying not to slip into the splits.

I kept doing this: trying to appear cooler or edgier in auditions instead of just being myself. A week earlier, before a *Beauty and the Beast* audition, I'd had a glass of white wine at the Wetherspoon's next door to 'loosen up'. Once inside, the wine convinced me to take off my heels and sing barefoot, hoping I'd come across as 'down to earth'. But all I'd managed to do was throw myself off completely and I forgot the words when I noticed the casting director staring at my bunions.

After tea at Grandma's, when I'd lied to everyone and said the auditions had gone brilliantly, I'd crept upstairs into Grandpa's quiet room for comfort.

I don't think he really knew who I was any more. A couple of weeks earlier, during one of our Sunday-afternoon concerts, Grandma had asked me to sing something. Halfway through, Grandpa suddenly stood up, pointed at me and said, 'I think that girl should sit down now and give somebody else a chance.' He used to love my singing. I felt mortified. Grandma had looked furious at the interruption.

As I sat on his bed, I noticed a packet of adult-sized nappies on the bedside table. So undignified.

Not knowing whether he'd still like it or not, I'd cautiously started to sing 'Somewhere Over the Rainbow'. He opened his eyes. I wasn't sure he recognised me – but he smiled. It gave me a lump in my throat. I couldn't finish the last line; my eyes filled with tears. Then the door opened a crack and Grandma came in. She walked over and hugged me, bringing with her that familiar scent of marzipan and cinnamon.

I smile at the memory and type ...

Me: Grandma would have been pleased wouldn't she. She was almost like Grandpa's agent!

Mum: She said he was too fine a pianist to be background music and should just be a soloist. Once he'd been stopped by HER from doing Barmitzvahs and Veddings, she expected the whole family and all their friends to come to his concerts.

She was very proud of his playing and quite frustrated and shouty when he forgot he'd already played a solo, as if any of the dozing alte kakers* would have noticed. Then after each piece she walked up and down the middle aisle clapping loudly and nodding at everyone encouragingly so they'd clap too – we called her 'The Clap Leader'.†

When he couldn't play any more she was of course very sorry to have lost this performer whom she lived vicariously through, and when he was gaga and put on his dinner suit in the night, struggling to get the front door open to get to an imaginary gig, she shouted at him, 'Ach, Jules, who would want you? 93 and you can't play any more,' or words to that effect 😖 She was a bitch.

Jojo was so kind when she looked after him. She'd say, 'Oh no, Grandpa, it's not time yet – you're too early for your concert. It's not until the morning. You go back

---

* Yiddish – meaning 'old fogies'.
† A role my mum has now taken on at all of my shows. I should probably be embarrassed but, to be fair, she's a really good hype man.

upstairs, take off your dinner suit, and I'll bring you a cup of tea.' And he would, every time. By morning, he'd forgotten all about it.

Stephie: ... hmmm that wasn't an easy read, sister ...! Bits of truth or not, do you feel better now?!

Mum: Not really –

———

I'm reeling. What just happened? It brings me up short to remember Jojo babysitting me so patiently, knowing that now, with her Huntington's, the roles have reversed ... But I also hadn't expected that sudden explosion of venom about Grandma.

In my shock I go to call my mother, but my phone pings with a new message.

Message from: Auntie Stephie

Thursday, 18 August 2022, 14:57

Stephie: How about you ask me things about Grandma on my personal text thingy, cos your mum's constant (and oftentimes vicious) tirades about Grandma make me so upset, that I feel ill in my tummy ... I don't care what's true or not, what's exaggerated or not. I don't know why she can't let it go now. It's over, done, finished ... and it's a vile way to carry on, in front of those of us left in this family. I don't want a part in it. Xx

Me: I'm so sorry Stemmie. Mum has always had that bitter 'slant' when she talks about anything to do with Grandma. I don't quite understand it.

Stephie: During the war years, our mum went around the country with dad to all the military bases he played at. She was young, happy and proud of him and her new life. She hurt for him when he had big disappointments, and she delighted in his successes. Mum always loved his excellence and technique in his jazz, even though it wasn't her favourite music (which was Classical) ... and she had to make a social life for herself, so as not to be alone at times like New Year's Eve. Most evenings he was out playing in the nightclubs till 2 or 3am!

Your grandma said she couldn't remember anything about Grandpa's funeral afterwards. She had taken a lot of 'calms'. She was frightened and very awkward at his funeral. She looked lost and sort of in a dream about it all. She always had a terrible fear of death and loss. The place was packed, standing room only. People cried, Jojo couldn't get through her little speech, without Katy lovingly taking over ... You sang 'Somewhere Over the Rainbow'.

Your grandma gave out a little cry and grabbed my arm as the coffin slid away behind the curtain ... I'll never forget all that. Xx

---

I think about Stephie's recollection of Grandpa's funeral (and grin in spite of myself as I remember Mum cringing at the way her younger sister (in her sixties at the time) kissed the coffin lid with one black-stockinged and stilettoed leg tipped up at the back – like Betty Boop).

Although my mum and Auntie Stephie had a very similar experience of Grandpa Jules – a gentle and sweet musical man with a silly sense of humour and a penchant for liquorice allsorts – they have completely different perceptions of Grandma Rosi as a mother. Of course, I've known this since I was a tween; our family isn't shy when it comes to talking about feelings, but the deeper I dig into my grandma's past the more and more glaringly obvious and unsettling this divide becomes.

My mum's the epitome of practicality and pragmatism. And although she can be outrageously naughty with her sense of humour, she's always busy, grounded and focused on what's next, marching ever onwards and feeling guilty if she rests for too long.

Auntie Stephie, however, lives in the moment and finds joy in the unconventional. She's a dreamer, a hippy. She's both strong and gentle … (I should probably find some better adjectives to describe her, though, as that makes her sound like a deodorant.) My free-spirited, bohemian 'cool auntie' has found so much comfort in uncovering Grandma's diaries, letters, photographs and documents, reverently touching her mum's handwriting as if in veneration – still able to catch the faint scent of her perfume. She says it brings her solace. She's quite literally the opposite of my mum – you can't be grounded if you live on a BOAT! The other day, my auntie told me how much she still missed her mother's arms around her and remembered their shared laughter. In that moment, I could still see the young girl she once was shining through her big, sad, brown eyes …

Mum, on the other hand, has taken on the enormous task of translating Grandma's old diaries – not out of any sentimentality or even a quest to know more about her own mother; but all for me. I keep hoping she'll find a love for my grandma that she's forgotten, but instead I notice Mum becoming increasingly hardened.

How could Rosi be two entirely different people to Mum and Auntie Stephie? Surely one of them is remembering her wrong?

And then there's the young Rosi in the diaries and letters, a completely separate identity; she's wide-eyed and bright, stoic and emotional all at once. One moment she's comforting frightened children like a mother, the next she's falling apart with fear. There's a rawness to her honesty, and a resilience that shines through – even when she clearly has no idea what's coming next.

It's all so tangled up. I feel dizzy and anxious and guilty because even though I know it's causing pain and anger, I can't stop picking at the threads. I'm determined to unravel them all.

Fuck. Maybe I am still as spoilt as I seem in my young diaries.

The irony of this multiple-personality situation isn't lost on me, considering my job as an impressionist. I've built a career on deftly slipping from one persona to another in a second, which can seep into every part of my life. I find myself code-switching depending on my audience. When I go to Vegas, I darken my Ls and soften my British Ts to Ds. But I'll drop my Ts and Hs while bantering with the guy at the garage when I take my car in for its MOT. For years and years, in a quest to be authentic, I've only succeeded in being authentically inauthentic. In other words, a bit of a dick.*

Is playing other people making me lose myself? Or have I always been a bit lost, finding comfort in impersonations because it's easier than figuring out who I actually am? Like a chameleon – or perhaps, more accurately, a hermit crab, swapping shells – I borrow other people's identities. I continue to hide behind these personas, each performance a shield against judgement. Is this a survival tactic or just a sign of my own insecurity? All I know is, my grandmother seems to have navigated multiple identities, and I have inherited the knack.

---

* Wow, I'm so profound!

Chapter 11

Diary of Rosi Schul
Sunday, 5 November 1938

I have not written for a couple of days because I have been so busy! After the first night in our room, I looked out of the window. There was a beautiful view of the lake. It reminded me so much of my beloved Esslingen. I got dressed and went straight out. While walking in the chaos around me and seeing the children all filthy and bewildered, an idea came to me to do something for them. At the corner, I saw a poster saying 'Punkt Sanitarny',* where the local Polish people had brought boxes and boxes of clothes and other useful things for the children. I walked in and asked what I could do for the children who were milling around me. There didn't seem to be anyone around who was 'in charge', so I asked for bowls of water, and with the help of some of the mothers, I washed the children and found suitable clothes for them. The poor things hadn't seen a drop of water in five or six days! I managed to joke and laugh with them and put them at ease. Later I took them for a walk to a lovely field – and as we walked, more and more children came to join! I felt like the Pied Piper of Hamelin. We played together, and I told my usual stories to an ever-growing crowd. It made me feel so good to see them happy and inter-

---

* Like a Red Cross centre.

ested. Since then I have been back every day. It feels right to fill my time this way.

Rosi with children (I remember her holding me under my head like that for photos; I probably made a similar face).

And guess what? My work with the children has now come to the attention of the Polish organisations, especially two members at the top of the newly formed committee, Schneider and Blecheisen. They have already organised a children's home in the local gymnasium, and they need teachers and other volunteers and they have asked me to join! I am to work with the Polish doctors, nurses and other personnel, who speak Polish and Yiddish only, because my Yiddish will come in handy to liaise between the Polish helpers and the children!

Every day I am to delouse the children using some water with chemicals mixed in. Then I can teach them, and play with them and find things to occupy them ... just what I have been doing all my life!

How quickly things can change – both for good and bad. Right now the future seems full of promise and I am told that one day soon we will be free to enter Poland properly.

Above: Rosi with children and staff/Red Cross volunteers.
Below: The Gymnasium. Bottom: Beds arrive.

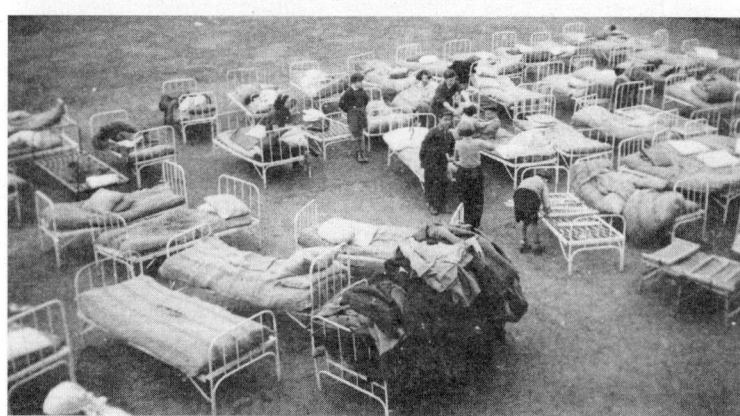

Diary of Jess Robinson
Saturday, 18 November 2006

Hello! I haven't written for ages. I've been a bit up and down and busy at The Parliamentary Yearbook, which is actually quite fun for a day job. I made £250 commission yesterday, so Rabbi and I went to the bar on the high street to celebrate and ... I met a guy called Michael Garner who is <u>a film director!!!!</u> He kept looking at me. Rabbi said he was a massive creep and he just fancied me (he was a bit old and sweaty), but when I told him I was an actress his face lit up! He said I have the right look for a film he's casting and he wants me to go to his place the day after tomorrow in West Hampstead. That's quite a posh area! Things are happening! WOOOO!!

He wouldn't tell me what the film was, but he hinted it was quite a well known franchise. Rabbi kept trying to guess and making silly suggestions like Care Bears and Pippy Longstocking and he got really annoyed. She didn't like him at all. She said he was dodgy. Oh, AND Rabbi told me she thinks she's a lesbian!!! HOW COOL IS THAT? We're going to go to some gay bars together. I'll be her wing woman. I'm excited for her ... And me.

Sorry, back to the screen test!! There's no script to learn, he said just come looking as glamorous as possible and we'll improvise some scenes. I'm going to wear my dress with the cherries on and Rabbi's knee high boots (if she'll let me). (I'll just nick them from her wardrobe if she doesn't.)

Love Jess

You can borrow the boots, you moron.
Love Rabbi
P.S. That guy is a weirdo!!
Xx

It's wild how quickly young Rosi seemed to pivot – from chaos and displacement to stepping into a position of leadership and care. One minute arrested and thrown out of her country, the next she's washing and dressing children, telling stories, and somehow becoming a bridge between languages and cultures. It's like she found a piece of herself again in helping others.

That ability to switch gears – to find purpose or light in the middle of uncertainty – feels VERY familiar … In our family, when emotional explosions happen and grievances are aired, we talk it out, feel our feelings, complain, and a few days later – max – there is a ceasefire and we Jew on with life. We're like the Real Housewives – fighting and making up within an episode or, at the very worst, a season. So it is no surprise that the upset from a few days ago isn't mentioned in the flurry of texts that arrive as I emerge from a dark recording studio and switch my phone back on after two hours of playing a pixie … (not too Jewish to be a pixie apparently).

Group Chat: Cool Bitches

Monday, 22 August 2022, 13:52

Mum: The police certificates are here!

Stephie: Mine too?

Mum: YES 🐱

Katy: Amazing!

Sasha: Amazing!

Mum: Stop saying everything is amazing! NHS

Mum: FS

Mum: Although it is amazing Stemmie got hers

Stephie: Alright sis! Leave it now 😡

Me: Hello!! That's brilliant.

Mum: How was your little Panda character, Jessie?

Me: Pixie today. Panda tomorrow.

Stephie: Is that a saying? Like 'here today gone tomorrow'?

Me: Ummm, sure!!

Katy: Are we all booked in for the Embassy?

Me: YES! I'm gonna send you all the instructions.
Please read CAREFULLY bitches.
You will all need to bring your ACTUAL passport AND TWO photocopies of it.
You will ALL need your police certificates WITH TWO photocopies of it.
I will bring all Grandma's documents.

Mum: Excellent efficiency! Just like Ze Chermans.

Sasha: Ja!!

Mum: Oh no! We've muddled our leggings, Jessie. These don't fit. Are they yours?

Stephie: Ach, hor bitte auf, ich have Gehirnschmerzen.*
I've used all my battery up trawling through these messages ... just tell me what I personally have to bring on Thursday xx

Mum: Yes. What do we need to bring? Can you just call me? Do you have my leggings?

Me: ARGHHHHHH

Me: OK. So we will meet for coffee at 11am, then Embassy, then I've booked us for schnitzel and apple strudel at a German restaurant around the corner!

Mum: Jessie, you took my leggings home. Can you bring them to the Embassy?

Me: OKAAAAAYYYYY!

———

I can't believe it! Soon the Cool Bitches will be raising a glass on a family holiday in our motherland. I'm looking forward to our outing to the consulate, where I'll finally meet my Embassy bestie, Matilda Koch, become German, and then we'll celebrate by stuffing our faces with strudel. JA!! Who knows, maybe Matilda will come too!

---

* 'Oh, please stop, I have a brain pain.'

Chapter 12

Letter from Rosi Schul to Theodor Rothschild – Thursday, 10 November 1938

Dear Herr Vater,

Thank you so much for the boxes of clothes for the children here. I adored your letter. I was bowled over with joy and I can hardly describe how much I loved the description of the concert at the orphanage. I can just see it all in my mind's eye – my lovely little girls and boys singing out in the sweet costumes you described. I was completely transported back to my beloved Esslingen – my home. I so long to be back with you all. If only I was there again, just for an hour …

It is hard not to compare the people and my surroundings with Esslingen, but as I continue with my work, it becomes more bearable.

The political situation in Poland? It is hard to know quite what is happening yet, but some of the locals were really astonished at everything I told them.

I am studying English as you suggested. Night after night I practise. Never in my life would I have believed that I could learn so much.

I have good relationships with the Polish doctors, nurses, and other personnel. Every day I am with the children. They all do exercise, singing and language lessons – especially English. Then, with the older children I do handicrafts, and they tell me their views. I have introduced them all to the folk tales I used to tell in Esslingen. There have also been some lectures from volunteers and teachers in the community, and afterwards we compose songs and make up stories inspired by these. I drain out the contents of my brain – and when I can't draw from my brain, I improvise.

Left: Rosi and children. She always cupped my head like this.
Right: Rosi at twenty-three years old (front and centre) with teachers.
(This is her handwriting.)

I will describe the facilities for you. There is a very large room in which the children live. It was a gymnasium. It now looks like a sanatorium. The living conditions are bearable for the children now, thank goodness. It is already quite pretty with white sheets on the beds, although it can feel cramped and at mealtimes the children eat on or under their beds.

Above right: View of the Gymnasium turned into a children's dormitory/living space. Middle right: Breakfast with no chairs. Bottom right: Rosi (third row from back, second on left) with doctors, nurses, staff and children.

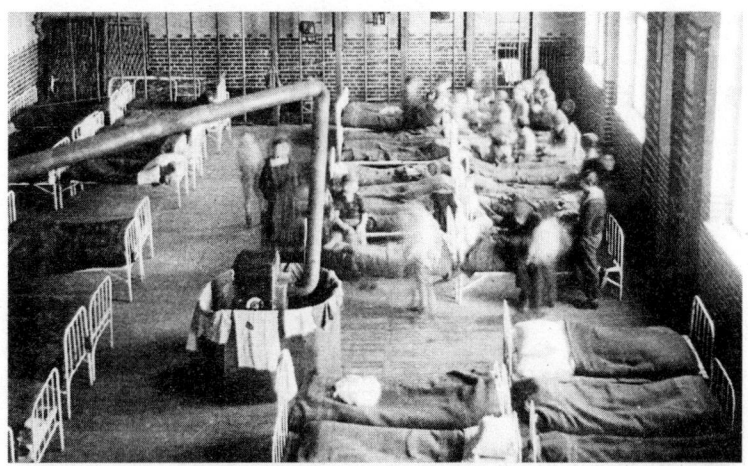

My work with the children has been very successful so far and is appreciated by the staff and committee members. Last night they gave a lovely performance in the barracks … an hour-long show of singing, dancing and playing percussion … à la Esslingen! Afterwards the Committee asked for it to be repeated in the big hall of a local hotel!

I am so grateful my work with the children is keeping them busy and happy. My singing, guitar and piano playing came in very handy … Well, what else have I done all my life?!

Please write back with more news and send my love to your wife, the teachers and of course the children, who I miss so very much.

With love,
Rosi

Diary of Jess Robinson
Sunday, 19 November 2006

I'm stupid I'm stupid I'm stupid I'm stupid I'm stupid. Rabbi is running me a bath. I'm on my second glass of wine. I'm a twat. I hate myself. I'm stupid. I'm a slut. I'm so naive. I'm stupid STUPID. Why am I so stupid? I can't believe myself. What happened?

When I got to the end of the road in West Hampstead, I texted Michael the director as we'd arranged, but just as I was pressing send I randomly saw him coming out of the chicken shop?! He saw me and waved and asked if I wanted any, but I said no. I thought it was a bit odd but I just played it cool.

We walked to his flat. It's on the top floor of this big posh mansion house. I expected it to be swish and spacious, but it was really dirty and small and it smelled musty like the shed in Grandma's garden and there was a layer of dust on the coffee table. I mean, it was all a bit disgusting and dirty, but I didn't want to be like mum so I ignored it and I just thought – well he's eccentric. I mean, directors are, aren't they? I sat on the leather sofa while he set up the camera and he said I should help myself to a drink. I just went for tap water, but the glass was a bit cloudy so I didn't drink it.

God, now I'm writing this down I can't believe it. STUPID STUPID STUPID.

Rabbi said I should have walked the other way as soon as I saw him coming out of the chicken shop. But I was all full of hope. I think it makes me blind sometimes. STUPID.

He still wouldn't tell me what the film was but he said we should warm up by just improvising a simple scene. So, he was behind the camera and my role was being a girl in a cafe and I basically had to ask him what he wanted, and make him a coffee. I felt a bit stupid.

I don't want to write any more now.

I will though. Because I AM STUPID and if it's here in writing I can't ignore it. Rabbi says it might help me process. Fucks SAKE.

He said 'you're very uptight.'

I said 'oh sorry – let me try again.'

He said 'are you nervous?'

I said 'A bit. I'm fine.'

He said 'if you want to make it in this industry you need to loosen up. This is a really big opportunity and you're getting in your own way.'

I said 'OK – let me try again.'

We did the scene again.

He said 'I think it's a waste of time unless you can loosen up. It's really disappointing to be honest. I had high hopes and I was really excited about you. I thought you'd have more about you. I've already bigged you up to the producers. Do you really want this? It's OK if you don't. We can just leave it.'

I said 'I do want it.'

He said 'Then prove it. Prove you can stop being so uptight.'

I said 'OK – how? Shall we do it again?'

He said 'I think it's a waste of time to be honest – I'm not sure you've got what it takes. What a shame.'

I said 'No, I really want this. Let's go for it.'

He said 'How the hell are you going to be on set if you're not confident and relaxed doing a simple scene here?' Then he said 'I think you should take your clothes off.'

I didn't know what to say. I thought I hadn't heard right or he was joking or something.

He said 'if you're uptight then we can't do this. I'm not being a perv. It's just a natural thing. It will help you loosen up. I can't recommend you to the producers in good faith if I can't see that you're hungry for the role.'

So I did. I took my dress off. I took my knickers off!! And I just stood there. I felt defiant. I didn't really feel like I was in my own body. I wanted to cry. I didn't though.

He said 'you've got a big bush.'

I felt stupid.

I said 'well, I wasn't expecting to take my clothes off.'

(I haven't done my bikini line for ages.)

He told me I needed to be more trusting and to sit on the sofa to do a relaxation meditation.

I had to sit up straight with my palms facing up and my eyes closed. He was telling me to breathe in for 8 counts and out for ten. I started to feel a bit light-headed. After about three minutes or something I was feeling more relaxed and actually really bored. I just wanted to leave and I was wondering when it would end when I felt something on my palm and I opened my eyes and IT WAS HIS DICK!!!!!!!!!!!!!!!! AND HE WAS NAKED!!!!!!!!!!!!!!!! He was disgusting. There was a drip on my palm. When I saw it I suddenly felt so SICK and horrified. I said

'I'm just popping to the loo' and I rushed into his dirty bathroom. I saw a makeup bag and hair elastics and a pink razor so he must have a girlfriend?? I didn't know what to do and I couldn't remember where I put my phone. I heard him put the kettle on so I peeked out the door and he wasn't on the sofa any more.

So I came out and he was in the kitchen wearing a silk dressing gown with his pot belly hanging out, casually making tea! He asked if I wanted one – like nothing weird had just happened. I said 'yes please' and while he was busy, I put on my dress and boots really fast, grabbed my phone which was hidden in the crack between the sofa seats and I KNOW I didn't put it there, and I took the chain off the door (WHY WAS THE CHAIN ON THE DOOR?), and ran into the street and all the way down the high street to the tube. I left my knickers. Is it all on his camera?? What if he blackmails me?? I AM STUPID.

I've got a blister on my heel now.

As soon as I sat on the tube I went all shaky and an old lady asked if I was ok. Now here I am. Rabbi opened the door and said 'why's your face all grey?', and I burst into tears.

She was really nice but she's SO shocked that I always manage to get myself into such stupid situations. She said I should be more careful and more cynical. She said I hope for the best all the time and I just see what I want to see and I always ignore the red flags. She's right.

I don't think I'm a very good judge of character.

She patted me on the back (which is really affectionate for her), and said 'Nevermind, it's all fodder for the memoirs.' Haha! Fodder for the memoirs! I like that. And we laughed. And I cried more and sort of laughed at the same time and a bubble of snot came out of my nose and she stopped patting me on the back and said it was gross and I'd made her feel a bit sick. So she went off to run me a bath. She's a good friend.

> Now I feel a bit numb. I'm so ashamed. I want to go home.
>
> I <u>won't</u> tell mum.
>
> Can you get thrush from sitting on a sofa? I hope I haven't caught something.
>
> I'm NEVER NEVER <u>NEVER EVER</u> sharing this.

So, while Rosi threw herself into caring for displaced children with purity, purpose and barely a trace of self-pity, seventy-five years later I remember sitting on my bed and rocking slightly, more for comfort than out of any kind of 'mental breakdown', binding my pretty diary with the gold gilt pages in Sellotape. Round and round and round I went with shaky hands until the entire roll was used up. A binding tantamount to a ritual – sealing, constraining the shameful secrets held within.

I did such an efficient job, naive little wannabe-witch, that until a few days ago I had managed to block out the entire incident. It only all came flooding back when I glimpsed the mockingly innocent multicoloured cover of whimsical birds and flowers peeking at me from the bottom of the box containing all my old diaries and school reports ('Jessica could do with concentrating more and showing off less'). And over the near twenty years it had lain in my attic, the Sellotape that ensnared the mortifying memory had sort of solidified. I'd cut it open with a bread knife on the kitchen worktop as Husband 2.5 (he took me out for a romantic dinner last night – lovely Simon, or … Derek?) stood by looking concerned as I gasped at the entry.

Now, he makes me a cup of tea and listens quietly as I discuss it with Rabbi (still my best friend) on the phone. She remembers it well, being utterly gobsmacked at the time that I was such a 'Pollyanna' (not the first time in my life I've been called this), believing the best of everyone … 'I just couldn't understand how a mate of mine could be so naive. But you just let yourself fall for what you hoped would be true. I would've got out of there as soon as I saw his flat,' she says, still in disbelief after all these years.

'You wouldn't have gone in the first place,' I say.

Rabbi recalls me telling her that I was on autopilot, as if I wasn't in my own body, just sort of looking down on myself, in a curious kind of way … 'You said you were detached … just seeing what would happen. But I think that's a pretty normal trauma response …'

'I know I'm not the only person this sort of thing has happened to, but I'm so stu—' I begin, but before I can get too far with the unhelpful self-flagellation, Rabbi says, 'Well, there's something I never told you that happened to me around that age …'

And my mouth falls open as my strong, savvy friend recounts her own 'casting couch' story …

'That's rape!' I shout in horror at the end of Rabbi's chilling revelation, as 2.5 hurriedly closes the kitchen window to avoid any neighbourly misunderstandings and goes into the other room to give us – well, Rabbi – some privacy.

'I did kind of say no,' Rabbi says, 'but in a really gentle, polite way, in case he got hurt and didn't cast me in anything again. In the end, I just didn't have the self-belief to get up and walk out.'

We're both silent for a minute … Each questioning what we would do if we were in that situation now? Whether we'd still sacrifice autonomy over our own bodies for job security – or whether, instead, we'd RIP HIS BALLS OFF …

'I finally confided in someone,' my friend continues, 'a guy who'd worked on the production at the time. And when I mentioned that it might feel good to get in touch with the director and tell him what he'd done, and how it had affected me, my "confidant" said, "Oh don't do that, he's very sensitive and depressed – it might upset him."'

Almost lost for words, I splutter, 'God! That's outrageous. I'm so sorry. God! Can you imagine if someone said that nowadays, after #MeToo?'

To which Rabbi replies, 'Oh no, it was only a couple of years ago!'

After we say goodbye, I reflect on it all with 2.7, who is running me a bath and has made me a hot chocolate. He adores my friend, but while he's upset and dismayed for her, he admits he's not shocked.

'It's just another disgusting example of a man abusing his power,' he says, looking grim as he goes to turn off the bath taps.

As I lie back in the bubbles, I muse sadly that my mum and Auntie Stephie (and probably Grandma Rosi if she were still here) would be united on this one. I know exactly what they'd say. They'd say it was our fault. We shouldn't have got ourselves into those situations in the first place.

We discussed a similar story last summer and things got pretty heated at the kitchen table when Mum said, 'When a man gets started you can't just expect him to stop.' And Stephie agreed. There was no amount of talking or reasoning that made them change their minds. I was so angry, and although they paused to listen, they didn't really 'hear me' … Maybe it's a generational thing? And that's fine, isn't it? Except it isn't. It's scary that Mum, who I love so much, and whose opinion I value and whose approval I have always (even now) sought, can think so differently to me. Men aren't *animals* – or maybe they are, but please – they have brains, they understand the words 'No' and 'Stop'. They don't *have* to keep going.

'Bloody hell!' I call from the bath. 'You don't have to be a bloody Nazi to be a predator!'

'No, thanks!' 2.7 calls back, who evidently thinks I'm offering to leave the bath water in for him.

'And also thank GOD,' I say to myself as I pull the plug out and wrap myself in the towel that 2.8 has left on the radiator (definitely worthy of an upgrade – gorgeous Sebastian/Muhammed), 'that however naive or numb or stupid young Jess was, at least she … *I got the chain off the door and got out of there with only a humiliation*' (*possibly caught on camera*). 'It could have been *so* much worse.' I shudder.

I didn't report it. Rabbi didn't report it. *Millions of us don't report it.*

A passage in my Grandma's diaries springs to mind: 'The lowest creature in the whole world is Man. Instincts, which lie dormant, emerge at the slightest provocation.'

'I've always been so good at ignoring red flags,' I think as I towel-dry my hair … Is there something in my DNA? Rosi ignored the chaos in Germany by diving into her work with the children, showing an incredible ability to focus on the good. She was busy sewing, storytelling and creating happiness for children in her internment camp, even as the storm clouds of war gathered overhead. She faced unimaginable challenges, yet her biggest worry was the snoring that accompanied her nights. Was her ability to focus on the positive ignoring 'red flags', or am I clutching at straws to make myself feel better and closer to her? It's not comparable, is it? Rosi was uprooted and traumatised for very different reasons and living a life of total respectability and purity. Unlike Rosi, there was no war around me; I was just a hopeful, privileged idiot.

I'm desperately trying to find patterns and connections where there aren't any. At least it's comforting to know that Rosi and I were united by our stubborn optimism: Rosi's relentless cheerfulness in a time of war, and my pursuit of acting dreams, despite the predators lurking in the industry. Both speak to the will to seek the good in a person or situation, no matter how naive it may seem.

'And is being naive really the worst thing?' I say to Brian the dog as he playfully tugs at the belt of my dressing gown while I try to wrestle it on. 'I mean, yes, if it gets you into danger … but isn't there something beautiful about believing in the goodness of people and the possibility of happy endings?' (Not that kind.) 'God, I sound like a Disney princess now,' I say, looking down to see what's jostling my feet – but instead of animated bluebirds helping me on with fluffy slippers, it's just Brian, humping them.

While my experience was far from a fairy tale, it's a reminder that we women must continue to support and protect each other. Let's look out for the next generation by not being judgemental when they fail to see the warning signs, and please let's help them not lose their hopefulness. In the end, we're all just trying to find our way, learning from the past and forging ahead with a little more wisdom and (hopefully) some compassion. 'So, here's to Rosi and to little me,' I think as I flop into bed; two women just trying to navigate our worlds, one diary entry at a time. 'Jew on,' I yawn as I switch off the light.

Chapter 13

Diary of Jess Robinson
Wednesday, 22 November 2006

The Parliamentary Yearbook is depressing. I haven't made any deals and I've been working really hard. I feel grey. Just meh. Dull. No energy.

I really, really miss Rabbi. She's started her UK tour. I'm going to see it when she's in Milton Keynes I think. Apparently the director is this up-and-coming guy and Rabbi gets on really well with him and he said he wants to put her in all of his shows.

I called mum on the way to work to see if she'd come with me to Rabbi's show in Milton Keynes. She kept asking if I was alright. I said I was fine but she kept pressing and then she said 'I think you're depressed'. I told her to fuck off and then I cried all the way to the office.

So, I think she's right.

I will call her later to apologise. I'm a bitch.

Diary of Jess Robinson
Wednesday, 22 November 2006

Just spoke to mummy. She said it was time for me to go to the doctor and that she'll take me when I come and stay next week. She also got me the number of John – a therapist in Woodside Park. I could get there and back on my lunch hour I think.

I love mum.

(Haven't told her about what happened. She'd be cross with me and think I'm stupid. I'm too disgusted and ashamed to tell her. Plus I don't want her to tell dad! Or the rest of the bloody village like I know she would.)

Diary of Rosi Schul
Thursday, 17 November 1938

I have had devastating news. My letter to Herr Vater may never reach him! I received an account of it all today from Samuel … Of course I already knew that all hell was let loose throughout Germany on the night of November 9th and into the early hours of November 10th … Some are calling it 'Kristallnacht'. It is all anyone can talk about here. Although we try not to do so in front of the children.

Firstly, thankfully – I am relieved to say that all my family have managed to escape to Belgium … fortune amid misfortune … But the beautiful school in Esslingen, where so many found solace, suffered a terrible fate. It breaks my heart. Everything was burned and destroyed! I cannot believe it. Samuel said the children were terrified. Some of them hid under beds or in closets and many ran into the surrounding countryside, fleeing anywhere they could to escape the horror in the cold and dark. Herr Vater did what he could to protect them, but to no avail. The children cried in fear and a Gestapo man told them if they didn't shut up, they would be thrown into the flames too. Monster! Samuel was beaten unconscious. And when he finally went back into the house there was glass everywhere.

Many of the teachers were manhandled and treated cruelly. Herr Rothschild was beaten, arrested and taken away immediately. Other members of staff were taken away and haven't been heard from since! It was a pogrom, just like the old days, only worse. I cannot imagine it.

And what of my three little companions who were taken away with me that fateful night, only to be happily sent back to their 'haven' …? Poor things. They would have been better here with me.

Life is full of such strange contradictions. The violence and destruction that ravaged my beloved Esslingen did not reach us here, and for that, I am grateful. What a twist of fate for us … being in Zbąszyń! We six thousand refugees escaped all that suffering. The children who were so deprived during our first days here are now safe, warm and, dare I say it, 'happy'.

How is it possible that amid such chaos we can still find the strength to sing and dance, to put on shows? We keep going, but what will happen to us? Nobody knows …

Embassy bound, I put down the last of Mum and Bruni's translated pages and stare out of the train window at the green smear of bushes speeding past. I think of these 'characters' in young Rosi's diary: her friends, her colleagues and those poor children whom she loved so much. Not 'characters in a story', I berate myself, *real people* who lived and breathed. Who had their own life ambitions and dreams – many of which would never get near becoming a reality. What terror and pain they must have felt. Rosi – stuck in this 'no man's land' as she'd often describe it to me … She must have felt impotent, grateful, horrified, relieved; a messy contradiction of emotions as she 'kept going'. On with the show!

Desperate to know what happened to Rosi's beloved 'second father', I search online and discover that Theodor Rothschild was allowed to return to the orphanage for a little while and then managed to continue his work with the displaced children in Stuttgart, until the Nazis came for him once more. He was deported to Theresienstadt (a Czechoslovakian ghetto established by the SS), where, on 10 July 1944, he died from malnutrition and severe pneumonia. He was seventy.

I also find out that around nine or ten days earlier than Rosi's last diary entry, one of her fellow refugees, Zindel Grynszpan, sent a letter to his son – Herschel Grynszpan – a Polish-Jewish student who was living in Paris at the time. Upon receiving the news about the violent deportation of his family to Zbąszyń, Herschel became so enraged that he went out and shot Ernst vom Rath, a German diplomat. (*Stay with me here.*) On 9 November, the news of Ernst's death reached Hitler, who then gave 'Minister of Propaganda' Joseph Goebbels the 'go-ahead' to gather a bunch of old storm troopers and urge them to retaliate – *violently*. This 'revenge' was staged to appear as a series of 'spontaneous demonstrations', but telephone orders from Munich triggered pogroms throughout Germany. The Nazis then used this as an excuse to launch more

Portrait of Herschel Grynszpan taken after his arrest by French authorities for the assassination of German diplomat Ernst vom Rath. Photograph taken in Paris, France, 7 November 1938.

horrifying attacks, burning and looting synagogues and Jewish businesses. Jews were murdered on the spot or taken off to concentration camps. This was *Kristallnacht*.

I take this in, stunned at the horrendous ripple effect a letter can have … the blank page, the damning ink, the innocent stamp … I also can't help my brain from wondering: what if it was *Grandma* who lent her refugee neighbour Zindel the stamp for his postcard, which led his son to shoot the diplomat, which started *Kristallnacht*? Then I think, 'Well, no. Hitler started it.' And then cringe at my playground idiocy. Dick.

Feeling fired up, and with all the important paperwork in my backpack (which is leopard print, to match my trainers so Mum can't complain too much about me not looking 'glamorous' today), I decide to walk to the Embassy from Victoria. Belgravia looks like it's been cut straight out of a postcard and glued into real life. I feel quite romantic – like an animal-print Eliza Doolittle – as I gaze at the streets lined with grand Regency houses, almost gleaming in the crisp sunshine. I stop by a patisserie and breathe in the scent of freshly baked croissants and overpriced coffee. Caught mid-sniff, I feel like a dirty street urchin when a sophisticated woman looks me up and down as she passes, the sight of me reminding her to tell her friend, whose face is stretched so tight it looks like she's trapped in a wind tunnel, that she thinks their Polish cleaner is stealing from them. I'm fooling no one.

This is the kind of area where a flat white costs £8.90, which I discover the moment I walk into our agreed rendezvous, Le Nepo Baby, and spot the Cool Bitches standing at the counter looking grim. But who cares? We're celebrating! This is a momentous day. We'll be German soon! A wrong will be righted. (Still, £9 for a coffee?)

While Mum, Stephie, Katy and Sasha clutch their extortionate drinks, I smugly hand out the A4 manila envelopes containing all the relevant documentation, which I've diligently assembled for each of us … in triplicate. The Cool Bitches murmur their thanks, eyes popping in surprise at my totally uncharacteristic organisational skills, and we make our way towards the German Embassy, passing other embassies (embassi?) with their native flags proudly billowing in the breeze. My lack of geographical knowledge quickly becomes apparent as I fail to identify most (*all*) of them. Turning the corner, we spot our destination. I do a double-take. 'Erch! Is that it?' Mum exclaims as we all check the sign.

The German Embassy is a hideous modern complex. It sticks out like a turd in a jacuzzi amid the classically elegant houses. 'Such an ugly eyesore!' Mum says, her loud voice rebounding off the Regency buildings, as though they're echoing their agreement.

'Maybe they got the shit building as punishment for the war, man,' Stephie muses as Sasha and Katy shush the septuagenarian siblings.

I look up at the black, red and yellow flag, committing it to memory and filing it away for pub quizzes. I wait to *feel* something … a recognition of *home*? The warmth of *belonging*? The pain of my people? But as the flag flaps half-heartedly in the breeze, nothing comes. The 'federal coat of arms' eagle is such an alien image to me. 'Why are its feet like that?' I wonder aloud, thinking they look a bit swastika-y.

The federal coat of arms of Germany, also known as the Bundeswappen.

And who is the eagle sticking its tongue out at? I'm reminded of nasty Lily Cooper in my village primary-school playground: 'My mum says your family all have big noses.'

I swallow.

I can't help but find it both ridiculous *and* sinister. Is it *meant* to be? I feel like I have to make fun of it, or it will fly into my nightmares, peck out my eyes and tangle it's spinning Stanley-knife claws in my hair.

We line up by the outer glass door, where a stern-looking German security guard bids us through. I solemnly nod at him and inexplicably say, '*Ja*,' in what sounds to me like Grandma's voice. What just happened? Is she here? Did she momentarily possess me? Katy catches my eye, grinning at my 'fluency'. Well, at least I didn't blurt out, '*Die Bratwurst ist sehr lecker*,' which I'd mastered during my Duolingo session on the train – just before realising my headphones weren't, in fact, plugged in. Nothing says 'Language Learning Champion' like gifting a free German lesson to the Quiet Carriage.

Our bags and coats are fed through the security scanner's open mouth, and we nervously shuffle through the metal detector, holding our breath as if it might sense some unspoken guilt. No weapons found – phew. Another security officer gestures to the lockers, her unsmiling eyes tracking our every move as we dutifully stow our phones away. 'Relax, Robinson!' I think, as I wonder why I feel as though I'm doing something illicit, like sneaking over the border, rather than reclaiming something that should never have been taken.

The inner door is opened and we're ushered into the central chamber of the Embassy, which Mum is disappointed to see 'is as ugly and unglamorous as the outside of the building'. I, too, had expected a grand interior: plush rugs, glistening chandeliers, dark wood and a warm welcome. Instead, we're met with a concrete waiting room, a dark tiled floor, rows of nailed-down plastic seats, and a faint smell of metal and disinfectant. It looks like a cross between a public swimming pool (which young Rosi wouldn't have been seen dead at) and a post office with digital numbers above the counters. We take our ticket and wait for our number to come up – 'like at the Waitrose deli counter, Mum!' Katy says in her most positive voice.

When it's finally our turn, I jump up, eager to meet my mate Matilda, who's been so helpful in her emails. But she's not there. Instead, a bored-looking woman unenthusiastically takes our meticulously gathered documents proving our right to German citizenship, as I proudly introduce each Cool Bitch. She stares at me blankly. Didn't Matilda tell her we were coming? I expect some reaction or spark of recognition. We're the Cool Bitches! I'd at least have appreciated a little gasp at the Gestapo's letter to Grandma or a single tear at the photo of Grandma's *Stolpersteine*.*

But no. Nothing. Clearly thinking we're mad, she tells us that we needn't have *all* come to hand in the paperwork before pulling down the closed-counter blind with a snap.

I feel like Dorothy at the gates of the Emerald City, until the woman lifts her blind again, and a brief flicker of hope appears. Then, almost as an afterthought, she announces matter-of-factly that 'Processing vill take et least two years.'

TWO YEARS????

I gape stupidly at my family, who are mirroring my own expression of disbelief … TWO YEARS! What a fool I am for merrily dragging everyone to London just to hand over some photocopies. 'Anti-climax' doesn't begin to cover it. Today is not at *all* the emotional, momentous occasion I'd been anticipating. What an expensive waste of everyone's time.

---

* A *Stolperstein* is a 10-centimetre brass cube set into the pavement bearing a brass plate inscribed with the name and life dates of victims of Nazi extermination or persecution. Literally, it means 'stumbling stone', and metaphorically 'stumbling block'.

It's starting to drizzle when we get outside, and the irritable mood is only lifted momentarily by Mum as she attempts to hail a taxi, oblivious to her diagonally straight arm as the wind blows her hair comically to one side. With her small chocolatey foam moustache from her artisan cappuccino, and the now fiercely flapping German flag behind her, it really is a thing of beauty. I quickly grab my phone, but just as I am about to take a picture, a cab appears and Mum hops in. Another wasted moment.

The ambiance of the German restaurant I so carefully picked out for our celebratory meal is about as cheerful as our mood – dim lighting and grey walls. Sasha has a headache, Mum and Stephie are beginning to look like the old lady text emojis we'd joked about, and Katy and I aren't in the mood for the *Bier oder Wein* we'd been so excited about, so we end up ordering tap *Wasser*.

Our schnitzel and potato salad taste a bit weird – what on earth have they cooked it with? It's almost fizzy … And the humourless waiter doesn't seem to appreciate our attempts at German conversation. When Mum declares loudly that the apple strudel isn't as good as the frozen one from Waitrose, the bill is plonked onto our table. Then, as if to add insult to injury, we find out that our waiter, who we've been practising our German on for the last hour, is in fact Swedish.

The rhythm of the train that rocks me home begins to soothe away the day's heavy disappointment. I dazedly allow my eyelids to close and as I shift in my seat, attempting to discreetly let out what I think will be a silent little *poot*, my eyes fly open as I realise with a sudden lurch of panic that apparently my day has not been soul-crushing enough. 'It's almost poetic, really,' I think as the ominous gurgle in my stomach jolts me upright. The universe has decided to humble me completely … the final blow comes not from stern security guards, but from what turns out to be a very dodgy schnitzel … I knew it tasted funny – and somewhere between East Croydon and Haywards Heath, disaster strikes.

Group Chat: Cool Bitches

Friday, 26 August 2022, 06:46

Mum: TWO YEARS!!!

Stephie: Morning.

Me: Hello.

Katy: I've been awake since 4:25 with a tummy ache :(

Stephie: I didn't sleep at all, and now I'm dog tired! Xx

Mum: Me too – 4am.

Sasha: Urgh

Mum: Jessie where was that lovely cream skirt that you were wearing yesterday from? Is it another Vinted purchase?

Me: Yeah, Vinted. £15.00 – but it's in the train bin now.

Mum: Why?

Me: Because I threw it away.

Mum: ??

Me: Don't ask. Thank God I forgot to give you the leggings back.

Mum: Oh yes, can you send them?

Me: ... You won't want them now.

Chapter 14

**Diary of Jess Robinson
Wednesday, 29 November 2006**

This keeps happening. I don't write for a few days and then EVERYTHING HAPPENS AT ONCE. Work had been going well and I even made a couple of deals which took my earnings to £400 for the week!! Mrs Moneybags or what?! Anyway, I had an audition on Thursday, which I'm not even going to bother writing about because it was so shit and then I turned up at work on Friday and the door was locked. Nobody was there. So I rang Layla (another out of work actress) who sits next to me and she said Marvin must have forgotten to call me, but they've moved out of the building and shut the office?!?!!?!?!?!?!?!

Everyone was in the pub around the corner, so we sat there and got REALLY DRUNK.

But it's TRUE. The actual Parliamentary Yearbook never actually existed!!! I can't believe it. Well I can.

Everyone was really upset because they're not getting paid for the 'deals' they made now. £400 DOWN THE DRAIN. I have to get another job asap. And it HAS to be one that doesn't make me want to DIE.

When we spoke earlier, Grandma said she would give me the £150 basic I would have earned, bless her. I feel a bit bad. I mean, that's not why I called her and told her about it ... I did that because mum reminded me I should call her, which is also shit of me. But when I told her, she offered straight away and said 'you'll always have your egg for breakfast', and so I said yes. I'm going to write her a little thank you card.

Diary of Rosi Schul
Wednesday, 30 November 1938

Life goes on here … I can truly say that at the moment, in spite of everything, I <u>love</u> what I'm doing, even with no social life outside of work! It does not matter to me that I am not paid. I have a purpose. And today someone gave me a lovely warm coat – now I won't freeze in the winter months. It fits perfectly! Wonderful!

Zbąszyń is as big as Esslingen with a wonderful lake and forest. You can't move beyond the borders but inside we have total freedom of movement.

I must write about this little community here. Peculiar and quite amazing! It is like a small communal state one lives in. We have our own law court, cobblers and tailors. Everyone who works is unpaid. It is the simplest life!

Through my work I have met many people, not least of all is Dr Raphael Broches, a brilliant violinist from Hamburg. He lives in one of the little rooms next to the Gymnasium, and whenever I have time, he will play some of my favourite music.

A Day in Rosi's Life

Every day, I make my way to the Stadium and on the way, I meet people from my home town – Hannover … But I have no time for them any more! My day really starts when I arrive at the Stadium. The children always greet me with enthusiasm. They run to me shouting, 'Rosi is here! Rosi is here'! It spurs me on to give them lots of love, both the eleven- and twelve-year-olds and the little ones too.

At midday, the children queue up for their second 'breakfast', and as there are no chairs, they have to eat standing in a row.

Upstairs in a little room, I have a sewing circle with the older girls ... knitting, embroidery and repairing clothes. If the weather allows, we all go into the large playing field, where we do running, skipping and all kinds of competitions, like sack-hopping, three-legged and egg 'n' spoon races ... They all enjoy it, and I love seeing them so happy. Then I visit those children who are ill, and I try to make them laugh and feel relaxed.

The highlight of my day is always 'Story Time'. In fact, as soon as I arrive there are shouts of 'we want a story today!' So I climb up one of the wall ladders and hold onto the rungs while they sit below me on their beds.

Because I have no books here, I make up funny and interesting stories. At the beginning of them I don't even know myself how each story will end, but oh! How I love the sight of the children's eager little faces, their wide eyes – so expectant for more twists and turns in the tale. Sometimes I get ideas from them, by asking, 'Well, what do you think happens next?' And when I leave, there are always more shouts of 'another story tomorrow, please'!

Later I help with lunch. I take mine in the kitchen with the adults, and there's always lots of fun and teasing. The staff are lovely, it reminds me of my time in Esslingen. The food is very good too. The last part of the day is taken up with board-games. Then I go to visit Dr Broches (he lives with a former matron from Hamburg Hospital – Thea ... I wonder, are they just friends or perhaps lovers?!). Anyway, I'm just so glad to hear good music, and be able to talk to this very intelligent man.

My day ends around 7 p.m. (or sometimes later), and by the time I get home I am absolutely exhausted! Grandma and Papa are already in bed and I fall straight into my space in the middle of the two beds.

I do dread the nights. I seem to slip into extremes – some nights with no sleep whatsoever, and then others where I am dead to the world for 12 hours! And each night my father and grandmother snore on either side of me.

How long will we be lodging here, I wonder? Who knows how much longer we have here in Zbąszyń ... and what then???

My luck is that this little Zbąszyń has turned out to be so much like Esslingen! When I look out of the window, I see a view just as pretty as the one I remember, with little houses and trees. Although, instead of vineyards, there is a wide landscape with a lake.

Because my work with the children is the same as in Esslingen, with the same love and affection from them (if not more), and the same good relationships with colleagues and staff, I don't feel the difference so much. Of course, Poland is not Germany, and the Stadium is not the Castle Wilhelms, and our cramped room is not my former lovely large room, full of my books and diaries and music, etc. ... Dr Bagnow is not our 'Herr Vater', and Wowa and Willy cannot be compared to Jonas and Fritz Samuel ...

But for now I am as happy and content as I can be, convinced that my work has to be with needy children ... whatever else the future brings ...

Diary of Jess Robinson
Friday, 1 December 2006

Last night, Omar – yes OMAR(!!), who is now working for a tv company that makes corporate videos, texted me out of the blue to ask if I knew any makeup artists cos he's been working with GAIL PORTER and they needed someone. And I wanted to see him again but also I knew I'd be able to do it and I needed the money, so I wrote back and said, 'I can do makeup.' And he said he wanted someone with actual training. So I said I did have training (which I don't, but I've done my own makeup everyday for years!). So he said great and that's what I went and did!!! I bought a couple more brushes from the Body Shop the night before and I cleaned all my makeup up – and at 7am I went into this rubbish little TV studio in Warren Street, which is basically just a skanky room with a camera. At least it was professional though and not like that other skanky room with a camera which we will never talk about again.

Gail was so nice and so pretty. I only remembered on the train that she doesn't have any hair because she's got alopecia. Thank goodness I remembered! Luckily we've got roughly the same skin tone because all through the filming, every now and then I'd 'step in' and powder her head so it wasn't shiny. I think I did a really nice job on her makeup. She was really pleased because we noticed that her eyelashes were growing back. She's very cool. At the end of the day, we all went to the pub. She is so down to earth. I hope she becomes my friend. At the end of the night I said 'I've got something to confess – I'm not really a professional makeup artist,' thinking she'd be impressed, but she just said 'I know!'

And on that make-up theme, as of JUST NOW, I've got another job!!!! I'm going to be selling makeovers! Starting tomorrow. Don't know much about it, but Rabbi got it for me and we'll be working together. Must go to sleep. Need to get to Pimlico in the morning!

Diary of Jess Robinson
Saturday, 9 December 2006

Bloody hell. I've left that stupid job.

Diary of Jess Robinson
Sunday, 10 December 2006

Rabbi has left too now.

We've just been drinking wine and we think it would be a really good idea to run a sex phone line. You can just sit there in your PJs and your phone is re-routed and the calls come in and you just talk to pervs while you're watching something on telly, or having a cuppa. We saw it on a documentary – there was an old lady saying 'mmmm oooooh yeahhh' while she was putting her laundry in the washing machine and eating biscuits in her slippers …

Just because I have to wait two years to be German (if they accept me), that doesn't mean I'm going to stop my diary studies. I'm too invested in young Rosi now, and I like receiving Mum's translated pages in the post. This afternoon, as I close my diary, I have the obvious thought once again that our lives couldn't have been more different – Grandma and me. Her entries radiate a sense of purpose, which I certainly did NOT have at that age. And that wasn't just to do with the unimaginable circumstances she found herself in. Rosi was always Rosi … She knew who she was, and what she was here to do – teaching, nurturing and giving her all to those children. Even her surname, 'Schul', means school in German. Her life, though difficult, was brimming with meaning.

And me at twenty-three? I'm more like a pinball, pinging around. No wonder I was depressed.

Rosi lived in a time when life didn't allow for much hesitation. Her circumstances demanded strength. She had to focus on survival and find meaning in the small, good things around her. Meanwhile, I had the privilege of choice. My struggles weren't about survival, but about figuring out what I wanted my life to be in a world that felt like it had too many options.

I think back to Rosi's entry as I open my laptop. Something about her mention of Doctor Broches piqued my interest. Expecting to find very little as I idly scroll through the search results, I feel a fizz of excitement when my eyes fall on a picture of this young man.

Raphael Broches, around 1930.

He seems gentle and kind and sensitive. I've got a crush like Rosi now. Actually, I think I love him. He could be a guy just walking down the street, couldn't he? I can imagine him playing in a trendy Hoxton bar, where it's cool to look a bit vintage. I feel heartened (and rewarded) to be able to put a face to another name in Grandma's diary. I close my eyes and imagine him playing the violin to her ... Did he get similar feedback to when *I* played the violin to her? I hope not. I wonder what he and my young grandma chatted about. Was Thea his lover?? (I can't find any trace of her.)

I hungrily read all I can find on him ...

Growing up in Hannover, he was thought of as a 'child prodigy'. In 1937, after landing a dream job in a prestigious Jewish orchestra in Palestine, he came home to begin a doctorate in philosophy, but just a year later he was expelled from Germany as part of the *Polenaktion*. Apparently, he was interned in Zbąszyń until the summer of 1939 – just a few months after Rosi's most recent diary entry.

I discover that in 1941, he was a member of an orchestra in the Warsaw Ghetto – I'm reminded of the musicians in the film *Titanic* – the show must go on, even when the ship is going down.

Hauntingly, after the orchestra was disbanded, all traces of him were lost, but it's most likely that this young man with the kind eyes was deported along with the other musicians of the orchestra to the Treblinka extermination camp and murdered there. He would only have been thirty-four or thirty-five years old.

I am heartbroken.

Chapter 15

Diary of Rosi Schul
Sunday, 11 December 1938

My work continues and is much admired everywhere just like in Esslingen. The children love me and I get on well with my colleagues; teachers and doctors. Each day is rewarding and full of variety, even though there seems to be no end in sight.

We've just put on an evening of entertainment and at the end, the committee decided it should be repeated in the barracks. My children's choir was a great success. It all worked out brilliantly and everyone fell over themselves to congratulate us. They dragged me to a little hotel where I played the piano and my guitar for everyone. We sang Yiddish and Polish songs.

I still think every day about Esslingen and the children and of course Samuel. He hasn't written again, though I have heard that he is safe and well. How I still yearn for him! It's ridiculous. I just know something would have happened with us, if the hell in Germany wasn't happening. There are real pogroms going on. Jews are rounded up every day. What will happen to them?

We have both good and bad luck to be here in Zbąszyń. At least we are safe for the moment.

But what will become of us? Who knows!

For now I am staying positive. And ... I seem to have a new admirer ... [Joseph] Cysner! Will it become a close friendship?

I wouldn't mind, or just a light flirt! He seems to like me and he's a very pleasant and intelligent man, but he's got a work-permit to go to Manila as cantor. It will not come to anything, I expect. But I do like him too …! Although he doesn't measure up to Samuel.

I will meet him tomorrow evening.

Diary of Jess Robinson
Monday, 11 December 2006

We looked into the sex line idea today and spoke to a woman at a company we found in the back of More magazine, but when we put the phone down Rabbi said it wasn't a good idea after all, because although it works out as about £50 per day, that's only if you're chatting to pervs nonstop for twelve hours or something. So that's gone out of the window.

BUT we did get interviews from the same company to be psychics on a psychic hotline!!!

It's much better money. Rabbi said no way because it's morally wrong as we're not actually psychic, but I did the interview anyway. Fodder for the memoirs! It was just over the phone. The man asked if I was psychic and I said I thought so. I mean I'd like to be!! I had to give the man a free reading. Rabbi was rolling her eyes and shaking her head in the background but I did really try and tune into him. I was a bit hit and miss. I knew the guy lived near the sea though?!!! Then I thought of the stuff that I've had said to me in my readings before. It was going OK until I said 'sometimes you look in the mirror and you don't like what you see' (which is what Kathy's aunt Carol said to me when she did my tarot and it really hit home), but the bloke got really angry and said he'd been born with a club foot and he was very proud of what he saw when he looked in the mirror. I hadn't meant to offend him and I felt terrible and I apologised and apologised, but he slammed the phone down. I was a bit shocked. Rabbi said it served me right.

I don't want to do shit things to earn money. It feels wrong. I don't want to spend my time like that. I really feel like I should do something a bit more 'worthwhile' as a job. Mum's a piano teacher, Katy teaches toddler music groups, Grandma was a teacher ... Maybe it's in my blood? Would I like it? I think I would if it was the right thing. i.e., not teaching maths ... or teenagers with knives. I think I'd actually love to teach singing and maybe drama too. I think I'll look into it.

Anyway, Rabbi's family is staying tonight and she doesn't have space for me, so I'm going to Gma's for dinner and to stay the night which will be quite nice. I hope Stemmie's there too.

Love Jess

———

I feel a little relieved that the young me might be showing a tiny glint of growth.

I'd always ignored the knot that formed in my stomach when I *knew* deep down things were wrong. My body could have been sending every signal possible, but if I thought I was making a choice that other people would disapprove of, I'd hit the 'bypass button'. The grand override finale was the moment Practice Husband proposed (something he later said he knew he should never have done ... so I guess we were at least matched on how well we ignored what was staring us in the face).

I will never forget that afternoon tea in the posh hotel. When I saw him get down on one knee, I froze. Everything inside me went cold. My stomach twisted. I had thought we were happy, and I knew marriage was the eventual plan. I'd been waiting for this! So why was my body reacting so strangely? I stuffed a finger sandwich in my mouth, hoping it would act like a cork in a bottle. I willed him not to ask it, but he did ... And instead of replying happily with a 'YES', or perhaps a completely out-of-character, 'Let me have a moment to think about it,' or an even more out-of-character, 'I'm so sorry it doesn't feel right,' I blurted out, 'I've got egg sandwich in my mouth!' – and a bit of crumb landed on his shoulder. As shocked as I was at my weird reply, knowing it wasn't a sufficient answer, I swallowed my very hard-to-go-down mouthful, which was less a reflection on the chef and more on my general state, and then said, 'Yes,' with tears of … dread (?) in my eyes. And then it was too late – the marriage carriage had left the garage. (Sorry, I was trying to find an alternative to 'the train had left the station'.)

Rosi, it seems, had no problem going with her gut. I wondered what did or didn't happen in her early life that taught her it was OK to follow her intuition. For her it was like a gleaming compass in the darkness. I also wonder what happened to make me so averse to listening to my inner voice. Too many other voices? Including all the ones I do as an impressionist?

And yet, when I think about one of the places outside my own home where I always felt completely safe – where I never had to second-guess anything – I think of Grandma's house.

I close my eyes and I can see myself there …

I must've been about eight, grinning at myself in the hallway mirror, a gap-toothed, lipstick-smeared mess, swishing around in Grandma's musical-note scarf. Auntie Stephie, my cool aunt with henna-red hair and a boat for a house, was visiting too. That afternoon, over tea and biscuits in the morning room, she had let me brush her hair. I got the brush stuck, of course, and as usual Grandpa had to come to the rescue with scissors.

At dinner, Grandpa Jules was in fine form. He tucked his napkin into his shirt and slurped his soup before anyone else had sat down, smacking his lips with satisfaction. Right on cue, Grandma screeched, 'JULES!' scolding him for his terrible manners, but I secretly thought it was brilliant.

Meals at Grandma's were always a three-course affair, and while we waited for the main course, Grandpa launched into his 'table entertainment'. First came the Napkin Puppet Show, starring Mouse and Rabbit. With a magician's flourish, he whipped his napkin from his collar and twisted it into a little mouse. He rested it in his palm, stroking it gently while we cooed over how sweet it was. Then, just as we thought the mouse had gone to sleep, it suddenly leapt up his arm, scampering towards his shoulder. Auntie Stephie and I squealed with delight.

Then Rabbit appeared – also fashioned from a napkin, but far naughtier. Rabbit pinched my nose, stole Grandpa's specs, drank from our water glasses and finally launched a full-blown attack, bashing Mouse repeatedly on the table until, at last, it was just a napkin again. I barely had time to feel sad for poor Mouse before Grandpa was on to Part Two of his Supper Cabaret: Jewish jokes – mostly lost on me, but Stephie was in stitches. I never got to see Grandpa's infamous 'Tribal Chief' finale, though, because the moment he reached for the wooden napkin ring and wedged it between bottom teeth and lower lip, Grandma would rush in and bark, 'Absolutely not, Jules!'

I remember this particular dinner fondly – not for the entertainment, but because the baked beans that accompanied our fish fingers and mashed potatoes that night had a distinct lemony tang. Auntie Stephie gagged dramatically, and Grandpa made the mistake of asking whether Grandma had remembered to rinse the washing-up liquid out of the pan. The look she gave him could have curdled milk. He bowed his head like a chastised schoolboy as she hissed something acerbic about him never lifting a finger in the kitchen. I kept eating, wondering, as I chewed dutifully, whether my tummy would squeak like the clean plate in the Fairy advert until Grandma, now foaming at the mouth (with soap or rage? It's hard to say), swept our plates away with a huff.

There were no more table tricks after that. Grandpa silently stared at his hands, while Auntie Stephie helped clear up in Grandma's postage-stamp kitchen.

Dessert was always the same: a little glass dish of sharp apple purée from the tree in Grandma's garden, topped with slightly stale almond flakes, cinnamon and sweet, fat raisins. But that night, there was an extra treat: a slice of mint Viennetta. Or at least, it used to be. Years of being frozen, thawed and refrozen had left it oddly deformed – its signature waves now lopsided and studded with ice crystals, like a fossil of its former self. I ate it slowly, savouring every bite.

After dinner, Grandpa gave me a goodnight kiss and headed off to the sitting room to watch telly and eat liquorice allsorts, while Grandma and Auntie Stephie cajoled me upstairs.

Her bathroom felt like another world – nothing like ours at home. The brown carpet was so old and scratchy it had its own personality, and the washing machine rumbled away in the corner. I loved Grandma's pale-blue bath. Especially the inflatable cushion she gave me to rest my head on while I sculpted a foam beard out of Matey bubbles.

As I soaked in the warm water, Stephie sat on the loo seat and Grandma on the edge of the bath, as they chatted away about this and that. There was something about hearing them laugh together that made me feel safe – and a little curious. Why didn't Mum and Grandma laugh like that? Sometimes, I wasn't even sure they liked each other.

Afterwards, in clean pyjamas, I snuggled into Auntie Stephie's old bedroom. Grandma tucked me in tightly, kissed my forehead and padded back downstairs, her slippers making soft scuffs on the landing. I lay there listening as Stephie's ancient car coughed into life outside. I traced the purple paisley pattern on the curtains with my finger while my Fisher-Price cassette player softly whirred beside me – Alan Bennett reading *Winnie-the-Pooh* in a voice that got slower and lower as the batteries began to run down.

In the morning, as always, *magic had happened*. A little saucer was waiting on the bedside table: one cut-up apple, a few raisins, some almonds, an After Eight and a tiny glass of milk. It wasn't there when I went to sleep, but somehow, it always appeared.

I knew the ritual. I'd nibble my snack in bed, then knock gently on the wall. If Grandma knocked back, it meant I was allowed to go into her room. I'd race next door, climb into her bed and try not to fidget as I counted the seconds till I could sit at the white dressing table with its princess mirror, layering myself in necklaces and scooping thick blue Nivea cream onto my face with grown-up precision.

Downstairs, after creeping past Grandpa's room, we'd sit at the garden table in the morning sun with Crunchy Nut cornflakes and raisins. And when Mum arrived – after the obligatory argument with Grandma – I'd proudly show her the tub of wild strawberries I'd picked from the garden.

This memory is so vivid, but what sticks with me most is that even at a young age, I feel I knew Mum and Grandma had a difficult relationship … I want to know more, but I'm not sure if I should open that particular can of worms. And anyway, maybe I've remembered things wrongly.

As I wonder if I might have fabricated these echoes of unease, my phone pings. A sign from the universe?

Group Chat: Cool Bitches

Sunday, 21 May 2023, 15:43

Katy: Have you been doing any German practice, Jessie?

Me: Naaaaaa, you?

Katy: Naaa. Got two years innit.

Mum: ... I've got an email in my computer, Jessie.

Me: 'on' not 'in'

Mum: From the German Embassy.

Stephie: Ooh er, maybe we've been rejected, man.

Katy: I got one too, it's just to say they've received our paperwork in Germany.

Me: Mum, while we wait (for two years), is it definitely still ok to keep translating the diaries, please?

Mum: Yes, if I have to, Dollydumps.

Me: And I was wondering if I could sort of interview you, about Grandma ... about what made her her. And your relationship?

Stephie: Well I'm up for it!

Katy: Can I be there too?

Sasha: I'm at Uni.

Katy: We could record it?

Mum: Ohh really?!!? Ach, yes alright then. Wednesday 21st June.

Me: 12pm – after your Keep Fit?

Mum: Well we always go to the pub after and then I've got to play for a quick funeral – so come at 1:30.

Me: OK, thank you!

Mum: No salmon, but I can dig out some sea bass from the freezer.

Katy: ?

Mum: Sorry, that was meant for Marywiththeleg. xxxx

I'm determined to keep going with Grandma's diaries – as long as my mum can bear to help me translate them. Thank goodness she has time in between all the 'quick funerals' she's attending. I think I'd hate it if my funeral was quick. Make it long. Make everyone suffer. Turn the heating up. A four-hour ceremony – that's what I want … (God, it would be so typical to find my backbone once I'm dead and it's in the coffin.)

Chapter 16

**Diary of Jess Robinson
Sunday, 14 January 2007**

So much to tell and I don't know where to start!!

Oh yeah, I am living in Finchley Central cos we bought a frigging HOUSE!!!! I'm just around the corner from Jojo and Katy and about 10 mins away from Grandma. (She's coming over for lunch later.) Basically I just needed to tell a few white lies about how much I earned per month and my accountant (who is definitely a bit dodgy) signed something and they think I earn £30,000 a year and it's a 100% mortgage and actually we don't own the house, Halifax does, but I'm on the property ladder in a HOUSE.

We moved in on January 3rd and it was SO fantastic. We drank lots of wine and danced in the garden. I slept on a blow up bed. And we have dad's wallpaper table in the kitchen til we get a proper one. And dad has been round most days since! Rabbi and I are paying him a bit to decorate. Grandma gave me a gift of £1000!!!!!!!!!!! Very nice!!!!!!!! So we're going to have carpets fitted and now I've got a mattress!!!!!!!!!!!!!

I still love Rabbi. She's my bestest friend. We've already had two great house parties. Need some more.

Also I ended up doing PANTO! Dick Whittington. I was the cat and I made the audience laugh every night by scooting across the stage like I had worms. It was a very short run, but I was really happy. I didn't like the guy playing Dick. He was an actual dick.

I have also been on SO many dates. I'm a total MAN EATER. Well I'm not. I'm very single. At Fiona's party I met a guy called Steven who was in a Tic Tac advert and I met a guy called John who was in a car advert. Steven Tic Tacs is really lovely and funny but I don't really think that he's sexy. Also he turned up on our date so hungover and low energy and then made me pay the bill. No thanks ... Car advert John was lovely and very handsome but on our date he casually dropped into the conversation after 5 minutes that he had a son which threw me a bit. Then we went back to his, and he played guitar and sang at me. It was SO CRINGE. So I got out of there.

Then there was Daniel. He's Jewish. He's a friend of a friend. I was quite excited about him. But he actually turned out to be not so funny and not so handsome and really quite boring. So after FIVE dates (because I thought I should try to fancy him), when he turned up at my house (I've got a HOUSE) expecting to sleep with me for the first time (and smelling of booze), I sent him home. Almost good, except I said Jojo was having an emergency and I had to go. And really I should have said 'Daniel, sorry, you're drunk and boring and there's no chemistry here and I'm only kissing you because I can't think of anything to say and I'm actually REALLY BORED. Can you go now?'

Oh well, at least I didn't sleep with him.

THEN, I met Nick on the tube after a drunken night out with Rabbi. And we just clicked. I saw him and his two band mates hitting each other with newspapers, and it made me laugh. He came up and spoke to me. We talked a lot – all the way from Leicester Square, and then he got off at Kentish Town. I knew then that he wasn't gorgeous but I was really attracted to him. His room is messy and his house is FILTHY. He's 32 years OLD – why is he living like that?? It's a bit studenty. He's got the kind of bathroom that when you've come out after washing, you feel dirtier than when you went in. Rabbi thinks he looks a bit rodenty haha. Maybe that's why he lives like one. I'm on FIRE!!! So I kicked him to the curb.

All in all, I don't think I want a boyfriend anymore. There are too many options and none of them are any good when you actually get to know them. Plus, I like flirting and meeting people too much. And I want to focus on my career.

And for someone who wants to enjoy adventures and FOCUS ON THEIR CAREER, I've spent way too many pages talking about boys!

Speak again soon.

P.S. I don't know why I've put this as P.S. I guess I don't want to get too excited about it, but – I GOT AN AUDITION FOR FIDDLER ON THE ROOF!!!!! Mum helped me write a letter to the director, saying I was Jewish and that Grandpa Jules's grandparents were part of the pogroms, and it worked!!!! It's an actor musician production so I'm going to have to practise up the violin and I'm going to play If I Were a Rich Man on the recorder. I will try to make it sound like a clarinet – klezmer style.

WISH ME LUCKKKKKK.

Diary of Rosi Schul
Sunday, 15 January 1939

Time has passed since I last wrote!

There is a good deal of news; both good and bad …

My grandmother has now been taken to an old people's home in Poznań, Poland. I'm so pleased she is out of this and being cared for.

Papa received a letter. Things in Belgium are very tense. Delli and Max are in prison in Germany! Ruthi is trying to get out and Mama is sick. Regina and Simon struggle on, and Berta doesn't earn a penny but runs a new, fantastic nursery in Belgium. Like her, I don't earn anything here. I work for nothing and pleasure. Yes, it's a pleasure. I still love it. This is what I'm known for, and it's very nice.

I appreciate every minute here ... the children are lovely. For Chanukah, they gave such a lovely performance, it could have been Esslingen! I was so happy with the reception we got from the parents, the audience at the Stadium, and the Committee.

Sadly, the relationship with Cysner, which was good for a while, is beginning to fizzle out. He is very preoccupied with his emigration and soon he'll be gone.

I still think often of Samuel. I know he is not 'the one' as he never writes back to me.

Will I meet the right man here ... or ever???

Joseph Cysner.

LIFE IS ROSI

I found Joseph Cysner! Bit of a cutie, no? He made it to the Philippines, where he became cantor at Temple Emil in Manila and taught music at two universities. He performed on the radio, gave concerts for the president, and then – just when life seemed settled – was imprisoned by the Japanese in the Santo Tomas Internment Camp. Imagine escaping the Nazis only to end up in another prison. You'd have to wonder, 'Is it me?' He survived, conducted services for US troops, and later settled in America. There was even an exhibition about him in 2017, and I found some excerpts from his memoirs online, describing his experience in Zbąszyń. I didn't see any trace of my grandma – but she might be mentioned somewhere … 'Things have ended with Rosi – I think she took it badly and tried to poison me. Though that could have just been her normal cooking …'

In the empty carriage on the train journey to Mum's the night before our family 'interview' about Grandma, I spread out across the empty table, examining the folder of pictures and family history Auntie Stephie gave me, every now and then checking details on a thread of emails from various cousins scattered across the world. I want to find out more about Rosi's family and what they were all doing at this point …

I discover a transcribed 'testimonial' by Grandma's youngest (and most beloved) sister Ruth – known as Ruthi. She describes the night when the Gestapo came to Hannover. With her mother, Sara, unwell in bed, her father, Baruch, was ordered to pack some warm clothes for himself and Ruthi – who was just twenty-two at the time. They were to be deported to Poland along with Grandmother Reisel (in this telling not eighty-eight, but ninety-six!).* One of the most haunting parts of Ruthi's story is what

---

* Quite a big discrepancy, so for argument's sake, let's just say 'twenty-one again'.

happened after they were loaded into a truck with 'old and young Jews' from their neighbourhood. They were taken to a concert hall in Hannover – turned, chillingly, into a *Sammellager*, a place to gather all the Jews before deportation ...

'At the *Sammellager* the Gestapo picked out six young and old women, including myself. We had to go through a pub in the basement, where the Gestapo and the SS men were drinking heavily. I was very frightened, as I thought they would rape us. They took us to a little terrace by the pub and made many photos of the group.'

Ruthi later discovered the pictures had been used in *Der Stürmer*, the notorious Nazi propaganda newspaper, where they published images of Jewish women as examples of 'typical individuals of the Jewish race'. Ruthi was convinced she'd be deported to Poland. And she might have been, were it not for her sister Adele, who with the help of the rabbi she was secretary to,[*] got permission to come into the hall and take Ruthi out. The rest – including Baruch and his mother, were put on sealed trains to Poland. Pieces of the puzzle are beginning to fall into place.

Upon finding their family's home sealed shut by the Germans, Adele (who apparently was warned about the deportation plans for the 27/28 October by a 'friendly' SS officer) and Ruthi stayed at an aunt's apartment.

Ruthi was then left alone in Hannover, while Adele and her brother Max (known as Menne) made a desperate attempt to cross the German–Belgian border. Despite travelling through the woods with a guide in the dead of night, they were caught. Adele spent three months in prison, and Max, six. Ruthi visited them often but couldn't help. Eventually, when he was released, Rosi's brother Max fled to Paris and was hidden there during the war.

My eyes fall on a smartly dressed couple staring back at me. I recognise the woman as my great-aunt Regina, Rosi's oldest sister

---

[*] Different from my kind of Rabbi but equally as invaluable.

(pictured here in her late thirties), and the man as her husband, Simon.

Rosi's oldest sister Regina and her husband, Simon.

Regina, who was living in Belgium, had connections to the Underground Resistance – specifically the White Army, which was instrumental in obtaining false papers that allowed her mother and her siblings to escape to Belgium, where the family were eventually hidden in Brussels and the children in the village of Orroir.

However, Simon was arrested in Antwerp in 1940 and taken away by the Nazis. He was never seen again.

Reluctantly, I turn to the next page …

Big sister Adele and her husband Eli stare back at me. They married in 1941 in Antwerp after getting those forged papers from Regina.

Eli tried to reach Switzerland but was caught on the border and taken to various French camps until he was deported from Drancy (near Paris) to Sobibór extermination camp.

Rosi's big sister Adele and her husband, Eli.

He was never seen again.

In Zbąszyń, Rosi, her father and her grandma were stuck in limbo: not allowed to go back 'home' to Germany, but not permitted to officially enter Poland either.

On 24 January 1939, there was an agreement between Poland and Germany, which allowed some Jews who had been kicked out of Germany to come back temporarily. The plan was to let them sell off their businesses, but there was a catch – the money they made had to go into special blocked accounts and, sadly, they never got access to those funds. Although she doesn't mention it, it's possible that Rosi's dad, Baruch, went back to do this at his shoe shop. I wonder if he did. Would anything have been left, or would

Left: Grandmother Reisel – twenty-one again. Right: Rosi's uncle Israel.

it have been vandalised and looted during *Kristallnacht*? Nobody in my family seems to know.

I study this amazing picture of Rosi's grandma Reisel, imagining that this is how she proudly sat on her suitcase that night in the stable, when she refused to lie down on the dirty straw. As I consciously put my hand up to my greying roots, I'm impressed she still had her thick dark hair, thinking with a mixture of disappointment and tenderness that I must have my dad's 'hair genes'. Then I feel like an idiot as it hits me that she would have been wearing a sheitel (a wig that many religious Jewish women wear after marriage). I know nothing about being Jewish.

Apparently it was in December 1938 that my great-great-grandma Reisel was supposedly taken to Poznan to the 'old people's home' young Rosi writes about ... But there's evidence that she was in fact reunited with her son Israel in Kraków.

According to the ID cards they were issued, Reisel and her son were still alive in March 1941, and were likely living together in the Kraków Ghetto, which had been established by that time.

Managing to get a sliver of internet signal on my laptop, I read that around 15,000 Jews were crammed into the Podgórze area of the city – a district previously populated by only 3,000 people! The ghetto was surrounded by walls to keep the Jews in and away from the rest of the city. The conditions were horrific; people frequently died of starvation and disease. From 30 May 1942, the Nazis began deporting Jews from the ghetto to various concentration camps, including Bełżec death camp, finally 'liquidating' the ghetto on 13 and 14 March 1943. Over a couple of days, the remaining Jews were divided into two categories: around 2,000 were deemed 'good for work' and transported to the Płaszów labour camp. The 'leftover' 2,000 or so (of which, if still alive, my great-great-grandma Reisel would certainly have been) were considered 'unfit for work' and either murdered in the streets, killed in their homes or sent to Auschwitz.

My stomach twists as I take in their faces.

It's harrowing, looking at these pictures. Staring into their eyes. Real people. Humans. Young men and women – my ancestors – caught in something unthinkable. Why is it only now, at thirty-nine, starting this project and *really* seeing these faces, that I feel the full horror of it?

Yes, I feel emotional. But more than that, I feel ashamed.

Ashamed of how small-minded and self-absorbed I've been. Ashamed that I've never properly explored my heritage and only half listened to the 'headlines' I'd been told. Ashamed that when I think of the millions who've been displaced, mistreated or have lost everything – then and *now* – it still feels too big to grasp.

Maybe that's the problem. A million deaths are a statistic. One face, one name, one story – that I can hold. That I can feel.

As I get off the train, I wonder why my grandma (certainly all through my life) described all of this as 'a big adventure' when these dreadful things had happened to people she knew and loved? I'm beginning to think she'd covered her memories in bubble wrap – softened them to make them easier to carry. So many of her diary entries after her deportation are still about teaching and boys … The few fragments of normality she could cling to in a life where she had little control over anything else?

As I see Mum's car pulling into the station, I hope that during our family chat tomorrow, if I just reiterate what young Rosi was blocking out, the irritation Mum feels towards Grandma and her diary might dissipate …

Chapter 17

Diary of Rosi Schul
Wednesday, 8 March 1939

I'm still here in Zbąszyń ... how much longer? The thought depresses me sometimes. I must not think about it. There are many good things; happy times and successes and of course low times. I have flirtations, but with no prospects, and I meet many lovely and interesting people – but only ever as friends!

My life is spent being with the children. They have so much love to give and receive. It's hardly technical but I really need it. The Stadium now has more staff, so at present my day begins at midday and finishes at around 7.30 p.m. I miss it so much in the hours and minutes I'm not there.

The performances are still my forte and the evening lectures are the greatest feats of organisation for me. In the morning to fill my time, I now take two English courses and I have also started teaching the language a little. On top of that, I'm working as a secretary for our Teachers Club. From this work, I get to know other people than the refugees – all different ranges of importance and value ... but still, why don't I meet the 'right one', my 'one and only'?!

There's Dr Tannenbaum ... he seems to like me, and we talk a lot together (he invited me to an important Committee meeting). Then there is 21-year-old Mendelson. He is extremely intelligent and friendly and seeks me out at all the shows and performances. What does he want with me – an old girl of 24 now?! He's a bit of a show-off. He tries to impress me but I know he is only interested because I'm unattainable. He plays quite a part among the top people of the administration of Zbąszyń, and I suppose it flatters me that he shows interest! There are handsome young doctors too!

Yes, I'm on good, friendly terms with all of them through my work and I do enjoy a little bit of flirting. They all seem keen, but I'm not interested.

A lot of people are leaving Zbąszyń daily – some through Germany or going directly to the countries for which they were lucky enough to get permits. Cysner, who things have completely ended with, is leaving tomorrow, and there'll be a farewell party for him. I will miss him, or rather the distraction of him. I know we weren't suited to each other, not really. But I do wish him well. It feels as if everything is moving forward around me, but I'm stuck. Frozen in time.

I have made attempts to get a visa for England and have received good letters of recommendation from different quarters, which should help ... but do I want to go there? I don't know! What kind of job would I have to take? I would rather go to Belgium, where I hear my family have found me a job in a children's refugee home. Now that would be just what I would love. My knowledge of English would benefit me in England, but if I go there, I may end up as a domestic servant! It's hell to contemplate!

I received lovely letters from Jonas from Esslingen – he's now a cantor in Sweden. He writes so lovingly, but I don't feel the same way about him ... I just don't have a special, close friendship with anyone ... will I ever find the right one, since I lost Fritz Samuel ...? Will it EVER happen?!

Israelitisches Waisenhaus
und Erziehungsanstalt
"Wilhelmspflege"
　　　　　　　　　　　　　　　Esslingen
(Jewish Orphanage and　　　　 7/3/ 39.
Educational Establishment)

    We hereby certify that Miss Rosi Schul has been employed in our institution for about two years.

    She had a deep influence over the children under her care whom she looked after with the greatest devotion and attention ; they trusted her implicitly.

    Miss Schul also showed an outstanding talent in organizing performances given by the children. She proved herself extremely versatile teaching handicrafts, needlework, gymnastics, music etc. Her natural abilities in managing and educating children made her particularly suited to such a position.

    Owing to political circumstances Miss Schul was regrettably compelled to leave us. Her departure left both staff and children with a great sense of loss.

    We can recommend Miss Schul with the greatest confidence.

(Signed: Dir. Rothschild).

Rosi's glowing reference from Theodor Rothschild – Herr Vater.

Diary of Jess Robinson
Tuesday, 13 March 2007

I got the job! The director – James – said he loved my letter. Yay. I love being Jewish! We start rehearsals in a couple of weeks. I must lose weight. Mum and dad and grandma are really pleased for me, though they're going to have to come all the way to Hereford to see it.

Also, I'm going to sign up to a Jewish dating agency on Tuesday. I just thought a Jewish guy might be a bit different from the idiot actors and musicians I've been meeting. And I am Jewish aren't I? I don't really have any Jewish friends apart from Rabbi. Not that we're religious ... We haven't even had bat mitzvahs and we can't speak Hebrew or anything. But it might just be nice to embrace that side of things more. Especially now I'm going to be in Fiddler on the Roof! ...

I feel positive and on top of my career and I'm ready to find the right guy!

I must remember this feeling and not just write all the shitty stuff.

It's funny, the things we both wanted at twenty-three ...

Rosi was longing for purpose, security and maybe a little romance – though not from the young show-offs who hovered around her performances. I was thrilled about a part in *Fiddler on the Roof* and daydreaming about finding a nice Jewish boyfriend. Different decades, different circumstances ... but something about that familiar blend of ambition, restlessness and romantic longing feels strangely universal.

On Wednesday, the sun is shining in Mum's beautiful garden and the mood is light as the Cool Bitches bustle around the wooden table, laden with folders, pictures and of course snacks.

Jojo is lying on the grass tickling Brian the dog, as Katy opens up the table umbrella and we squeak as a plastic spider on invisible thread dangles down from the centre. Dad's little joke still gets us every time. I now refer to it as 'a legacy trick'.

I have high hopes as I open my phone's voice memo app, having agreed we should record the conversion for my niece Sasha, who's studying biochemistry at Manchester Uni while dreaming of being … a singer-songwriter.*

Stephie pours the colon-cleansing coffee as Mum hands out ice lollies. I'm under no illusions that Mum will be frank about her relationship with Grandma, but I'm hopeful that this will be good for her. A therapy of sorts. I steel myself. There'll probably be laughter, irritation … maybe even a few healing tears. I reckon that ultimately Mum and Auntie Stephie will find some common ground – a meeting of minds. I press record.

'OK, Mummy,' I begin cheerfully. 'First of all, tell me – what are your nice memories of Grandma?'

Mum seems caught off-guard. 'Oh!' She pauses, thinking. 'Nice memories …' She gazes at dad's spider as she racks her brain for what seems like ages. I catch Auntie Stephie's eye, and I'm about to change tack when Mum says, 'Well, I must have been about twenty-one at the time.'

'Twenty-one?!!' I think, disconcerted that the first twenty years of Mum's life seem to have drawn a blank …

'Your grandma and I had a lot of fun being in the chorus of *The Gondoliers*, which was on at the Hampstead Institute in Hampstead Garden Suburb,' Mum continues. 'We got the giggles in rehearsals every time we had to sing a particular song. It was "List and learn", as in listen and learn … Only, there was a woman next to us who had a very pronounced lisp. So she said "Litht and learn". For some

---

* I'm telling you, however hard we try in this family, we can't ignore the call of music, even if we're on the path to doing something 'sensible' …

reason, Mum and I thought that was so hysterical that we could hardly sing our parts.' Mum starts laughing at the memory and imitates the lisping lady, swaying and swooshing her skirt from side to side as she skips around the garden table, causing the next-door neighbours to smirk as they peer at the Jackie Show over the fence.

'Bit mean!' I say, trying to sound virtuous for the sake of the recording, though I know I've mocked people myself. I mean, it *is* my job. Which is a flimsy excuse. I'm an arsehole.

My sisters and I laugh at Mum, who is now bowing for the applauding neighbours. Once they disappear inside talking animatedly about their fully bonkers friend, I continue, 'So she had a sense of humour then?'

'Yes, she did.' Mum pants as she rearranges her breasts, which have tried to escape their M&S underwired cups during all the skipping. 'Well, sometimes ...' she corrects herself, sitting back down with her coffee. 'I have a picture of her laughing so hard her false teeth nearly fell out.'

Grandma laughing so hard her false teeth nearly fell out.

'We were all at Grandma's for lunch, sitting around the morning-room table, and Grandma asked' – Mum adopts her familiar impression of Grandma: a cross between a German witch and a Gestapo officer – "Und how iss your friend Janet?" I told her that Janet had come to the organ just before church started, given me a big hug and said very loudly in my ear' – Mum's voice turns breathy and earnest as she impersonates the vicar – "I've got terrible constipation!"* ... and Grandma just laughed and laughed, till her teeth dropped down,' Mum finishes as Stephie and Katy pass around the blurry photo of Grandma – a second of total joy caught forever.

The atmosphere is buoyant. This is going to be fine! Encouraged, I press on. 'And what about as a child? What was she like as a mum? Do you have early memories?'

'Well, there was always ...' – Mum launches back into her Grandma impression – "You'll do your piano practice before you go out to play!"'

The way Mum delivers the line is suddenly so full of venom, it's as if the rug has been pulled out from underneath us. The mood shifts immediately. Stephie fidgets in her chair, staring at the spider, which swings in the breeze that has picked up ... (No, don't be stupid, Jess, Mum's mood does not have the power to change the weather.) I sit forward.

'That started from when I was five or six years old,' Mum continues indignantly. 'It made me so upset. And I cried because I could hear my friends playing in the road. That was another thing she stopped me from doing,' she spits, adding, 'like me not letting you play on the village green.'

'Well, you *didn't* let me,' I counter mildly, thinking to myself, 'So what?! That's a pretty mild bit of parenting to still be holding

---

* That's where I get it from, I think ... the impressions, not the constipation. I'm very regular, thank you.

on to with such anger.' 'How come, Mum?' I ask, now annoyed. 'It segregated me. The kids from the council estate said I thought I was too good to play with them.'

'I thought it might be dangerous down there. I didn't know who all the men were, and it didn't seem responsible to let you out of sight,' Mum says.

'You made me practice too,' I remind her. 'You made me practice before I was allowed to go to my own birthday party at Pizza Express.'*

'Well, maybe it was the only time of day it was possible. I was *furious* when you came home with that scratchy violin. I wanted you to play the cello, but you came home from school one day with that little violin case, swinging it proudly. That was my hope – gone out the window,' Mum says dramatically.

'Your *hope*?' I ask, baffled. This is getting bonkers.

'I thought if you wanted the violin so much, you'd want to practise, but you hardly ever did. And when I accompanied you on the piano, if you made a mistake, you'd poke me in the back with your bow.'

Shit, I did. I quickly apologise, feeling ashamed and wishing we weren't recording this stupid conversation. I'll have to edit it before we put it in the 'family archives', I think, conceding that poking someone with a violin bow is quite an effective way to stop a conversation – maybe I should carry one to boring social events.

Mum has zero trouble remembering unpleasant memories about Grandma Rosi.

'She was always doling out punishments for something. I remember one summer's day at primary school, at the end of term, there was going to be a party. The long dining tables were set up with paper tablecloths, plates and little cups of orange squash.

---

* Tell me you're middle class without telling me you're middle class.

Then Grandma arrived, looking very smart, to pick me up. She wouldn't let me stay for the party. Instead, she wanted me to go with her to a function in London where I was supposed to play the piano. I cried the whole way in the car because I didn't want to miss the school party with my friends. I just wanted to stay with my ordinary friends, drinking orange squash. But Grandma made me go to this Jewish function, where she could show me off.'

'She was proud of you,' I say, glancing at a resigned Stephie.

I feel annoyed at Mum. 'So WHAT?' I think again ... Imagine if we all hated our mothers because they didn't let us do everything we wanted to do when we were kids. Imagine if they'd *let us* do everything we wanted to do as kids ... 'We'd all be dead!' I think, remembering not wanting to hold Mum's hand when we crossed the road, and the time she yanked me back before not one, but two buses could hit me. (It *is* true what they say about them, isn't it?)

'She just wanted to show me off,' Mum repeats bitterly. 'That's why I had to play the piano for visitors in the music room every Sunday afternoon. Every. Single. Time.'

'Did you have to do it too, Stephie?' I ask, remembering my own experiences of Grandma's music room and beginning to feel a bit of sympathy ...

But before Stephie can answer, Mum jumps in: 'Every time your grandma asked Stemmie to do something she didn't want to do, she had a little petit mal attack. She had epilepsy. I don't think she could induce it,' she adds quickly in her little sister's defence, pre-empting my next question, 'but the second Mummy said, "Und vot are *you* going to play, Stephanie?" Stephie had an episode. It was awful to watch, and Mummy was so horrified she didn't make her play.' My mum's face softens as she remembers ... 'From about five years old, Stephie wrote the most amazing stories. She has an imagination like Enid Blyton. Her stories were always about little animals or princesses … and all kinds of dramatic things would happen. Mum was very proud of her.'

'So, she was proud of *both* of you,' I say gently. Turning to Stephie, I ask, 'What was Grandma like as a mum to *you*?'

Stephie sits up straight, smiling fondly as she thinks for a second and says confidently, 'My first memories are very loving. I was sick as a child, yeah? So I got all that attention. Mummy and I were instinctively close. I remember a lot of cuddling, her fussing over me, worrying … I went to the nursery where she worked … I was with her all the time.' She looks at my mum and says, 'But it was different for Jackie …'. Her voice trails off a little. '… I have these Red Cross letters from before I'm born. They're all about Jackie. I know Mum loved her – she absolutely adored her.'

Katy nods encouragingly. 'So, what changed?' I ask carefully.

'It's when I was a teenager,' Mum says. 'That's when everything changed.'

'I think it was when I came along,' Stephie adds guiltily. 'We didn't play together. There's such a significant age gap – five years. But it was the time too. Jackie's childhood was what I call "postwar". By the time *I* was a teenager, it was the 1960s. Pop culture exploded – fashion, music, everything. It got me, completely.'

I smile at my auntie in her embroidered flares with her wild Kate Bush hair, and think, 'It's *still* got you.'

'Not that Jackie didn't have all that,' Stephie continues quickly, 'but by the time I was fourteen, Jackie was nineteen. She'd already had sex!! She was looking for her freedom. It's also first-born syndrome,' Stephie adds thoughtfully. 'Everything is learnt from parenting the first child.'

'Was Grandma strict with *you*?' Katy asks.

'Our household was strict,' Stephie says. 'Mummy and I fought when I started hanging out with boys or lying, or when I didn't wash. I was a thief and a liar,' she says matter-of-factly. 'Jackie had more discipline and more focus. I wasn't even made to learn the piano. But I was so close to Mummy. My bedroom was next to hers, and at night I'd knock on the wall, and she'd knock back.'

Katy and I share a smile, both of us remembering the sleepovers at Grandma's. 'What did you understand about Grandma's expectations of you when you were growing up then?' I ask Stephie.

'To be successful, do everything, have children, have a husband ... she would have loved me to have a baby,' Stephie says a little sadly.

'For me, it was to study and to go into further education,' Mum replies. 'The Royal Academy of Music was acceptable because she compared me to her siblings' children. All my cousins were at university – they're scientists, doctors, businessmen. I had to keep up the standards. She wrote to them all the time about me. "Jackie got into grammar school," she'd tell them. "She's performing this, she's doing that, she's passed her exam." But at the same time, she'd take it all away by saying, "You know you only got into grammar school because your daddy played the piano for them." It was always a kiss and a slap. A kiss and a slap. It was constant ... And things were never forgotten,' Mum continues bitterly. '"My mummy sleeps in the kitchen."'

'I'm sorry?' I say, confused.

'Every time you said something outspoken, she'd go, "My mummy sleeps in the kitchen,"' Mum replies.

'You know about that story?' Stephie asks, seeing my bafflement. 'We lived in a flat in West Hampstead when we were little. It had two bedrooms and a large kitchen.'

'Yes, and it was big enough to fit a divan bed against the wall,' Mum adds. 'Mummy worked at the nursery in Wembley, and Daddy was still playing in nightclubs and coming home at four in the morning. Stephie and I shared a big room, and Dad slept in the little box room. And Mummy slept in the kitchen on the divan bed because she had to wake up early to be at the nursery ...'

Stephie takes the baton. 'So, we were at this posh hotel in Cliftonville and Daddy was playing in the band, and we were sitting at the table having afternoon tea. A very posh lady, a friend of Mummy and Daddy's, was sitting with us and talking about her flat in St John's Wood. She was saying, "Oh yes, it's very spacious. There's a lounge, a dining room, two bedrooms, and a maid's room behind the kitchen." And Mummy, wanting to sound equally grand, said, "Oh, yes, we too have two bedrooms and a kitchen." And little Jackie pipes up, "My mummy sleeps in the kitchen!"'

'I must have been about eight,' Mum says. 'And Mummy laughed it off at the time, saying, "Oh, children talk such nonsense!" but later on she was *furious* with me. After that, it became shorthand for putting your foot in it. "My mummy sleeps in the kitchen."'

'We did grow affectionate of that phrase as the years went on, didn't we?' Stephie says, smiling, but Mum is like a runaway train as she ploughs on …

'All of Grandma's punishments came in the form of stopping me from going out. If she poked her head into the room and saw me watching TV, she'd say, "Jackie, will you lay the table, please?" I remember once saying, "Do I have to right now? I just want to see the end of this programme." And she answered, "Right! Now you don't go out on Saturday." If I asked what's for supper, she'd say, "*Scheiss mit Ei*" [shit with egg].* If I asked to do the washing up *later* so I could meet my friend, she'd say, "No, you stay here and do your duty." She knew it'd make me late. She knew what she was doing.' Mum's voice is bitter, her words spilling out like a dam has broken. 'When I desperately wanted to move in with three other

---

* A note on *Scheiss mit Ei* (shit with egg): having sampled many of Grandma's creative culinary concoctions over the years, I would imagine *Scheiss mit Ei* to be more palatable than some.

music students, she refused, saying I'd be promiscuous and get pregnant, even though I'd been with one boy for three years. Later, when I was married to my first husband and deeply depressed, I decided to have psychotherapy. I told Mum, and she said she was amazed I had the cheek to spend my husband's money on therapy. She said I had a simple mind and there was nothing to analyse. Then she suggested I read her diary to "understand more about myself".' Mum's voice sharpens as she recalls, 'I told her, "Your diary is *your* reality and your truth, not *mine*." But she insisted, "No, it's all facts – just facts." So I opened a page and read a paragraph from when I was three years old. It said, "Jackie is the sweetest little thing with her black curly hair and button nose, so gorgeous you could eat her up. However, she has no interest in books whatsoever. I think she is going to be as stupid as her father and his family."' Mum pauses, shaking her head in disbelief. 'I said to her, "Is that supposed to help me with my psychotherapy? Is that supposed to show me something good or helpful about myself – that you wrote that when I was *three*?" She just shrugged and said, "It's only the facts."'

My mum's expression grows even darker as she turns to Katy and Jojo. 'The last entry I read was about me marrying your father. It said, "Jackie gets married tomorrow to Robin Miller, a lovely, lovely boy. Poor man, with that fishwife!" She called me a *fishwife*! Her own daughter. It is so insulting and cruel. I told her, "I'll never, *ever* read your diaries again." I said, "You might as well burn them because they're nothing I'd ever want."'

There is a silence as Mum's words resound in my head ...

'That's horrid,' I say, fumbling ineptly for a response, as I notice Stephie staring up at the sky, visibly upset.

'Was she jealous?' I venture cautiously.

'Yes,' Mum says firmly. 'I think it was something like that. But I was very angry. I was often very angry with her, and when I found my voice I'd shriek at her.'

Stephie turns to Mum, saying softly but emphatically, 'You have to think about it in the context of the age you both were. Mummy was about fifty, and you were around twenty-three at the time. You were the same age she was when she made her big journey. She was probably menopausal by fifty.'

'She always denied it,' Mum snaps. 'She said she had no symptoms at all. No hot flushes.'

'I don't mean just the external symptoms,' Stephie explains patiently. 'Menopause can affect your psychology as well. Think about it, Jackie ... When *you* were fifty and Jess was twenty, were there ever any arguments?'

'God, yes!' I exclaim, almost fondly recalling the screaming matches Mum and I used to have and picturing my dad retreating into the garden to escape the atmosphere.

'And you didn't say nice things about Jessie at that time either, Jackie,' Stephie points out.

I'm inwardly both horrified and totally accepting of this, knowing what a treat I was. Stephie continues, 'So I think it's *crucial* to consider how Grandma felt at that time. Can't you zoom out and say, "This is how she was at that point in her life"?'

'No,' Mum says bluntly. 'She said those things about me at *all* ages. It was a permanent state. She was always that horrible. I remember her Teutonic sneering. "You're not a hard worker; you don't practise enough." But the minute I got enthusiastic about a piece and started practising for hours, she'd poke her head in and say, "Oh, vot's come over you, practising for vunce?" Well, it was enough to make me stop. She was so withering.'

'I think that might be a German trait,' Katy offers. 'There's this funny Instagram account where a daughter imitates her German mother –'

'She said it to Daddy too,' Mum interrupts. '"Oh, vot's come over you! You laid the table for me today." She couldn't just say, "Thank you, darling, that's so helpful."'

'Is it a German thing? Or a Jewish thing too?' Stephie muses. 'It just snatches the carpet from under you ... But she didn't do that with me,' she adds sadly.

There is a long pause and then I ask, 'Do you think that was just her character, or could it be because of the war and what she lost? Did she maybe feel like you had all the opportunities she didn't, and you weren't living up to what she could have done?'

'It could be,' Mum concedes reluctantly, while Stephie says hopefully, 'That sounds like something!'

'I don't know,' Mum says. 'Maybe she was hungry to relive the youth she didn't finish having. I remember when I had my music groups in my bedroom, all my school friends, their boyfriends and people who played instruments or wrote poetry came over. I'd play the piano, someone would play guitar ... It was all very cultured. And she'd always come into the room and sit on the floor against the wall to be part of it.'

'Well, that's nice, isn't it?' Katy says hopefully, looking at Mum as I remember Grandma's description of her evenings with teachers at the orphanage in Esslingen.

'There were maybe nine or ten people crammed in my bedroom,' Mum recalls. 'And when they started talking about politics – socialism, Ban the Bomb, all that – I had no opinion. I'd just sit there quietly, listening, trying to take it all in.'

'God!' I think as Mum says this. 'That's what I did ... still do!' I can't imagine Mum having no opinion. It gives me hope ... She continues, 'And then Mummy says' – cue the impression, which has now escalated to something between Hitler and a Dalek – "Und vot do you think, Jackie? No opinion ... *again*?"'

'In front of your friends?' Katy and I say in unison, appalled.

'Oh, that's so diminishing.' Stephie sighs.

'Demeaning,' Mum says bitterly. 'Why did she do that to me? I don't know whether she thought she was encouraging me. Maybe she did,' Mum says thoughtfully. 'But then, when I started to have opinions as an adult she'd cut me off and say, "Thank you, Doctor Robinson." And despite the criticism, I needed to be approved of by her, I felt I had to do my duty and go there at least twice a week to give her some sort of social life and look after your grandpa with his dementia, and I felt guilty about not wanting to go and I felt resentful about her expectation. Duty, duty, DUTY!' Mum exhales what seems like seventy years of anger in one long breath. Like an exorcism.

Desperate to pull the conversation back to a more pleasant footing, I say, 'She was a very nice grandma,' and Katy nods in agreement.

'I took Katy to see her after a drama exam once,' Mum offers. 'Katy got 98 per cent – a distinction. I told Mum, "She's got a distinction! She got 98 per cent!" And Mum said, "Is that because you've got a little squeaky voice?" I called her later that day and said, "Don't you ever put my children down with sneering comments like that." She took everything away. A kiss and a slap.'

There's an awkward silence, which is suddenly filled by Brian barking at a stolen pair of Mum's tights floating in the pond. As I rescue them with a stick, Jojo's laughter prompts Mum to say, 'Your grandma was proud of Jojo when she could play for her friends and entertain at tea and dinner parties. She had her over almost every Sunday until Jojo had the courage to say to her one time, "I'm not coming, Grandma, they're not my friends and I want to see my own friends." Grandma was very angry.'

'I called her Adolf!' Jojo says loudly, suddenly fully alert and engaged in the conversation. 'I used to say I had to go to tea with Adolf!'

Katy grins and I try not to laugh, but Mum continues. 'I remember your grandma was meeting friends in Golders Hill Park. She'd only take Katy – who was of course very advanced and articulate; they were only three and four years old at the time. Jojo heard Grandma's voice when she came to the front door to collect

Katy, but Grandma didn't want Jojo to see her, so she quickly took Katy and closed the door and Jojo hurried so desperately to see her that she fell down the whole staircase and I had a terrible fright. I picked Jojo up, went out to the car and told your grandma she was a fucking bitch not to take Jojo as well and how little extra trouble she would've been. I think actually I might've called her the CUNT word.* I was so angry, and she said to Daddy, "Just drive Jules, she's not well." Then, when Jojo's psychosis and paranoia were brought on by her Huntington's and she believed she had to go to the toilet every ten minutes and she was very troubled – believing she had a tarantula on her back – Grandma didn't want her at her house at all any more. I said to her, "I can't see you then. I choose Jojo if you're going to put me in that position." She answered me with silence. Stephie explained that she was very upset to see Jojo so unwell, but of course it was completely self-centred of her not to be able to tolerate Jojo's presence in her house with me and Stephie there as well, and very unsupportive to me.'

Jojo strokes Mum's arm, saying, 'Ahhh, poor Mummy.'

Mum sighs. 'She was disappointed. Disappointed with her life. A proud, disappointed woman.'

Stephie shakes her head. 'It was her pain. I think behind all her outbursts and vitriol was a little person. At home she could at least control everyone and be the matriarch because no one challenged her ... except you, Jackie. She was terrified of anyone in the family making a fool of themselves because she thought it would reflect on her. Her pride hid this little girl. I can see it in her photos. Maybe I'm looking for it, but I see it. Even when she's nine, her eyes look different from everyone else's, like she's already carrying something heavy.'

---

* My mum might be the only person not to say 'the C-word' but instead say 'the cunt word'. I love her.

Mum rolls her eyes, but Stephie presses on. 'I played the daughter very well, even though I didn't have children. I'm still childlike and I was easy, and I felt safe with her. She had a daughter in me.'

'She always felt you needed her,' Mum says, pouring the now-cold coffee.

'I did ... I do,' Stephie admits sadly. 'It was a flattering comfort to her. But you didn't need her, Jackie. You have always been so independent.'

Everyone looks a bit drained and pale, despite the summer warmth. Wanting to end on a positive note, I say, 'Mum, what do you think you got from her? What traits did she pass down?'

'Apart from vitriol and resentment? Ha-ha-ha!' Mum quips bitterly. Then, noticing Stephie's sorrowful look, she clears her throat and says, 'The value of culture. She taught us the importance of culture above religion. A love of classical music, art, books, exhibitions. And self-respect.' Mum pauses and then, as if she can't stop herself, continues. 'But also, and I know this is unhealthy – I know it's wrong – but the *anger* she stirs up in me energises me so much. Even now, at seventy-eight years old, I'm still upset about her not letting me leave home at twenty-three. That rage *fuels* me. The way I live my life now feels like ... like revenge. Now I do whatever I want. If I want to be lazy, I'm lazy. I'm my own person, my own judge ... So, yes, what I got from her is a love of culture and classical music, which she surrounded herself with, but I also got a rebellious determination to *not* be like her.' Mum's voice crescendos. 'So when you girls asked me to pick you up from the other side of London at midnight, or come and get you from school, I'd *always* go. I'd *always* help you. I never said horrible things or held grudges or threw your mistakes back at you. That anger she gives me fuels my determination to be different, because I HATED HER!'

The last three words hang in the air. The truth is stark, raw, undeniable. Mum's confession lands heavily.

'Can't you just drop it now?' Stephie says, standing up, her huge eyes wet with tears.

'No!' Mum spits back, her breathing fast and sharp.

'What about …' I begin, but Mum snaps, 'If you want fluffy memories of your grandma, *don't ask me.*'

And just like that, the interview is terminated.

Chapter 18

Diary of Rosi Schul
Sunday, 19 March 1939

There is a constant stream of people leaving now through Germany to other countries.

Two more nice young men leave tomorrow, no future for us. One of them loves a beautiful 18-year-old girl.

I think I will go to England now. I have references from here; whether it will help, I don't know. Or perhaps I should still go to Antwerp to set up my own nursery, with no one telling me what to do, but I don't speak any French, so it makes little sense.

The ideal situation would be to work in a refugee home. I could do that in England and my English would help. But I'll have to take what comes. I might have to be a maid. Arghhh!

I feel old. Will I never have a truly fulfilling relationship?

Yesterday I slept in a young woman's place. She lives with a man, but they're not married! It's very modern and free-thinking. I'm just a baby compared to her, even though I'm only one year younger.

She believes Mendelson is a good match for me because he's so young and clever and she's a good judge of character. No – he's too clever for me. And there is no spark. Nothing doing!

My friendships in the Stadium are good. But still, just friendships. I don't expect much to keep me happy. A little flirtation would be nice. I hear nothing from Samuel these days. God! How I suffered over him to no avail.

Why do all my relationships have so many problems? They're never equally balanced. Oh, if only something could change!

Diary of Jess Robinson
Monday, 19 March 2007

I'm such an idiot. The woman at the dating agency in Temple Fortune was SO sneery. Apparently I am not Jewish enough to be on their books! They said they would have made an allowance if it had just been the fact that my dad isn't Jewish, but because I also didn't have my bat mitzvah, and I don't speak Hebrew and I don't belong to synagogue means I'm not right. I feel like a fraud.

And I feel SO angry with mum. I want to SCREAM. ARGHHHHHHHHHHHHH!!*

I hate her for not bringing me up to know more about Judaism. Why didn't she??? I have no Jewish friends. I can't call myself Jewish. Although I bet the Nazis would still want to gas me.

Maybe I'm not meant to find the right guy. Maybe I should just look for someone normal like daddy. Wahhhh! I want to go home. I'm going to go home to mum and dad's ... I know I mustn't take it out on mum. I won't. But I do feel SO SO SO cross with her!

One minute I'm too Jewish, the next I'm not Jewish enough. Who the fuck am I??? I'm just a dick. In fact, I am closer to being an actual dick hanging between someone's legs than I am a Jew. And – I wouldn't even be a circumcised dick.

GOODBYE

---

* My pen has ripped through the page here.

P.S. Really looking forward to Fiddler on the Roof. I won't tell anyone about not being Jewish enough for the dating agency though, or they might fire me.

There aren't that many translated pages of Rosi's diary left, but as I read our two diary entries side by side, I'm struck by Rosi's 'Argghh!' For the first time it reminds me a bit of my own writing. I mean, I complained about boys and Mum, and said 'I want to die!' Rosi was less dramatic and a bit classier, but still … I feel I definitely inherited my grandmother's skill as a diarist.

'Will I never have a truly fulfilling relationship?'

and

'I am closer to being an actual dick hanging between someone's legs than I am a Jew.'

See? It's hard to tell who wrote what, isn't it?

I am still reeling from our 'interview'. Mum, still 'stirred up' by the conversation, is having a break from diary translating. Who knows if she'll want to continue at all? I can't blame her. Maybe I'll have to pay to get the rest done professionally.

There hasn't been much chat in the Cool Bitches group since then, aside from a few terse messages cancelling our next meet-up. I almost changed the group name to *Not Cool Bitches*.

Katy and I have decided not to share the recording of the interview with Sasha – at least not now. Maybe not ever.

I keep thinking about how subdued Stephie looked when she drove off in her old Vauxhall covered in Beatles stickers.

Worrying that I've traumatised her, and imagining her on her houseboat, alone and isolated, I reach for my phone …

Message to: Auntie Stephie

Wednesday, 21 June 2023, 20:30

Me: Hello Stemmie. Are you ok?

Stephie: I'm OK man. I've been thinking about it a lot and I think sometimes 'a picture says a thousand words'. Jackie was very happy in her childhood, and she and Grandma got on famously ... lots of love and fun together:

Text by Auntie Stephie: 1. Rosi and Mini-mum stroll along the seafront in Brighton. 2. Grandma and Mum, who is looking so sweet and happy here. 3. Another sweet mother-and-daughter pic. Also love Rosi's dress.

When I came along, Jackie was five and suddenly she had to begin to be the 'big sister', cos I was ill with my Petit Mal, so I got most of Grandma's attention (which made Grandma and me so close). This next picture tells a story. Look at our faces; Grandma so peaceful and genuinely happy, Jackie, somewhat subdued, uncomfy, and almost a bit tearful, and me, a bit 'duh'? and innocent.

Five-year-old, uncertain-looking Mum, glowing Grandma and baby Auntie Stephanie.

Then, in these next two photos, you can see a 'tension' creeping in between Grandma and her. The first pic she would have been around eleven or twelve, and I would have been about six or seven. She was pressured to succeed at school, and the piano, etc., despite not really having the confidence or wish to 'stand out' or 'perform' in front of people … (maybe cos Grandma didn't think I could be the one to do that, what with my illness), and she needed a 'mensch' of a daughter to be proud of …

Photos from Stephie illustrating a growing seriousness/coldness between Mum and Grandma over the years.

Because it's so entrenched in your mum's head and memories of memories of memories of the bad stuff; the arguments, the discipline, the expectations laid on her, I believe she can't (and WON'T) see anything loving and sweet that Grandma did and felt for her. It's as if she thinks Grandma ruined her life with all that horrid stuff between them ... But no, that is absolutely NOT true! Your mum has a ton of things to be grateful to Grandma for, and Grandma WAS proud of her, and grateful for all the things that Jackie did to help out, when Grandma was old ... but it wasn't said out loud, cos NEITHER of them had the right words to say to each other anymore.

What is it, ultimately? Chemistry, circumstance, or just rotten communication?

Who knows! It wasn't my experience with Grandma — even when we fought. I loved her sense of family, her spirit, her knowledge, and her sense of adventure. I loved her for everything she did for me, even when I hurt her at times with stupid talk or bad behaviour — there we were together. I would still sit on her lap, or we'd be in her beddy together, talking and talking and laughing and crying. She said I was her 'rock', but really she was mine, all through my life, one way or another.

I feel that somehow it's all my fault (coming along when I did) that formed the different dynamic between your mum and your grandma. Katy was so much older when you were born, AND you had BOTH your 'proper' parents when she didn't cos your mummy and her daddy split.

I wonder if there's a parallel between yours and Katy's relationship, through the years, and mine and Jackie's?

Some envy? Maybe jealous 'irritation' that raises its head every so often, coming from vying for attention from our

> parents, and, dare I say it, being perceived as the 'favourite' in our respective cases?
>
> I repeat again, what was it? Chemistry, circumstance, or just a deeper connection?
>
> I think, out of everything I got from mum, we have the same heart ... xx

---

Oh, MAN, I love my auntie Stephanie so much I could cry. She has a HUGE heart. And she feels things *deeply*. Mum has sometimes written her off as silly or dramatic, but I love seeing them together. They're a brilliant team – chalk and cheese in the best way. Mum the realist; Stephie the dreamer. Both open, both talkers. I don't know if it's down to all the therapy we've all had, but when it comes to feelings, we are a family of talkers.*

Grandma was fascinated by psychology too. She never went to therapy herself – and discouraged Mum from going ('They always blame the mother'; something my own mum repeated to me) – but her shelves were filled with books by Freud and Jung.

My husband (proper, not Practice) and my dad, who came from very stiff-upper-lip British families, were both taken aback when they joined our family. They appreciated all the talking to varying degrees: my late dad, a quiet man (possibly because he couldn't get a word in), often opted for the back garden rather than talking about emotions, but my husband is amazed by it – he finds it refreshing compared to his own family's British bottling. Is it a Jewish thing?

Stephie's wisdom still surprises me. Sure, she might talk to her stuffed pig, Rosie (who has her own passport!),† and she once

---

* And essay texters – thank God texts aren't 10p a go any more – we'd be bankrupt.
† SHIT, I forgot to apply for her pig-passport.

rescued a turkey from a farmers' market, named it 'Kissy Face' and let him sleep in her bed, but she's not silly. I think she'd sometimes rather hide away in her sanctuary of a houseboat, full of curios and incense and the Stones on vinyl, than face the harsh realities of the world outside. And honestly, I get it.

She often feels like the black sheep. When Grandma was alive, Stephie knew her place; she had her routine, which she both loved and resented. Grandma expected her daily, relying on her for help, errands and companionship. Stephie is strong – at five foot nothing she can shift a grand piano. But now Grandma's gone, I think Stephie feels unmoored. Mum is the matriarch now, with her three daughters in orbit. And Stephie isn't quite in the middle of that constellation.

I think Grandma knew that. She'd always say to me, 'Don't forget to give your auntie a call.'

I send out a silent prayer – well, more like a wish, or 'vibes', as Stephie would appreciate – hoping she can somehow feel it from Brighton to Rickmansworth. 'You're part of the family. A big part. And you are so, so loved. And I promise to do right by you, and make sure the Stones and the Beatles and Kate Bush are always playing when you are too old to wipe your own bottom.'

Reflecting on all of this – on what Mum and Auntie Stephie shared – I'm left with a tangle of feelings: guilt, sadness, a desire to 'get it right'. I feel this is an important aspect to Grandma's story, but the idea of sharing the rawness, the contradictions, makes me anxious. Isn't it disrespectful to portray a Holocaust survivor in anything less than a saintly light?

But the truth is rarely tidy.

Rosi was complicated. She was light and dark. Kind and sharp. She had a steeliness that could cut, and a warmth that could hold you like no one else. She was, in other words, human.

Hearing Mum's and Auntie Stephie's stories side by side, I'm struck by how differently they experienced their mother. With

Mum, the relationship was steeped in conflict, criticism, control and impossible expectations. I believe her. And Stephie doesn't deny it. As a daughter, Mum was held to unreachable standards, trapped at the piano while her friends played outside, constantly put down. Her scars run deep.

Stephie's version is gentler. A mother who adored her, who let her sleep in her bed, who fussed and nurtured her. Two sisters. Two truths. The kiss and the slap.

As RuPaul or Jessica Fletcher or someone once said, there are three sides to every story: there's your side, there's my side, and then there's the truth.

I acknowledge both the love and the pain, the tenderness and the harshness – or, as Mum puts it, the kiss and the slap.

This search for meaning isn't about painting Grandma Rosi as a villain or a saint, but about seeing her as a whole person. Flawed yet resilient. Loving yet strict. And maybe, just maybe, the Bitches and I can still find a bit of peace in that understanding ...

Which leads me to think about my big sister and Auntie Stephanie's question: 'I wonder if there's a parallel between yours and Katy's relationship, through the years, and mine and Jackie's?' ... The beginning of an answer forms, making me squirm. Nevertheless, I take a breath and hop on a Zoom with Katy, first of all to get *her* take on Grandma. I want to know if she remembers her the same way I do, or if, like Mum and Stephie, we're carrying different versions of the same woman.

As she talks thoughtfully, new bubbles of memory float up and pop in my mind ... jam sandwiches, copper coins tipped from a leather wallet, sewing cards with holes and bright wool. I smile. Fifteen years after Katy, I was there too, threading that same chunky needle in the morning room.

'She was incredibly enthusiastic,' Katy says at one point, her face lighting up. 'She didn't just like things – she loved them. Books, table tennis, bridge, backgammon ... She didn't just consume culture – Grandma wanted to connect through it. She'd even jot down a book's synopsis in her diary so she could remember to discuss it later.'

I'll leave a big old space in the book here so *you* can write some thoughts about it, which you can discuss with your family at a later date:

_____

_____

_____

_____

_____

You're welcome.

'And it wasn't just her own life she kept tabs on. She kept track of everything,' Katy says, and we laugh at the memory of her full diary, which contained not just *her* appointments – but everyone's.

'She'd write it all down so she could remember to ask about it next time.'

It's true. I'd mention, in passing, that I had an audition coming up, or was going to visit some friends, and two weeks later, she'd bring it up, unprompted: 'Did you get the part?', or 'How was your friend's play?'

'She did also have a temper,' Katy says, sitting up straight, no hint of drama in her voice. 'You really didn't want to get on the wrong side of it. And she could be very critical – of Mum, of people in general.' Then she adds, still calm, still measured: 'I think she had a lot of anger in her. And I feel like I've got a lot of that anger too. Which is strange, because I haven't lived through anything like what she did.'

I realise I'm holding my breath … it's not that I'm surprised by what Katy's saying – I've always known she feels things deeply. It's just rare to hear her say it out loud. Outwardly, she often seems so composed, so rational, so in control, that when she does express something emotionally raw, it takes me by surprise. And I never know when the explosion is coming or what might trigger it. 'A kiss and a slap' creeps into my mind again.

She'd be mortified to know it, but there's a part of me that always feels like I'm walking on eggshells around her. Like one clumsy comment could open a crack I don't know how to mend. So I tread carefully. I always have. And now, as I'm becoming more outspoken, I feel there's been a change between us. I don't think she's used to hearing me this way. I'm not sure she likes it either.

I'm not sure she likes *me*.

Cautiously, I ask whether she thinks we had the same experience of Mum.

'No,' she answers immediately, without hesitation. We laugh, but her eyes are sad. We talk about grief. About how things shifted when my dad died. As horrific and utterly traumatic as it was to watch him die – drown; I wouldn't wish lung cancer on my worst enemy – it brought Mum and me closer. It was just the two of us there. We stood side by side, and now there's a softness between us that wasn't there before. But as things shifted between Mum and me, it seems to have unsettled my relationship with Katy, who, along with my half-brother Gideon (Dad's son), was forced to watch the whole gruesome scene unfold over Zoom thanks to the Covid lockdown. They were kept at a distance by circumstance; physically removed. While Mum and I lived it in the flesh, they were spectators – present but impotent. Watching a death in pixellated silence.

'For me, it's gone the opposite way with Mum,' Katy says. 'I've been quite depressed about it. It's really difficult to talk about. I'm actually thinking I probably need to go and speak to someone.'

It's layered, of course. Katy and Jojo have a different dad – he left when my half-sisters were five and six, moved to Scotland and started a new family. My dad, Brian, became more of a father to them than their own dad – especially to Katy. And I know she loved him. I also know that grief, for her, came tangled in something complicated – the surprising weight of her emotion, the regret that she never expressed her love for him out loud, and anger at her 'real' father. She lost another 'dad' all over again.

The distance between Katy and me isn't new, but it has grown, stretched quietly over the years, like elastic that's been tugged too far and never quite snapped back.

When I was small, she was a big sister to me – at least, that's what I've been told. By the time I had real memories, she was already away at university. We lived in different worlds.

I was essentially raised as an only child. My two teenage sisters felt more like visiting cousins than siblings. I grew up in a house with just Mum and Dad, while Jojo and Katy had a whole different era, a whole different father.

We had a brief patch of camaraderie when I was in my twenties. We ran holiday theatre schools together in the village. We were a good team – her steady, me silly. But when I went ahead and ran one without her, she was hurt. I was baffled; I saw it as me being proactive, needing the money. She saw it as disloyalty – me taking the reins of something we'd built together.

Today we both admit that there's a distance between us. Calmly, politely. We acknowledge that something has been broken. We don't trust each other. We've both heard things, relayed through Mum.

Katy once told me – again, calmly, in one of those rare, emotionally honest exchanges – that she thinks I sometimes take things that aren't mine to take. That I charge in, claim the space, the story, the emotion, while she's still quietly trying to decide what she feels, wants and what's fair.

And she's not wrong. I am impulsive. I do leap. I feel things out loud, I act fast, I want to make things happen. She deliberates; I declare. She's still drafting the email; I've already hit send and signed it off with a kiss and a flourish.

I used to get annoyed when she said I was like Mum – I took it as a criticism, but lately, I've started to see it differently. Mum is gritty. Mum is resilient. I'll take that.

Katy is thoughtful, analytical, kind. She weighs everything. And maybe my momentum makes her feel powerless. As we think back to Grandma's Sunday-afternoon concerts, Katy reflects that in our family the arts are held up as the pinnacle of achievement. 'If you don't "perform",' she adds, 'you're a bit worthless and invisible. Put on a show, have an art exhibition, play in a concert, perform for an audience, otherwise no one's interested … I was proud of being an actor, but I stopped performing when Sasha was born.' It's a telling comment – one that reveals more than it seems to intend. Does Katy feel invisible? I can see where she's coming from and how she might feel that, but if you ask me, the real pinnacle of achievement in our family wouldn't be a standing ovation, it'd be someone becoming a doctor or a lawyer … or at least marrying one.

Like Mum and Stephie, we've both inherited different pieces of the same story, and we're trying to stitch them together with entirely different thread.

Katy and I are as chalk and cheese as Mum and Stephie, but the difference is, certainly since Grandma died, Mum wants the best for Stephie. She looks out for her in that bossy, big-sister way. There's care in it, even when it's clumsy. With Katy and me … it's harder to find that care. Sometimes, it feels like we're from different planets. And sometimes it feels like she doesn't even want to be orbiting mine.

Cool Bitches? More like Broken Bitches, I think as the Zoom ends … but I reach for my phone one more time …

Message to: Katy

Wednesday, 21 June 2023, 22:40

Me: I do love you and I'm sorry we're in a tricky place x

Katy: It was good to chat xx

———

I switch off my phone.

I do want us to find common ground again. I want there to be a way back. And maybe, just maybe, this strange journey we're on – becoming German, retracing Grandma's steps – might help us get there.

I feel I'm just scratching the surface. The story isn't over. Not for any of us. I just know there's more to discover, and my mind turns back to how I'll coax Mum into another conversation.

'Maybe a new pair of leggings will butter her up,' I think as I turn the next page in Rosi's diary.

Chapter 19

Diary of Rosi Schul
Thursday, 13 April 1939

Whenever something really lovely and exciting happens, I reach for my diary ...

Noah Nachbush, a great Yiddish actor who I first met three months ago, came to Zbąszyń again. He recognised me straight away and couldn't have been sweeter towards me – he commented on my sparkling eyes! At every function he kept me by his side, with remarks like 'Liebike mit Deine lechtige oigen' (dearest with your bright eyes). I can't believe it. He wrote something similar on the back of a photo he gave me. I cannot read his Polish writing, so somebody had to translate it for me. He attended one of the children's performances, and loved it, as did the large audience of parents and Committee members ... the children were fantastic! He walked me home afterwards.

And in the evening, to another hall with all the VIPs! I had the best seat, between Mendelson and Nachbush. He said to me, 'I'm so attracted to you, I must cuddle you!' and 'Come and sit with me – Ich liebe Dich, let me kiss you!' Well, I couldn't believe it! Mendelson was so cross, and the result was predictable. We were turned on! He walked me home, and became very loving, with hugs and kisses ... I thought to myself, 'Why not? ... it won't lead to anything serious!'

I found Noah Nachbush entertaining refugee children! And look, there's Grandma in the front row! Appearance organised by the Relief Committee for Jewish Refugees Expelled from Germany.

Diary of Jess Robinson
Sunday, 15 April 2007

Fiddler on the Roof has opened. I love it. I get on really well with the two girls playing my big sisters. Apart from Zoe who plays Hodel, I am the only Jewish person! I didn't expect that. They were all asking us for advice and what it's like to be Jewish. I let Zoe answer mostly and I was pleased she knew the prayers! I've learnt them now (although I pretended I already knew them too). I have a crush on the actor playing Motel the tailor, but Lucy shagged him on the first day so I'm not going there. Mum and Grandma came to see it the other night. They said the Jewish accents were dodgy (apart from mine and Zoe's). It's true. Helena sounds French and Lucy sounds like a pirate for some reason. I keep expecting to see a parrot on her shoulder – Ha!

> Mum and Grandma weren't sure about James the director when they met him. He's not Jewish, but that's not why – it's because he got a bit pompous and sneery when Grandma said setting the star of David on fire at the end was quite shocking and in bad taste. I mean she doesn't mince her words, but she is Jewish and she DID survive the Holocaust – so it was a bit cunty of the director to tell her she doesn't understand the art and symbolism. I felt weird. I wanted to say something, but I didn't quite know how to voice it. Plus I don't want him to think I'm difficult …
>
> I feel Jewish. (Even though I wasn't brought up in a Jewish community.) Zoe says she does too, but there's a time and place to admit it. She said she often doesn't tell people because they'll judge her. It's sad. She said sometimes she feels ashamed of being Jewish.
>
> I just thought WHAT?!
>
> I feel ashamed that I am Jewish but I don't really know about the religion. I don't know the holidays or prayers and I wish I did, even though I don't believe in God.

I feel a weird mix of connection and disconnection with Rosi at the moment. On the one hand, I feel linked to her through our shared love of performing – the way she lit up when organising a show, the joy she found in expression and audience connection. I recognise that feeling in myself every time I write a new show or step on stage – the experience letting me be bigger, brighter, louder than real life allows.* On the other hand, maybe Mum's reflections on her childhood are tainting things.

---

* Not that anyone in my life has EVER accused me of struggling to project … bless you if you're listening to the audiobook of this – THIS IS HOW LOUD I CAN SIIIIIIIIING!

I still wonder what it's like to have the deep grounding in Jewishness that Grandma did. Rosi's Jewishness was just there – a constant, unshakeable part of her life. For me, it's always felt more fragmented, like I've been trying to piece it together with scraps. Not pork scraps, obviously. At twenty-three, I was ashamed of how little I knew about the prayers or the holidays. Decades later, that shame hasn't fully gone away. Especially now, with the world as it is, holding pride in being Jewish feels complicated. Anti-Semitism hangs like a dark cloud on the periphery, and people make assumptions, pass judgements, or even grimace at the mention of it. I understand now why Zoe in *Fiddler on the Roof* felt the need to downplay it, but that understanding makes me angry too. And uncomfortable.

And yet, here I am, tracing my Jewish heritage as I wait to see if I'll be accepted for German citizenship through Rosi. It feels ironic – uncomfortable, even – that I'm seeking citizenship from the very country that uprooted and exiled my family. There's something absurd about it, like a cosmic joke I can't quite laugh at yet. A German and a Jew walk into a bar and sit at a table for one. It's the same person. It's me. But at the same time, it feels necessary. Not because I *feel* German – I really don't – but because it's part of our story.

I do *feel* Jewish, though. It's in the echoes I hear in klezmer music or the taste of certain foods. Sometimes I fantasise that there's a dormant ability to speak fluent Hebrew just waiting inside me. Maybe it'll be unlocked with the bite of a particularly chewy bagel, or a certain clarinet melody … maybe I just need a bump on the head.

As a grandmother, Rosi didn't keep kosher or go to synagogue, but I know that as a girl, she was deeply religious.

Later in life, her Jewishness wasn't about ritual. It wasn't performative. It was cultural, emotional, cellular. Something indelible.

Her accent was German. Her tastes were German. But that part never felt as alive to me.

Jewishness has always marked me out, made me feel 'other' – both in my small English village, where we were the only Jews, and later in London, where I was suddenly not Jewish enough.

Jewish feels familiar, even in its contradictions.

But German? German is a stranger – even though it's been quietly threaded through my life since I was born.

Things have gone back to being cool between us bitches … Katy and I continue to rub along together, fine on the surface of things. We take Jojo on sisterly outings and pretend for her that 'life is rosy'. And just like the good-quality knicker elastic she covets, my mum bounced back from the uncomfortable garden interview. She's been Jewing on with village life, piano teaching, social engagements and generally being a pillar of the community.

Group Chat: Cool Bitches

Saturday, 21 October 2023, 14:21

Me: Hi Bitches. Happy Saturday. Question of the day …

Mum: Uh Oh – Poopie, don't ask something about Grandma that will make my stomach churn with anger please … I've got 2 play 4 a christening in a minute.

Me: It's not directly about grandma and you don't need to text back immediately – definitely not during the christening.

Mum: OK congregation coming in.

Me: Enjoy. Switch your phone to 'airplane mode'.

Mum: OK Dollydumps xx

Me: My question is ... Do you feel German?

Katy: At the moment I find it impossible to forget how Grandma and her family were kicked out. Worse, what the Germans did to everyone they didn't want in their country. So I feel nostalgic for Grandma's early life, and all the Germanic traits that remind me of her. I think I have inherited some Cherman traits but personally I don't feel connected.

Mum: Ja, ich transkribiere immer noch ihre Tagebücher – Scheiss mein Ei – I'm very connected to ze lengvidge!

Katy: That translates as Shit my Egg.

Me: Google translate says it's 'fuck my egg'.

Mum: Mit. Scheiss mit Ei. Service is starting.

Katy: 😂

Katy: I think I feel about 55% English, 30% Jewish, 10% Scottish (from my dad), 5% German.

Stephie: Cooee. No, man. I don't feel German, but I do feel connected to the language, there's something familiar and comforting about it, having heard it spoken all through my childhood, by aunties and uncles etc ... xx

Me: That's interesting. And do you feel Jewish Stephie?

Stephie: Yes, totally xx

Sasha: I'm glad I learned to speak it at school but I don't feel German. I think I feel a bit Jewish though.

Mum: Well the baby is sweet, but there are too many children at the Christening. So noisy! Got 2 play hymn in a min, but I'll quickly say – I don't 'feel' German, but I love being able to speak it and understand most of it – and like Stephie, it's the familiarity of it from childhood – even hearing Yiddish is nice and also fascinating. Do I feel Jewish? Yes, especially in Church!! But when a Jewish person like my friend Nicola says derogatory, insulting things about NON-Jews, I am disgusted and feel very disconnected from that type of Jewishness. I'm very anglicised. One moment – got to play 'Morning Has Broken' …

Me: You can answer later.

Katy: I hope she at least remembered to put her phone on silent today.

Mum: Terrible singing from the choir!! They're so out of tune and feeble. One more verse.

Sasha: How is she texting and playing?

Katy: Maybe she's using her feet?

Sasha: Flexible, grandma!

Mum: As I was saying. There's an automatic connection for me with the two Jewish girls in the village. But just going about my life, wherever I go, I feel 'different'. I don't feel connected to my German heritage – the Teutonic, severe, strict elements which came to England with Grandma – the need to be the BEST – to be so revered and respected – no thank you. Hitler wanted the best and purest German race. If THAT'S German heritage ... Nein danke – nicht für Mich xx

Mum: Why did Siri just say 'Hitler' out loud? I didn't ask him to. Now everyone is looking at me.

Sasha: Hitler is at the christening?

Me: Jesus! 😂

Mum: No, Hitler. Hang on. Got to get ready for 'Jerusalem'. What a silly choice for a christening.

Katy: So why the question, Jess?

Me: Just looking back over my old diary from when I did Fiddler on the Roof. Plus I was speaking to a German girl at the gym the other day (a sort of friend), and she laughed at me for wanting a German passport but not being able to speak any German. I mean I kind of made a joke of it myself ... but really I felt like a dick and a fraud. I'm sure she didn't want to make me feel that way. Then when I asked if she wanted to come and see some Comedy that night she said 'British Comedy isn't funny!' I don't know how to feel! Maybe she just didn't want to hang out with me.

Katy: 😖

Mum: Ach – these fucking superior Germans!!! It must be bloody genetic!!

Ze only Cherman who had any right to be cantankerous and superior was Bach!

Was the German sense of humour better when they stood laughing at Jewish people in the streets – watching their shops smashed up, their books burned and millions starved, tortured and gassed when they thought they were having showers? Was it not ze Germans who are the reason we're even getting citizenship on behalf of grandma?

Katy: You made a joke of it though, didn't you, Jessie?

Me: Yes ...

Sasha: We should use the word they use when we tell people about it, which is reparation.

Mum: Yes.

Me: I did make a joke of it, you're right. Because I feel silly.

And mum, just because they're German doesn't mean they're anti-Semitic or Nazis! They're probably beaten over the head with the Holocaust again and again, aren't they? It's my own fault – I wanted to make light of it because it's such a horrible big thing, and I feel ashamed that I don't know German. Mummy, why didn't you teach us??

Mum: Dull readings in this service today. Terrible! Why don't they speak up?

Me: Was there ever a conversation about me learning German? When I was a kid, I mean? Did they just teach French at school so that's what I learnt? Did you wish for me to learn a different language, like you wished I would learn the cello instead of the violin, mum?

Mum: I hardly spoke it til after mum died – other than if I was in Germany.

    Ah you should see this baby – so sweet! Just got to play 'Shine Jesus Shine'.

Me: BANGER!

Sasha: Yeah! I love that one.

Katy: I hope they do the claps.

Stephie: It's all still so fucked up that people (like your gym buddy) miss the point … it's absolutely NOT about speaking the language, but about remembering and reparation on behalf of Grandma (who survived the Holocaust) and all the millions who did not … who lost their homeland, just by being Jews … the shame is your girlfriend's. This sort of thing follows us all our lives, and each time the point gets missed, we must try and find our voice to say, 'Hey, NO'! xx

Mum: Yessss! I agree absolutely. That girl probably didn't mean to make Jess doubt herself – but we all go round with teeny bits of vulnerability – Henning Wehn lives here and loves English humour!

    They were good at that hymn. It's a younger crowd here.

Me: Well you'd think so at a christening.

Sasha: Haha 💀

Me: I often betray myself to make other people more comfortable or happy. Did grandma? Do you?

Mum: No she didn't – yes I do – I'm very keen to not be huffy and make atmospheres.

Katy: I think Jess is talking about 'people pleasing', mum. Like when you find yourself giving or doing more than you'd like, or biting your tongue, so as not to upset someone else. In the end you feel that the other person took advantage of your niceness, even though they often aren't aware of what it cost you, and would probably be mortified if they knew.

Me: Yeah. That's it.

Mum: Ladyfingers!

Katy: Was that meant to be an insult?

Mum: ggggggggggg nn

Sasha: I think she sat on her phone again. 😂

Mum: You can take the piss. But I have been multitasking all morning; reading and taking Marywiththeleg for her colonic procedure, playing the Organ and answering your texts. After this, I am going to take back my Sainsbury's knickers SUCH DREADFUL QUALITY! and buy some better ones from M&S. Marywiththeleg says the knicker elastic is MUCH better.

So I shall not be answering texts between 3 and 5 pm.

Mum: Knicker elastic

Mum: Sorry FFF

I feel a wave of love for Katy's understanding of me. Maybe we aren't such strangers to each other. There must be a chance for us, surely? God, this has been a rollercoaster – in the sense that I've felt sick throughout.

Chapter 20

Diary of Rosi Schul
Monday, 1 May 1939

Is it really possible that spring here in Zbąszyń is as beautiful as spring in Esslingen? Spring is the season that makes me the happiest. I remember walking to school in Hannover through the cemetery, or zooming about on my bike. Such wonderful memories. And sad.

But now I'm sitting at the window of my room, and the sun shines brightly, just like in Esslingen. There's a lovely lake to my right, woods on the left, and the countryside all round. I can hear the familiar sound of the train line. Now, I can be outdoors all day with the children in the sun. Is it a great blessing, or have I become so easily satisfied that even Zbąszyń can make me happy? Everyone here is so friendly and warm towards me. I want to stay here through the spring ... How can it be that this 'no man's land' has become a sanctuary for me? How much longer will I be here though? And what then?

Diary of Jess Robinson
Friday, 11 May 2007

I have had the WORST night. I am writing this in bed.*

I'm a bit shaky. I feel sick and sad and so full of rage. WITH MUM.

I went to Zoe's mum's Friday night dinner in Hampstead. There was a guy there – Simon – who Zoe wanted to introduce me to. He works for Foxtons estate agents and has his own car. It was SO awkward though. First of all – I brought Zoe's mum a box of Dairy Milk chocolates for after dinner, which we OBVIOUSLY couldn't have because they don't mix meat and milk and some people there are properly Kosher.

We all stood up when the red wine was poured and I said cheers and knocked it back cos I was a bit nervous but I got a shock because it was so so sweet. Zoe rolled her eyes at me and had to pour some more because you have to say the prayer first. She and Simon kept having eye contact. WHY DIDN'T MUM TEACH ME THIS STUFF??????????? Then when we'd had our wine, we had to go and wash our hands and then go back to the table. But silently? When we were back sitting at the table Zoe's dad farted when he stood up to do the Challah blessing, which made me get the giggles, but we were supposed to be silent before we'd taken a bite so Zoe was looking at me crossly. I couldn't help it. It was the worst feeling. I couldn't believe no one else heard it.

Simon and I started to have a nice chat, and for a bit I had a really nice time, until I burnt my lip on the chicken soup which was so bloody hot it made me flinch and dribble it down my chin. I've got a red mark there now. I think it's going to blister. It was all so embarrassing. Why can't I just be normal? After that, whenever I

---

* Never a good sign.

tried to make conversation with Simon, he just gave a one word answer and turned away to talk to Zoe, who I think he fancies.

After dessert I said I had a headache and went home early. I was quite tipsy, and I was going to walk to the station at Golders Green, but I took a wrong turn and got lost. A black cab was coming down the road though and he stopped and asked if I needed to get somewhere. So I got in.

As soon as I shut the door I burst into tears. The driver asked me what had happened so I told him everything. And he was being really nice and telling me to keep my chin up like Dad does. I felt so much better, and more hopeful. But when we were nearly back in Finchley he turned onto an estate near Mill Hill East.

He got out of the front and opened the back door. He said 'Don't worry it's nothing dodgy, I know you've had a tough night. You remind me of my daughter and I just want to give you a hug.' And I thought it was a bit weird but I needed a hug and he was being so kind and fatherly. He sat on the back seat and he hugged me and I hugged him back. And then I stopped, but he didn't let go for ages. For a second I thought he'd fallen asleep!! Then suddenly he pushed me back and stuck his fat tongue in my mouth!!!!!!!!!!!!!!!!!!! It gave me a shock!!!! He tasted of cigarettes and dog shit. It was DISGUSTING. I couldn't believe what was happening. I felt myself freeze. Then something in me kicked in and I pushed him off really hard and said 'no thank you'. No thank you?! I should have said GET THE FUCK OFF! But he was bigger and I was scared and I didn't want to offend him. I was REALLY frightened he would overpower me. So I tried to be polite. And then luckily a woman walked past and looked in the window and it must have spooked him cos he got out really quickly and then drove me home in silence.

I didn't pay him. I jumped out. As I was opening the front door to the house, all shaky – he shouted 'Frigid Bitch!' out of the car window and then he drove off ...

I feel a bit tearful. It's my own fault I know. Rabbi isn't in. I've had some tea and LOADS of chocolate (I brought the box of Dairy Milk home). But I AM SO ANGRY AT MUM! This would never have happened if I could speak Hebrew and I knew how Friday night dinners went. Then I wouldn't have made a fool of myself and had to leave early. I'm also really angry at Zoe. I wonder if Simon would give me a second chance? I might text her in the morning. But she's probably snogging him now.

I hate myself. I want dad. I want to go home. I want to get off the ride. I don't like it. At least I didn't have to pay.

I want my mum.

Jess x

Oh my GOD! That's another bloody 'incident' I'd completely blocked out. Reading about my experience with the taxi driver brings a familiar flood – the hot flush of shame, followed by that strange, cooling relief that nothing worse happened (again) …

But something else creeps in now, something that doesn't usually come with memories of foolish young Jess narrowly avoiding disaster or doing something naive. It's a feeling I recognise, but here, it lands differently. It's unmistakable.

Rage.

Not just the simmering, fleeting kind, but a full-bodied, smack-you-round-the-chops, roaring rage.

That night I'd blamed myself: I was naive, stupid, too drunk, too awkward – too something to have avoided what happened. I'd replayed it over and over, picking apart every choice I made, as if there was some magic formula I could've followed to avoid the situation entirely. That was how I coped. How I have always coped. By turning all the blame inward. By carrying the shame so I didn't have to confront the truth: some men are just predators. I'm furious at men like him who prey on vulnerability, who manipulate moments of trust. He saw a young woman in distress and seized the opportunity to push a boundary, to take something from me. Even as my instincts kicked in to push him off, I was so scared of offending him that I said, 'No thank you.' No thank you. I want to scream at younger Jess to shout, to fight back harder, to get out sooner.

I can't change the past, but maybe something I can do is stop seeing myself as stupid. I wasn't stupid. I'm not stupid. I was doing my best to navigate a world that didn't teach me, and still doesn't teach us, how to deal with monsters who disguise themselves as 'nice guys'. Young Jess deserves my compassion, not my criticism. That moment wasn't a reflection of my weakness; it was a reflection of his monstrosity.

As I sit with this rage, a memory prompted by something in my diary entry pops into my head ... this one much earlier and less insidious: I was nine, standing in a Jewish deli in Edgware with Mum. She was picking up goodies for tea at Grandma's, the air thick with the warm, sweet smell of challah. She ordered rollmops, bagels, cream cheese and smoked salmon. Then she turned to me and smiled. 'Want anything else, Poopie?'

I pointed at a tray of glossy, golden patties in the window, my mouth already watering.

'Can we get some of those little Scotch eggs?' I asked.

Mum froze. Horror flickered across her face. Behind the counter, the old Jewish man raised a single, disapproving eyebrow.

I had no idea what I'd done wrong – but Mum recovered quickly, laughing like I'd made the funniest joke in the world.

'Oh, Jessie!' she said brightly, rushing through the rest of the order and ushering me out of the shop at top speed ... All the way to Grandma's, I stared out of the car window in silence, puzzled, trying to work out what on earth I'd said.

My faux pas was met with great hilarity when Mum relayed Scotch Egg Gate to Grandma and the next-door neighbour that afternoon, and it was explained to me that Scotch eggs weren't kosher, as they contained pork – something that Jews NEVER eat. But Mum wasn't laughing at the time, and it only occurs to me now that she would have felt embarrassed in a space where she felt the need to 'perform' her Jewishness. I didn't have the context then, but I also didn't have the context for what that moment was teaching me: about the unspoken rules of belonging, the quiet tensions of identity, and the sense that I would always be a little bit outside.

It's a feeling I carried into that Friday-night dinner years later, awkward and nervous, trying so hard to fit in. I didn't know the prayers or the traditions. I knocked back the wine at the wrong moment, got the giggles at the worst time, and ended up embarrassing myself over and over. By the time I left, I felt small, humiliated and invisible. The same feelings followed me into the taxi. The shame of not belonging, the exhaustion of trying so hard and the vulnerability that predators like him seem to sniff out.

The truth is, none of those moments were my fault. Not the confusion in the deli, not the awkwardness at dinner, and certainly not what happened in the taxi. Maybe this rage is what's been dormant in me … and now it's finally helping me to see it all differently.

I think about Rosi, sitting by the window in Zbąszyń, finding peace in a no man's land. Her resilience feels like a lifeline reaching out across time. Perhaps I'm guilty of looking for connections where there aren't any. Of being overly simplistic or romanticising it all. She didn't shrink under the weight of her circumstances; she found a way to hold on to herself. Is that something I've inherited? Even if I didn't realise it until now? Maybe this rage is my strength; it certainly became Mum's. Perhaps it became Rosi's strength too; overtaking, turning her into the woman that Mum knew as a mother. For now, I hope it sticks. I like the feeling. It's powerful, burning away the old stories I've told myself about not being enough. It's what is finally letting me stand up for younger Jess.

The silly girl in the deli. The novice at the dinner table. The – I don't want to say 'victim' – the Jess in the taxi. Not stupid, or shameful. They deserved better then. They deserve better from me now.

I think something is shifting in me ... Am I finally growing into the woman I should've been for them? I feel a bit empowered! ... And also a bit like I need to have a nap.

Chapter 21

Diary of Rosi Schul
Tuesday, 16 May 1939

I had some more mail from Jonas. I hear Samuel is going to England. He hasn't written to me at all! I hear nothing from my old friends. I'll certainly never go back to Esslingen.

Thankfully Max and Delli are out of prison, but not her husband yet.

Yesterday at the performance for the Committee, the children played in the little band so well. There was accordion, saxophone (which was combs with tissue paper), triangles, spoons, drums, tambourines and a washing board. There were choral groups too and I included two rounds. It went down beautifully. The performance was a triumph!

Afterwards Mendelson walked me home and there was much PG!*

---

* Does PG mean what I think it means? Snogging? Touching? SEX??

John Jakob Mendelson, Labour MP and Rosi's suitor.

OMG, I found him!! Not to be confused with Peter Mandelson (different spelling, different century), Grandma's Mendelson – the one she got 'turned on' with after the Nachbush drama – was John Jakob Mendelson. He survived the Holocaust, studied at the LSE and later became a Labour MP for Penistone (yes, Penistone).*

Reader, she PG'd him – and then he went off to persuade Harold Wilson to run the country.

---

* Sounds like an illness that your doctor should treat. And also the brand name of medication they'd prescribe for you: '10mg of Penistone, direct to the area. May cause blindness.'

Diary of Jess Robinson
Sunday, 27 May 2007

Things have turned around again! Tonight at Layla's party, I met a really nice guy called Aiden who is an actor as well. And he can unicycle!* He's blonde, and his hair is a bit thin, and he's almost got buck teeth. He kind of looks like a pixie, but he's really charming and funny and he bought me loads of drinks and put his jacket round my shoulders when we walked out into the street – like in a film. He's 27! He's not my type AT ALL. BUT he sang 'Crazy' by Gnarls Barkley on the karaoke and talent is a turn on. I just want somebody nice to look after me. Someone to sit on the sofa and watch EastEnders with. We're going to go on a date at the end of next week!!!

I must be myself.

Mum said I am striking and vivacious. I wish she just said I was pretty. But I know I'm not.

I need to go on a diet.

Love Jess

P.S. I have an interview at a teaching agency and for Stagecoach Borehamwood to teach singing. I hope I get them. I would like to have day jobs which I actually enjoy and I am good with kids.

Last night I called Mum – surprised to find her home on a Saturday evening – and we giggled as I read her the entry from my diary ...

Mum has always been excited about my love life – well ... the bits I told her about. When I was fifteen, she'd often pick me up from Visage night club in Hemel Hempstead, which, firstly, was

---

* The fact that I wrote that Aiden could unicycle as a POSITIVE makes me spit my tea out. Ha-ha-ha!

very *un*-Cool Bitch behaviour from me; who gets their mummy to pick them up from a club? But secondly, I now realise since her tirade about Grandma that it was a hugely supportive liberal gesture and her own rebellion against *her* mum. As soon as I'd get into the car she'd ask excitedly, 'Did you do kissing?' Do kissing! DO!!!!! What a cringey, childish way of phrasing the question.

She'd obviously not come to terms with the fact that I was growing up. It felt like I'd just come out of nursery – though, to be fair, the teens outside were all staggering around like giddy, red-cheeked toddlers.

The question always rubbed me up the wrong way, because inevitably, no, I had *not* 'done kissing'. No matter how hard I tried, I had never done kissing. OK, once, but we'll discount that, because the boy had kissed me as a dare, evidenced by the cheering and laughing and the way he swaggered back across the half-empty dance floor while he mimed vomiting.

No matter how much I'd crimped my hair (and then brushed it out because I didn't like it, which made me look as though I'd just put my fingers in an electric socket), no matter how much Body Shop White Musk I'd sprayed on, no matter how many spots I'd managed to cover up, artfully using my tea tree medicated concealer, I could not attract the opposite sex. My train-track braces were to blame. I know – loads of people had braces and still managed to 'pull', but Mr Killick, my orthodontist and member of the Aldbury Church Congregation, had advised my mum that I should have white braces, so they didn't show when I sang my 'lovely Ave Marias and Panis angelicuses in church'. He even gave Mum a special discount, because 'he knew she'd appreciate such a gesture – wink-wink'.* When they were

---

* He thought she'd appreciate it because she was Jewish? Is it a micro-aggression if it's generous? Yes? No? Don't Christians like a bargain too? Jesus famously turned water into wine – a very thrifty business.

on, we were all very pleased (although I couldn't show it, because it hurt to smile).

But what Mr Killick had neglected to tell us was that when I went to a club (heaven forfend!), my white braces would glow as brightly as an acid-yellow highlighter under the UV lights. This meant that every time I smiled at a boy, I looked like a flirty Skeletor.*

It's devastating to admit, but I don't think I'll ever fulfil my teenage fantasy of standing on the sticky dance floor of the Hemel Hempstead leisure-centre club and snogging to Chumbawamba.

Off the back of sharing subsequent diary entries about my love life in my twenties – similar to greasing a fortune-teller's palm with silver – Mum has agreed to meet me for coffee and cake today. And with the promise of more greasing (i.e. me doing her Waitrose shop), we're going to have a chat about her own experience with boys during her twenties.

Mum's relaxed as she sits back, dusting the almond croissant flakes off her breasts, and says, 'So, you want me to tell you about Grandma talking about having sexual intercourse before marriage, do you?' Her voice carries in the quiet little café and I look around, embarrassed.

'Um,' I falter, noticing the gaggle of pensioners who glance up from their cuppas and crossword puzzles … that isn't exactly what I asked, but … 'OK,' I say quietly, hoping she takes the hint from my 'indoor' voice while thinking to myself, 'OK, Mum, I'll let you lead this.'

'Well, she never spoke to me about her own experiences, but she did say' – Mum begins her familiar German-witch impression, still not lowering her voice – '"If you were in a serious, long-term relationship, it would not be unusual to have sex before you got

---

* A very effective form of contraception by the way.

married. But it is not something to do in a casual relationship, because if the man gets what he wants, he will no longer be interested, and the relationship will finish." My school friends talked about that a lot in the cloakroom at school ... From about the age of fourteen we'd sit together at lunchtime and talk about what we would or wouldn't do with a boy before we got married – y'know, how far we'd go.'

'Right,' I say, catching the twinkly eye of the elderly lady at the neighbouring table, who smiles cheekily and nods. I bet she wouldn't nod at my recollection, I think, remembering how from the age of fourteen in our school cloakroom, my two best friends and I took turns to demonstrate *More* magazine's 'Position of the Fortnight', using, instead of another person, the 30-litre bin as the male counterpart. I grin at the mad memory, which Mum takes as encouragement to continue ...

'It was around 1963 when I met this boy named David Chambers' – 'Sounds like the name of an estate agent,' I think to myself – 'I was nineteen and I thought he was a very lovely boy and very lovely looking,' Mum says dreamily. 'He went to the same parties that I went to, and to the campaign for nuclear disarmament meetings that I went to, and finally, after a year of longing for him to notice me and wanting him to be my boyfriend, he came to my school and saw me playing a Beethoven sonata on the piano at the end-of-summer concert. From then on, he became my boyfriend, coming to the house quite often to have piano lessons with Dad. By the middle of August, I was as much a part of his family as he was ours. When we first slept together that summer, Mum was away in Europe with one of her sisters, so she didn't know anything about it. From then on, if we wanted a night together, I stayed at his mother and father's house – they were very open – and pretended I was staying with my friend Jenny when actually I was staying with him. Either way, Mummy never knew.' My mum pauses to take another bite of her croissant while the elderly lady, now rapt, moves her chair closer. Mum smiles at her and pivots slightly to include our new friend in the conversation and, for the millionth time in my life, I think to myself that Mum should've been an actress. 'A good year on,' she continues, 'I was helping Mum with Sunday lunch, and she asked me if I had had a nice evening after staying out at David's. "Yes, very nice," I said, and she said to me …' – Mum adopts 'the voice' – '"You wouldn't sleep with David, would you? You wouldn't have sex with him, would you? Because you know, he wouldn't know what to do. He's just a schnip* of a boy …"

'My mother was German,' she adds to the room by way of an explanation. 'Of course, I fell straight into the trap and said, "No, he's not a schnip of a boy, and he does know what to do!" And your grandma replied, "Ah, no vonder you look so tired. You look as if you have been whoring all night!"'

The young mother on the table behind us gasps, though I'm not sure if that's because of Mum's language or because she's so wrapped up in Mum's tale.

Mum absentmindedly pops an almond flake into her mouth. 'Another year passed, and by a terrible mistake, Mum found out that I had accidentally got pregnant. I had been trying for two or three weeks to lose the baby – to make my period start – but nothing had worked. I went to see an old backstreet abortion lady in Norwood three times. Poor David and I were very desperate for me not to be pregnant. We were both very worried. He had just started at the architectural school, and I had a place at the Royal Academy of Music. I had absolutely no doubt that I did *not* want to have the baby, even though David's mother knew and had offered to look after the child if we got married.'

The café is silent. Nobody is pretending not to listen, and Mum adjusts her top and sits up as she looks appreciatively at her audi-

---

* A Yiddish word meaning 'insignificant person'.

ence. 'The backstreet lady's treatment didn't work, but I was still hoping. I called David to tell him that I had a tummy ache and thought maybe my period was coming, but Mummy had picked up the phone in her bedroom and was listening in without me knowing. That's how she found out that I was pregnant. From then on, it was in her hands.'

'Oh dear!' says the elderly lady, now fully sitting at our table.

Mum nods. 'I had to go and see a psychiatrist and a doctor in Harley Street, and I had to pretend that I would kill myself if I had to have the baby; otherwise, it wouldn't have been legal for me to have a private termination. The operation was in a little clinic in West Hampstead.' As Mum pauses to take a sip of coffee, I recall driving down a West Hampstead side street with her and her pausing outside a residential house and saying matter-of-factly, 'That's where I had an abortion when I was your age' … so this story isn't exactly a revelation, but still, I feel shocked to hear it in its entirety.

Putting her cup down, Mum continues. 'I arrived in the morning and came home in the evening. It cost Grandma £100. I wasn't upset. I was just so relieved not to be pregnant any more. I was looking forward to getting on with studying music full-time. But Grandma never forgot that mistake. From then on she used it as her reason for never letting me leave home. She said, "You vill just get pregnant again!" She always, always threw my past mistakes or experiences at me. She stored my comments to use against me … as in "My mummy sleeps in the kitchen,"' she adds, as if in explanation to the elderly lady, who stares back at us, unblinking. 'Achh, this all stirs me up too much!' says Mum, coming to the end and leaving the crowd both slightly confused and wanting more. Like watching Madonna live.

Things have become clearer, I think, as I drive home to Brighton that night with a fresh folder of papers … It's hard to stomach these stories about Grandma, but my God, I have such love for my mother. Yes, she can't let go of her anger towards her mum, but I'm so grateful that she came back into the conversation and, despite that anger, has continued to translate Rosi's diaries. My mum is open and strong and full of resilience and courage. She'd do anything for me.

Chapter 22

**Diary of Rosi Schul
Sunday, 28 May 1939**

We are working on quite an ambitious children's show at the moment, which will take place in the 'Schützenhaus' (club-house). I manage to produce a new performance at least once a month, which keeps the children fully occupied – they love it as much as the parents and the large audience of people from the mill and barracks, etc. This time there are other people working with the children too …

This is a description of the programme:

It begins with the children aged between 7 and 13 years old, in what I call a 'Spoken Choir'. They perform a very moving poem, 'We weren't always the people who cried'.

Then they sing Hebrew songs led by Ingale Weindling, a young cantor, and I do the Canons, which have up to four parts, sung in a round … they're lovely, if they come out right! It's not easy for such young children. The percussion band is slightly different from the one I used to lead in Esslingen of course, as we have to improvise with anything that makes a different sound. It's all quite funny and inventive! Wilhelm Busch's 'Max and Moritz' is a sweet duet, which I used to sing with my sister, Ruthi … it's been performed many times before and it's always a great success. Then there are little plays and poems and solos. The children show great talent and musicality with whatever I give them to do, and there's enough material to fill a two-hour programme ... In the past, we've even had to repeat pieces twice because the audience loved it so! It brought me a lot of appreciation, in particular from Sally Strumfeld, who worked professionally on the radio in Frankfurt, writing and producing programmes for children. Yes ... Strumfeld ... tall, dark and handsome ... it's too good to be true! He loves me, and I love him ... what more can Zbąszyń bring me ...?!

The only picture I can find of Strumfeld was this old one, tucked in the back of one of Grandma's albums.

Diary of Jess Robinson
Saturday, 2 June 2007

I am teaching at Stagecoach Borehamwood! She needed someone to start straight away! I LOVE TEACHING! The principal, Brenda HYMAN (Hyman haha!) is pretty mad. She's really highly strung but so nice and wears blue eyeshadow and pearly pink lipstick. Really 80s! She's Jewish. She lives in Edgware one road away from where we lived when I was born. Funny!! The drama and the dance teachers are lovely. We watch Brenda when we're having our tea and biscuits at break time and try not to giggle. She literally follows the kids around with a dustbuster in case they drop crumbs. They said I fit in straight away. We're a good team. We're putting on a show in July and then we're all teaching on the summer course too, where the kids put on a show in a week. We're going to do Annie. So, that is my new Saturday job and I wouldn't change it for the world! Well I obviously would if I got an acting job, but I would miss it.

THEN, during the week I have a placement being a teacher's assistant up the road in a school for children with special needs! The woman at the agency said that lots of people on their books only want to work with 'mainstream' children but if I chose to do special needs I'd get a lot more work and £10 extra per day – so £75. I said I'd give it a try and I LOVE it. I LOVE the kids so much.

At the moment I am working in a class with five children who are all autistic. One of them is also in a wheelchair. She needs help when she goes to the toilet and she is quite big so I've been trained to use a hoist, which was a bit scary at first. I didn't want to go too fast or make her go into the wall or anything. I'd be mortified. But actually it's very easy to control and be gentle with. It helps lift her onto the bed, because she is still in nappies. Her name is Keisha and she's a really sweet, gentle girl. She doesn't speak usually, and is very withdrawn, but today I sang to her. Songbird. And she looked straight at me and clapped her hands and the teacher, (John), couldn't believe it, so he got the headmaster and videoed it for Keisha's parents who cried when they saw it at the end of school. They said Keisha has chosen me. It made me cry. We all cried a bit. Not Keisha. She was back in her own world again. I wish I knew what goes on in her head. I think she's amazing. Now it's been decided that every morning I am only going to work with Keisha. I can take her into the sensory room for forty-five minutes – which I love. It's full of fairy lights that change colour, and 'spa music' plays and there are bean bags and glow in the dark stars on the ceiling, so we sit there and I massage Keisha's hands and feet with cocoa butter. I can also do 'music therapy' with her – I mean I'm not a music therapist am I? But I can sing to her in the music room and we can play the piano and bang the drums and stuff. She does NOT like it when I sing Amarillo.*

This sounds so stupid, but I feel full. I feel whole and happy and like I'm doing something decent and good and kind. For her obviously, but it feels kind for me too.

And fuck me, it's better than telesales!!!!!!!!!!!!!!!!!!!!!

Love Jess

P.S. Date with Aiden went well. I was myself. He is really romantic. He bought me flowers and he kissed me at the end of the night and we're going to the cinema in a bit!!

Teaching and working with kids is in my blood – an unbroken thread running through the generations of my family. I remember vividly a lightbulb going off: 'Ohhhh, this is what I'm meant to do with my time.' At least, I knew that's what I was supposed to do to balance out my urge to be a performer, which I was still very much

---

* Everyone's a critic.

working towards. Teaching became more than just a day job to fill the gaps; it grounded me, pulled me out of my own head, and pulled my own head out of my arse – I sound like a contortionist, but I did tie myself in knots of anxiety and ego. It made me more empathetic, compassionate and, I think, a better person.

Along with young Rosi, my mum's father Jules also set the tone. Grandpa Jules even invented his own 'Play-a-Note' sight-reading game.

Grandpa Jules' Play-a-Note cards.

No wonder Mum found her place as a music teacher. Like Grandpa, she taught the piano, and like Rosi, she put on school shows and shared her passion with kids. There's an old photo of her with my sisters Jojo and Katy, long before I was even thought of.

My sister Katy went on to teach the piano and flute and run baby and toddler music groups. And my sister Jojo worked as a nursery nurse and a jazz pianist, composing her own music, until her Huntington's disease made it impossible for her to continue.

Now, she can't even play the piano. It's so upsetting to see such an unfair cruelty happen to the kindest, most gentle soul of us all.

Left to right: Jojo and Katy deal the cards as Mum (I didn't know she could play the flute, but I'm not surprised) plays a note.

Working with kids, and later adults, with special needs taught me what real care and kindness looks like. It's also where I stopped being 'squeamish'. Doing nappies (not just children's), and feeding, and hoisting, and bathing people has a way of stripping things down to what matters. Now, when I help my sister Jojo with something as personal and basic as visiting the loo, I think about how she did the same for me when I was small and she'd babysit. That cycle of care is humbling, and it's taught me a lot about what it means to show up for someone. I should call and visit her more.

I keep thinking about how transformative teaching and caregiving can be. In some countries, young people are expected to spend a year in the army or doing national service. I guess Austria's model, with its options for social care, feels closest to what I'd imagine making policy if I were in charge here. I'd make it a law for every young person to spend a year working with kids, or the elderly, or supporting people with disabilities and special needs. Stepping outside yourself to focus on someone else's needs builds character and empathy in ways that nothing else can. VOTE JESS! You can trust me! I wouldn't lie to you – I've already confessed to shitting myself on a train!

As I dig deeper into Rosi's diaries and talk more with Mum, I'm starting to unravel the tangled threads of our family's history. It's not a tidy tapestry. Not yet. Perhaps it never will be. Rosi's resilience and creativity are inspiring, but the stories my mum has shared about her own experiences paint a different picture. For all her romantic adventures, Rosi could be incredibly hypocritical when it came to Mum and her relationships. In fact, the more I learn about how Rosi treated my mum, the more conflicted I feel. On the one hand, there are her incredible children's performances, the creative programmes she devised and the joy she brought to so many young lives. On the other, there's a far colder side she showed as a mother. Reconciling those two versions of her feels impossible. Is this project bringing me closer to her, or creating a rift between us?

Chapter 23

Diary of Rosi Schul
Monday, 5 June 1939

Spring in Zbąszyń is as wonderful as in Esslingen and I have a fulfilling relationship! What more could I want?

The concert was a huge success. Everything was fantastic and people were bowled over with my work. It made me feel as proud as a toreador. The manager of a Polish children's theatre was impressed, and other professionals were very enthusiastic. It is quite amazing to me – I know that the most serious people here consider me as one of the most gifted people in Zbąszyń. It is unbelievable that people see me this way – how can I deserve it? I think I must have become very good with people because I have learned self-control and do not put myself first.

Now, straight to the point – the new relationship! With much PG! Yes PG!* It was just an episode, but without commitment, which I have always loved. And that's as far as it goes. He's a fantastic guy, possibly the most educated and cultured and sophisticated person in Zbąszyń! He writes plays for radio and for theatre and puppet shows, etc. He's a good-looking guy, tall, dark and slim – just the type for me in the short term. Between us there is never a dull moment! Our meeting and connection was through working with children.

---

* PG! There it is again!

We have a mutual respect and I have had many wonderful evenings with him, including great conversation and loving (which is good for both of us).

I'm frightened of marriage. I know I would never be happy. One could marry so quickly, and then there could be deadly boredom. But Strumfeld is unusual!

At the same time I'm carrying on with Mendelson who is 21, although he has the mind of a 31-year-old. But oh my! Handling the two of them is difficult!! They hate each other and don't speak to each other – lucky for me! Apart from these two there is Zalner.

I will be faithful to <u>myself</u> and solve the dilemma in my own time.

Diary of Jess Robinson
Friday, 8 June 2007

Hello. I've been a bit up and down ...

I have been on a special diet lately. I saw Dr Roberts on Harley Street. It cost me £140!!!!!!!! But I could afford it because I've been working hard and not going out much.

I was 9st 13 and he said for now I am only allowed to eat protein (meat, fish, eggs) and citrus fruits. It's been really difficult. He also gave me pills to take ten minutes before meals – I think to speed up my metabolism. Then I take more pills 20 minutes after I've eaten. Anyway, it <u>really</u> worked. I have to go and see him tomorrow as it'll be the end of the diet period. My target weight is 8st 10 pounds. I really hope I've made it. I have been quite strict with myself. I'm just so scared I'll put it all back on again.

Mum and grandma said I was overweight when I was there for tea a few weeks ago. It was just as I was taking a second bagel and it made me feel so ashamed. I haven't spoken to mum since.

HOW DARE SHE? I was so cross with her for saying anything. In this family, everyone is obsessed with weight and food and eating. Well I've lost about a stone so I've shown her. I resent her a lot for that. I think she should mind her own business and know better after Katy went anorexic!

A few weeks ago when we were in the garden, mum looked at Katy (who is still always sooooo slim) and said 'Look at her body, Jessie, we'll never have that.' Why would she say that??? Even if Katy isn't anorexic now it's MAD OF HER. I feel ashamed of my body when I'm with mum, but I also want her approval. Why is it even a subject? She's fucked me up.

Anyway – This is the diet:

Special Diet

It is best to avoid peas, beans, bananas, avocado, pears, grapes, dried and tinned fruits, and foods which contain flour and milk, yoghurt or cheese.*

In the second week increase the variety of your diet but still avoid starchy foods such as bread, pastry, potatoes and the well-known fattening foods.†

I hope I can do this.

A cup of coffee or tea with a biscuit between meals may well make a pleasant break – but it will start a habit which might become difficult to control.

If you have a large or fattening meal, be abstemious‡ on the following day in order to allow your body to compensate for it.

Never eat bread, biscuits or bread substitutes.§

---

* So all food? Avoid all food?
† That famous food group: the Well-Known Fattening Foods.
‡ Abstemious! Dr Roberts clearly spent all those £140 on a big old thesaurus – what a great word!
§ I know this is a book about, for some parts, the Holocaust, but I think this sentence is possibly the bleakest one in the entire story.

Don't take alcohol everyday & avoid spirits & beers. In the immediate premenstrual phase you should restrict the fluid intake to 5 cups daily.*

If you gain more than 4 pounds, diet strictly for 2 days. It is probably best to eat only meat these 2 days.

Two days of dieting should be sufficient to remove the regained weight, and you could then return to your normal diet.†

THE END

So – wish me luck! My farts have been TERRIBLE. I accidentally did one a couple of nights ago when Aiden (WHO IS NOW MY BOYFRIEND) and I were watching Friends. He spent about ten minutes looking around and sniffing.

There's a side to Aiden that I'm not sure about though …

Like, a couple of days ago we got on his moped and went all the way from West Hampstead to Southend. It was really fun being on the back of his bike to begin with, but after about 30 minutes my arms were tired and my body ached from holding on. He kept telling me I was holding on too tight but I was a bit nervous, especially when he was weaving through traffic.

When we finally got there I was really tired and achy. We got some sandwiches and we were going to spend the day on the beach. It was all nice and fun. He was really funny when we were in the sea, which was FREEZING. But when he came back from getting us ice creams and I was just relaxing, he said he could see my cellulite and that I'd put on weight. It made me feel AWFUL. I got a knot in my stomach and I felt sort of sick. It made me want to cry. But I didn't.

I thought I'd done well with my diet. I'm only just getting back to eating 'normally' again – I only reintroduced brown rice and

---

* Jew on!
† There is nothing normal about this.

vegetables, and this was supposed to be my one day off that I'm allowed per week.

I didn't want to eat my ice cream then, OBVIOUSLY, because I felt crap and he had such a go at me because he'd 'wasted his money' on me. People were staring. Then he sulked because I didn't want to go in the sea again. Why would I????!!! I just kept my T-shirt on and wrapped my towel over my legs and waited for the day to be over.

On the way home his moped broke down. Rabbi said it was karma.

She's not sure about Aiden. Apparently when I'm with him I'm much quieter and I'm always checking to see if he's OK or needs anything. But I want him to feel comfortable. Sometimes when I'm around him he does make me feel a bit stupid. It's probably more to do with me. I still haven't learnt to love myself. I'm an idiot a lot of the time. I won't admit that to Rabbi, but this is my diary. I can write whatever I like. Sometimes, well most of the time, I write this as though someone might read it one day, so I'm worried what I write might be too intimate. Or if my spelling is shit (which it is) or my grammar is crap which it is.

Rabbi thinks my diet is expensive and crazy. She said I go from one extreme to the other in everything I do. She said sometimes she thinks I'm like Judy Garland. An old fucked up star. It made me laugh but she said she felt sad for me. I am quite tearful a lot of the time. Rabbi says I need to respect myself more and not put myself in weird and dangerous situations. When I finally told her about the taxi driver, she said she couldn't believe that a friend of hers would keep getting themselves into situations like that.

I'm SOOOOOOO hungry and I've got a headache. Or maybe it's because I have only eaten a boiled egg, 2 × black coffees and ½ a chicken breast. Rabbi wants me to go to a party with her tonight, but I mustn't drink. It's 5pm now. So I'm going to try and go to bed at 7pm and sleep through the hunger.

I AM SO ANGRY AT MUM!

Also, how did Katy manage to be anorexic for so long? It's really tiring and hard.

Night Night,

Love Jess

I love how my grandma was such a PLAYA! It makes me feel much better about the diary entry of mine where I was dating about six different guys. I still haven't managed to find out what 'PG' stands for, but the code 'PG' does appear throughout Rosi's diaries whenever her lovers are mentioned. I suggested 'Penis Groß' but Mum and Bruni – my wonderful diary translators – doubt it very much. They say that aside from the fact that it would be impossible for *THAT* many men to *ALL* possess big willies, Grandma would only have been kissing and cuddling! And I *think* I believe that, seeing as how shocked she was in an earlier diary entry about that unwed couple living together.

The crazy diet I did in my twenties was shocking to read about, but sadly it was one of many I embarked on to try to make myself smaller. When I see the Cool Bitches for Sunday lunch, it's still playing on my mind, so I decide to open up a new conversation as I continue to grapple with my German-Jewish roots.

Once again, I record the conversation – like a spy. But a terrible spy, because my voice memos app is clearly visible on the table.

'Did Grandma cook a lot of Jewish food?' I ask, wondering whether her odd concoctions came from some weird tradition I don't know about or if she invented them herself.

'Oh, no,' Stephie replies. 'No, the only Jewish food she ever made was chicken soup with matzo balls, butter beans and pearl barley – cooked from scratch in that tiny kitchen. My big sister always helped, didn't you, Jackie? Otherwise, it was German food.

Or corned beef,' she says, grimacing. 'I used to shove it under the lettuce leaf and give it to Coley the cat when Mummy wasn't looking.'

'She knew!' Mum chimes in. 'And she'd make you sit there till you'd finished.'

'Yeah, I hated it!' Stephie exclaims. 'But anyway, your grandma was a feeder.'

I nod, remembering the spoonfuls of food plopped on my plate whether I wanted them or not.

'And cheese had to be covered in jam. But that is a German thing,' Stephie adds.

'I learnt to make a Sunday lunch and a full English breakfast by the time I was eleven or twelve,' Mum says, spearing a bit of parsnip. 'She went away on holiday a lot and left us all behind, so I'd invite Auntie Hilda or Auntie Gwen and make a whole roast lunch.'

'When you were *twelve*?' I manage, my mouth full of potatoes.

'Yeah, she could, man,' Stephie confirms.

'And I had to look after you,' Mum says to Stephie, who nods. 'You were six or seven, and you had the most frightening nightmares. We'd be at home alone because Dad was out playing, and Mum was in Spain or Germany. Suddenly, I'd hear the most terrible screaming, like in a film. I'd rush to your room to soothe you, saying, "It's only a dream, it's only a dream."'

'Jackie looked after us when Mummy wasn't there. And *she* didn't force me to eat corned beef.' Stephie beams.

'And …' I begin, glancing at Katy, who knows from past post-therapy heart-to-hearts what I'm about to ask, 'what was Grandma's attitude to dieting and, um … diet culture?'

'She had very large, cellulite-y legs,' Mum says bluntly.

'Yeah,' Stephie agrees. 'She was very self-conscious about them, always.'

'She hated them,' Mum says simply.

'That's so sad,' I say.

'Oh, well, the stars then didn't have large legs,' says Stephie.

'So you were taught it was a "bad" and "wrong" thing? Even though cellulite is normal?' I add, as much for myself as for the table at large.

'We just knew – you shouldn't be fat.' Mum nods. 'We'd sit there on the couch watching *Sunday Night at the London Palladium*, and Anne Shelton would come on. Mummy would say, "My God, is she fat?!" Well, we'd all do it then.'

'Our Uncle Harry married a woman quite late in life, and she was probably a size sixteen to eighteen,' Stephie says, taking a sip of her whisky.

'Big arms,' Mum chips in. They're starting to remind me of the two old men from *The Muppets*. 'He was a very handsome Jewish man, a bit of a … what do you call it? A grey … a grey …'

'Gandalf the Grey?' Katy suggests.

'No!!' Mum laughs, still searching. 'A handsome grey? A grey wolf? A snow wolf?'

'Do you mean a "silver fox"?' I say, filing away *a handsome grey* for later.

'Yes!' Mum says triumphantly.

'Well, anyway,' Stephie continues, putting down her glass, 'Grandma – and, well, everyone in the family – called him a pervert for marrying a much larger woman.'

Katy and I gasp. Feeling horrified and triggered, I'm beginning to think I shouldn't have started this conversation after all.

'Yes! They really assumed he was perverted to find her attractive,' Mum reiterates.

'That's terrible,' Katy says, appalled.

'So backward!' I agree in disbelief.

'Well, you say that *now*,' Mum replies, 'but it was the culture. But you're quite right, of course. Mum had a thing about it. She'd *feed* us.'

'Yes, feed, feed, feed, eat, eat, eat,' Stephie says.

'And then she'd say, "You know you are fat?"' Mum slips into her familiar Grandma impression.

'So she criticised you girls?' I ask.

Mum looks at me. 'In my teens, I was hungry all the time. And I was a bit plump. I remember one day I came home after school and I was bloody starving – I'd been out since eight in the morning. There's one meatball, a bit of mashed potato and some peas on the plate. No seconds or anything. I said, "Is there another meatball, Mummy?" And she said, "You've had enough, you fat pig!"'

'No, are you sure?' Stephie asks, shocked.

'Yes, I am!' Mum's voice rises.

'OK, OK!' Stephie says, making calming motions with her hands.

'And then the diets started,' Mum says.

'Endless diets,' Stephie adds.

'There was an obsession with cottage cheese,' Mum begins. 'It started appearing because Rosemary Conley or somebody said it isn't fattening.'

'Yes,' I remember. 'You'd eat it all the time when I was growing up. And the Cabbage Soup Diet? And WeightWatchers?'

'Yes,' Katy chimes in. 'When I was growing up in the Seventies there were always books around or diets cut out of magazines, like the F Plan.'

'Yes,' Mum says, almost defensively. 'Because I was a fat pig, and I was worried about being a fat pig. She criticised my body. There was a time when I came round, and Grandma's sister Ruthi had just arrived. I heard her say to Auntie Ruthi, "She's put on a lot of weight." And I had. I see it in the photographs – I'd gone up to ten stone or something.'

'But she didn't have to say it!' I say, feeling cross about all the times Mum had commented on my body.

'No,' Mum admits. 'But we all do.'

'We all do,' Stephie jumps in. 'We all do it. I do it, don't I? It's new thinking to not have the right to comment on someone else's body.'

'Yes!' Mum says gratefully. 'In fact, I said to Lisa's daughter the other day as we were walking through Hemel Hempstead, and a girl with the most enormous bottom in a pair of leggings and a terribly short T-shirt passed – I said, "That's not a good look, is it?" And Lisa's daughter said, "Why would you say that? It's nothing to do with you!"'

'Well, she's right!' I say, feeling vindicated.

'Am I allowed to say, "Isn't that tree big?" Or are we allowed to say a dog is overweight when we see them on those dog programmes?' Mum asks, with a combative glint in her eye.

'You can say what you like', I reply trying to stay calm and articulate. 'But what someone looks like is generally the least interesting thing about them and NONE OF YOUR BUSINESS and it's small minded and cruel comment on their body in a disapproving way. It's about your *own* insecurities. When you're negative about people's bodies, you're measuring yourself against them to make yourself feel better. And it's none of your business. They might have an illness! Many people who are really large have been abused, and it's a subconscious way to keep people at a distance. There are all sorts of reasons why people look the way they do. And there are also plenty of people in bigger bodies who are totally comfortable in their skin, and proud of who they are and love themselves and are way healthier than thin people who fit a certain ideal. It's diet culture and society that say they're wrong, because men have decided what's attractive, and the diet industry – worth millions – preys on people's insecurities to make money.'

I finish my speech, pleased with myself, but knowing it's probably fallen on deaf ears. 'And it's not just a neutral, "Look at that tree, it's big,"' I add, trying to drive my point home. 'It's not neutral when you're talking about someone else, it's approving or disapproving. You say it because "big" to you equals "bad", or "lazy", or "unsuccessful".'

'So I have to relearn?' Mum asks, irritated and exasperated.

'Absolutely relearn!' I say.

'But you can't stop yourself from thinking,' Mum begins.

'Yes, you can,' I snap militantly.

'If you educate yourself', Katy says gently, 'you can change your thinking. You can say "the way they look is none of my business" and stop. Acknowledge the judgmental thought and let it go – you don't *need* to say it.'

I nod, grateful that my big sister is backing me up.

'So I have to bite my tongue? Unlike the woman in church the other day who described a Jewish person by miming having a big nose?' Mum asks, visibly annoyed now.

'Maybe it's a *Jewish* thing to talk about what everyone looks like,' Stephie muses.

'We've definitely inherited a very judgemental side,' Katy adds.

'Grandma was very meticulous in her dressing,' Stephie says. 'She always knew the right colour necklace to wear with every shirt or dress. She looked gorgeous in the Forties and Fifties. Her hair was long, sort of Rita Hayworth. She always had her lipstick on. And she wore mules because of her bunions.'

'We inherited those from the Schuls,' Mum says as we all assess our feet.

'Did Grandma's mum criticise her body at all?' I ask, glancing at the dessert options.

'I wouldn't think so,' Stephie says.

'No, she was a very kind lady …' Mum agrees, perusing the menu and adding to herself, 'Now, if I have the cheesecake, I'll have to only eat lettuce for the next week.'

In the car home I reflect on how that deeply rooted toxic diet culture shaped the lives of the women before me – and, inevitably, my own.

Mum was right all those years ago when I first went to see a therapist. As she (and Grandma before her) suspected, my therapist said it was her fault. But only *partly*. The media is definitely to blame, along with the diet and beauty industry, the patriarchy – yes, I said it; I'm a feminist (I think) – oh, and showbusiness, and people who don't know any better.

It baffles me to think that Grandma, having gone through such life-changing hardships – questioning whether humans are innately good – still bothered to place so much importance on appearance and weight. You'd think surviving would be enough, that she'd be too busy celebrating life and freedom to care, but maybe looking a certain way was part of her survival strategy, a way to camouflage herself in the British landscape; to fit in. I remember a line in an early diary entry, when Grandma admired the teaching assistant Samuel had fallen for … 'Her legs and hips are unbelievable. Again and again I catch myself looking at her. For example, on Friday in the bath, I waited to see her beautiful figure. It's a fantasy image. She has a perfect body.'

Poor Grandma. Who told her cellulite is 'wrong'? Not sure Hitler can be blamed for that one. Hey, Grandma – leave those legs alone!*

I get it, though. Mum's beliefs are shaped in part by Grandma's harsh criticisms, and she projected those anxieties and fears about weight onto me. Growing up, I felt constantly scrutinised and judged for my weight and appearance. Once, I was in the kitchen talking to Mum's friend when Mum came up to me and, without warning, pulled my tracksuit bottoms down, saying, 'Look at those thighs, Joan. She doesn't get them from me.' Mum felt sorry for me, dismayed because my thighs were 'wrong'. They 'go forward' (I now know those bits are called quadriceps). She even spoke to my dad's sister about it and found out it's a Robinson

---

* Now repeat that to the tune of Pink Floyd's 'Another Brick in the Wall'.

trait – so not her fault. No wonder I fantasised about leg surgery. MAD.

I'm no different from millions of women, I had/have a tricky relationship with food. I've done it all (bar surgery), by the way: diet pills that make you shit oil and accidentally follow through when you cough (VOTE JESS!); weight-loss injections bought off the internet; wearing a damp rubber suit while standing in someone's dingy weight-loss clinic as electric currents pulse through me to target my 'problem areas'. I've tried every disgusting fad diet that promises a smaller body – all in a desperate attempt to meet unattainable standards and, perhaps more painfully, to seek Mum's approval. To finally have the 'correct' thighs. Honestly, if I'd put as much effort into learning the violin as I did into dieting, I'd be in the Royal Philharmonic by now.

Mum's actions weren't born out of malice, but from a place of wanting the best for me. I do believe that. She genuinely thinks slim, pretty girls do better in life. And, sadly, in the West, that's often true. It's led to a damaging cycle of self-loathing, disordered eating followed by years of therapy, learning to set boundaries and stints of avoiding her while I work through my anger.

I still feel angry and irritated when Mum makes insensitive comments, but I realise now that my anger is misdirected. Well, *partly*, because she does know better, and being nearly eighty now is not an excuse. If she can use the internet, she can educate herself. But diet culture and societal pressures are the real culprits, making women feel inadequate.

To think of Great-Uncle Harry, who married a larger woman, being labelled a pervert by his own family simply for finding her attractive – that's abhorrent to me. Yeah, it was a different time, but the impact of those attitudes is long-lasting.

Now, at forty(ish), (playing age eighteen to fifty), I'm finally coming to terms with my body. It's hard. These toxic ideals surround me, staring back from billboards, TV shows, social media and everyday conversations overheard while I'm just minding my own business.

Breaking this cycle is daunting, but it's so necessary. It's one of the reasons I've decided to have a dog instead of a human. I'm learning to embrace my body and reject the toxic ideals that have haunted my family for generations. I'm learning to forgive myself, forgive my mum and forgive Grandma, understanding that we are all just doing our best within a flawed system.

It's funny, but I think I might be growing a pair of flaps. I seem to have plenty of opinions I didn't know about. I think I might be finding my voice. I'm like a caterpillar transforming into … my mother?! Actually, maybe I should write a book. It can be aimed at Jewish daughters. I'll call it *The Very Guilty Caterpillar*.

Chapter 24

Diary of Rosi Schul
Sunday, 18 June 1939

The weeks are flying by and I am happy, and not least because of my continuing success with my lovely work, and wonderful relationships with my colleagues and Strumfeld …

Does this sound big-headed? But this is just my diary, and I consider it to be a mirror of my life. I have been writing diaries since childhood, from eleven years old right up until now. Most were left in Esslingen, and I hear to my deepest regret, they were all taken from my room and burned by the Nazis on that fateful night.

I have decided: it is Strumfeld! Sally Strumfeld is the man for me! Strumfeld is my man. Zalner is immature and Mendelson too young, but Strumfeld is a man! It is a great mutual love! The evenings are wonderful. What an experience! We have had twilight meetings. We weren't supposed to be together all night but we went to a fairy-tale garden with a bridge, and we sheltered under it when the rain came. So romantic! We picked strawberries, we played chess and we had much fun and PG in the dark.

Diary of Jess Robinson
Sunday, 24 June 2007

It's been a shit day. I'm writing this in bed.

I'm back from going to the cinema with Aiden. He's being horrid. Stupid balding bucktoothed pixie.

He gets in bad moods quite a lot. Not working really affects him. I'd been staying with him for nearly a week up until this morning. He wants me to move in with him. But I get really affected by the nasty atmosphere he makes. It's like he turns into a teenager and the thing that bothers me the most about it is that I can see myself in him. It's how I used to treat mum and dad, so not only is it crap to be around, it also makes me feel ashamed of myself. Also, he swears at me. Maybe it's because I'm not used to it, because although we swear in my family, we never swear AT each other. It feels aggressive – even though afterwards he always says it's just words and he doesn't mean it.

Rabbi hates him. She said I should kick him to the curb. But he can be soooo lovely and funny. I just want him to go back to the romantic, kind boy I had my first date with. I can't stop hoping that he will change back again. Maybe he just needs to get a job he likes and then he'll be happier and nicer.

On the way home his stupid moped broke down again. When I called mum, she said I should get on the train and come here. So that's where I am. Back in my old room. Mum and dad don't really like him either. Dad thinks he's stupid because he's got a moped but he doesn't know how to change his own spark plugs.

Mum says he's got a nasty streak and next time he's making an atmosphere I should just be bright and breezy and say, 'I'm going out for a coffee now.'

But they don't see his lovely side.

I really was looking forward to today.

I usually love going to the cinema.

He just rang. I'm not picking up.

It'll be OK, Jessie.

Will it?

Yes. Go and watch telly with mum and dad.

OK.

Bye.

Love Jess Xx

Letter from Rosi Schul to Samuel – Sunday, 25 June 1939

Dear Samuel,

There you are! You are a <u>naughty monkey</u> for not writing to me.

You have been on my mind for a long time. If I'd written as often as I thought of you, you'd have received a million letters from me.

I am so glad to hear you are now settled and building a new life.

My grandmother has been in Kraków for many weeks now. My father is trying to go to Belgium. In the meantime I am still in Zbąszyń but now I wish it was over. I have been here for a long time. Frozen, while others move forward. All was fine until recently. I have been in a dream and it is as if I have suddenly woken up! I look around me – as if for the first time – and observe how others cope with these experiences, and how they have been affected through these times – the impact. The old people are quite resigned & it hurts to see them so apathetic. What do they still expect of life? Some children are intended for refugee transport to England, Australia and elsewhere, and their parents are totally despairing and distraught. When will they see their children again? They will have to give them up after nine or ten years of being with them … and yet they queue for hours to register their children for travelling away. Unthinkable!

As for the youths (10–17), they are so demoralised. They are thrown together with little distraction other than dancing in a very tiny place once or twice a week. I talk to them when I see them on my way to the children's wing. They used to be so enthusiastic. Now, I hardly recognise them, partly because they have grown up, but they are all so disillusioned now. They just hang around on the streets. And whenever a commission arrives from Warsaw to check on numbers & examine the situation – we put on a show and the inspectors are pleasantly surprised & think things are nice. The young people sing and then the committee delivers a load of meat for these few thousand humans & it seems to them that life can't be bad here. I do know it could be much worse ... But in the long term what will really happen to us?

Who knows the reality?

There is a hallway where I meet my neighbours to exchange news. One hears that 500 Jews will be going to Poland and others are going back to Germany. All the elderly will go into inner Poland, and all the young men will be called up into the army. Zbąszyń is to be cleared by 1st February. The army barracks will be cleaned by the SS and they are going to build a new camp.

Your letter was an epistle – almost too much to read, and although I was very happy to receive it, I would have preferred half as long and face-to-face contact with you.

If only I could be more positive myself. You'll certainly be cross that I still haven't taken on your suggestion. I just can't believe in it. The point is, I've become disillusioned about going to Palestine.

I remember how enthusiastic I was when I was 15 about this search for the truth. But what has become of it? Well, I have searched for the good and the pure, and I read about socialism, but the more I see, the more disappointed and disillusioned I have become. One talks and discusses too much. We were idiots to believe that our theories were possible. Today I know from my experiences that one must live in such a way as is right for oneself. As your heart tells you. Ideas of world improvement should be dismissed.

Let's leave it to those who haven't come to that realisation yet.

Nothing can force me to deceive myself any longer.

Do you remember the night we said goodbye? How earlier we'd played doubles ping-pong and lost. And we were so angry we gobbled up all the chocolates. We listened to Beethoven's Appassionata – drinking punch, which we'd made in my room. Chasing each other around your room. Dr Rothschild laughing. Jonas dancing and asking different people for more brandy. Our discussions of emigrating to America.

Ruth Gold, Aunt Adele, Mutti Reiz, Kätchen, Schmiel, Tante Rosanna. Jonas. Everyone. It was so, so lovely, wasn't it? Now Everything has gone. Gone forever.

I am now the old auntie hanging onto memories.

Rosi x

Diary of Jess Robinson
Saturday, 29 June 2007

I've just come back from grandma's. I'm FURIOUS with Aiden. It was the first time she'd met him and I really wanted him to be 'charming'. We were supposed to leave from his flat at 12.30 to get to Hendon for 1pm but he was still in bloody bed when it was time to leave. So I left on my own. I was so embarrassed when I turned up without him. I know she likes to sit down to eat at 1pm and she'd made roast lamb!

Aiden didn't get there till 1:45! Sometimes I HATE him.

Grandma was very nice to him but she obviously thinks he's a schnips. I felt ashamed and stupid. She thinks I'm wasting my time, I'm sure.

On a high note though, I had an audition for a production of Little Voice yesterday and it went REALLY well! I had to imitate Marilyn Monroe, Judy Garland, Marlene Dietrich, Shirley Bassey and Billie Holiday for the audition. And I could actually do it!!!!! HA!!!!!

Grandma and her bridge friends were really helpful when I found out about the audition so I practised at hers. They gave me a lot of confidence when I sang for them in the morning room last week. Aiden said all my impressions sounded like Mr Bean but he was in a shit mood (what's new?) because he hasn't had any auditions for ages. But Grandma's friends thought they were excellent. And they should know – cos they were alive at the same time as all those singers. They're all about a million years old. I left there feeling really confident and the next day I turned up at the audition in my Cancer Research charity shop outfit with mum's frumpy navy slip-ons only to see three Jane Horrocks lookalikes sat in a row. I was so ready to be told I looked too Jewish for the role.

The audition was basically a whole day's workshop. We all went in together and watched each other audition – quite unusual and a bit intimidating! They were all blonde and really pretty and they were really astounding actresses – one of them was just so so so so so so so good!! I don't have much confidence in my acting so I felt a bit worried.

After lunch we went in to sing one by one. I'm sorry, but I know my voices were far, far better than the two girls before. I did my Marlene Dietrich with the German accent just as Grandma had taught me and Terry the producer looked over at Stella the director and grinned.

Afterwards the musical director gave me a hug(!) and said 'I can see how hard you've worked, well done!'

So FLAPS CROSSED. I reeeeeeeeeally like being other people. At the moment I prefer it to being myself!!!

Rehearsals would start pretty soon and the run is only a few weeks but I would LOVE LOVE LOVE IT. PLEEEEEEASE LET ME GET IT!!!

Blimey! What a rollercoaster. Things are shifting for both of us, aren't they?

As I read Grandma Rosi's diary, I'm struck by the sweet, unfiltered hopefulness of her youth. She was so full of life and optimism, even as the world around her fell apart. Her love for Strumfeld feels pure, and untouched by cynicism. It sounds magical ... filmic even, like something from an animation: the twilight meetings, strawberry picking, sheltering under the bridge from the rain. How gorgeous! I can hear the swell of the orchestra and see the little animated bluebirds and mice and squirrels as they surround young Rosi.

Reading my own diary now, and trying to practise a bit of self-forgiveness, I see someone who was also trying to protect herself – though not very successfully.

That year chipped away at me in ways I didn't understand at the time. Like being picked last on the netball team at school: 'Oh, are all the good ones gone? I guess I'll have Jess then.' (To be fair, unlike Rosi, I was shit at all forms of sport.) It was only natural that I'd never been anyone's 'first choice' of girlfriend. When Kelly went off with Omar on my birthday, I was sad, but I don't think I was surprised.

Dating always felt a bit like the club in Hemel Hempstead with my hideous glowing braces. God, I didn't even 'manage' to lose my virginity till I was eighteen – and it was not for want of trying. But I realise now that 2007 was transformative: the 'director', the taxi driver ... those moments left me feeling exposed (literally), stupid, ashamed and diminished. By the time Aiden came along, I was clinging to the idea of being wanted, being chosen. Being the princess in my own fairy tale. I ignored all the red flags (as I did with Practice Husband) because I didn't want to face them. Aiden's sulking, his temper, the way he made me feel small – or rather, too big – it was all there, but I excused it. I kept hoping he'd change back into the funny, romantic boy I'd first met. I couldn't believe that maybe that version of him didn't exist any more. Or, more accurately, probably never did.

What strikes me now is how similar that is to what Grandma might have felt. Did she cling to the magic of her twilight garden, even when life turned harsher? Did she try to hold on to a version of love that no longer fitted the reality she lived in? It's amazing how much we try to shape ourselves around the love we think we deserve, even when it hurts us.

Grandma's letter to Samuel feels like such a turning point. She's shaking off some of the romanticism she once had. Her words carry weight – she's starting to see things for what they are. The idealism and dreams she held on to just aren't possible any more. She's no longer the hopeful girl imagining a better world; she's hardened. It's painful to read, knowing what was to come, but maybe this is where the woman Mum remembers – the sharp, guarded one – begins to emerge. Maybe it was the only way to survive.

And then there's young me. I can see myself shifting too. I still remember that lunch so clearly – sitting with Grandma, watching her take him in with her sharp, silent judgement. She didn't have to say anything. I already knew.

At the same time, something else was growing: my sense of self, of what I could achieve without Aiden's approval or anyone else's. The audition for *Little Voice* was exhilarating, one of the first times I felt truly proud of my effort – and my talent. Grandma and her friends helped me feel that confidence. Their encouragement was validating. For a moment, I could set aside all my self-doubt and just be those incredible women – Piaf, Garland, Bassey. There was freedom in that.

It's ironic, really. Grandma was beginning to turn inward, away from her youthful ideals, while I was looking outward, trying to rebuild a sense of who I was through teaching and performance and creativity. Both of us were grappling with identity in our own ways: she was narrowing hers, dismantling core beliefs, painfully letting go of dreams, while I was expanding mine – being other people to test the limits of who I could be.

The question I'm left with is this: was Grandma's disillusionment a necessary step for survival, or did it rob her of something vital? And for me, was hiding behind other personas perhaps a way of finding myself after all? Or, in fact, a way of avoiding the parts of me that felt broken? Maybe it's both. Maybe, like Grandma, I was just doing what my heart told me to survive.

God, what a cringey sentence.

Chapter 25

Diary of Rosi Schul
Sunday, 9 July 1939

The Kindertransport has started, and I've been promised the chance to be a chaperone on one in the near future! Yes! Thanks to my work with the children, it has been arranged that as part of my job, I can also go with many of the Stadium children on a boat to London, England! Papa has been lucky enough to get a visa to London through our relatives in Antwerp. However, I do not have one and I have no permit to stay in England, so I must return to Zbąszyń, along with the two doctors and two nurses who will also come on the boat. I do not want to leave my Strumfeld – but I know I must, and he will do all he can to wait for me here till I return.

My uncles and cousins here in Zbąszyń have nowhere to go, poor things. I don't know what will happen to them. And what has become of my eighty-nine-year-old grandmother in her old age home? 'A safe haven' they said … 'SAFE'?? She has never been heard of again …

Diary of Jess Robinson
Sunday, 15 July 2007

I
LOVE
THIS
JOB
!!!!!!!!!!!!!!!!

I love the cast. They are so supportive. I love my role. I love singing with a FIVE PIECE BAND. The director is lovely. The musical director is brilliant. We get standing ovations every night. I feel like I am HOME!! I just wish the run wasn't so short. I'm just getting into it and it's going to be over before it's begun.

The woman playing my mother knows the producer of Dead Ringers! I recorded a cassette tape of myself singing Judy Garland, Shirley Bassey, Edith Piaf, Billie Holiday and Marilyn Monroe and I sent it to his BBC address yesterday.

Aiden isn't coming because he says can't afford the train fare. I said I'd pay for it, and Mum said he could go in the car with her, but he doesn't want to. He said he's 'too proud'. He's a fucking DICK. I don't care. I don't have time for him right now. I'm focusing on me and I love every moment in this wonderful bubble land.

But I have to diet. Yesterday I had a Slim Fast and an apple for breakfast, a Diet Coke for lunch and some spinach and Ryvita for dinner. Today I had an apple for breakfast, salad and tonic water for lunch and spinach and 1 Ryvita and jam for dinner.

Written down it looks good. I might treat myself to a couple more Ryvita and jam later.

I don't want to get obsessed, but I'm trying not to eat more than 800 calories a day. I got some scales from Argos yesterday. They're really cheap, so they're telling me I'm 8 stone, which I know I'm not cos on Friday on the shopping centre ones I was 8.13 and at mum's on the weekend hers said 8.10, so I've set mine at 8.12. Today they said I was 8.9 but it's hard to tell.

See ya later!

———

There it is! The Kindertransport. This chance to escape was born of Grandma's love for children and teaching, and her need to 'Jew on' instead of wallow in despair. Like for me, her work with children wasn't just something she did to pass the time, it was what gave her purpose. It brought her joy even in the darkest moments, and throughout her diary I can feel how deeply it sustained her. It saved her life, stopped her from going the same way as her uncles, cousins and grandmother, who were all 'never heard of again'. Those words are a gut punch … a brutal reminder of how fragile everything was for her.

In 2007, fully caught up in the whirlwind of *Little Voice*, it's alarming to see my mad dieting, terrible maths (which has never improved) and how many times I managed to write Ryvita in one sentence … Maybe I should send the CEO of Ryvita a pic of that diary entry and ask for a sponsorship deal.

Despite the disordered eating, I can feel the joy in my writing. For the first time, I felt like I was doing exactly what I was meant to do. It's such a contrast to the doubt and insecurity I'd been carrying around for so long. I was starting to see my own worth, not through someone else's eyes, but through the work I was doing and the way it made me feel.

Even in such different circumstances, it's joyful and it's comforting to see how similar Grandma and I were in these moments …

Chapter 26

Diary of Rosi Schul
Monday, 24 July 1939 – Warsaw

The day has come! With many of my children from the Stadium I boarded the train to Warsaw. The parting of the children from their parents was utterly heartbreaking. One of the cruellest things I have ever witnessed. Why couldn't they come? Or at least the mothers? I can't understand it. I do not think I will ever forget the anguish on their faces, the tears. It tore at one's heart. Now, I must do what I can to be a mother figure for these bereft children. Poor things.

At present, the children, the other four members of staff, Papa and I are staying in a home for disabled children, in makeshift dormitories. Every day one of the rooms is disinfected, because the infestation of fleas and lice is so bad.

Strumfeld is also here in Warsaw! We have the best and most rewarding friendship. Our love has blossomed. My hope now is that somehow I will get papers to stay in England and Strumfeld will find a way to follow me there.

Diary of Jess Robinson
Monday, 13 August 2007

Haven't written in ages. I'm depressed. I'm missing the show so much. It was too short. I'm missing the people. Aiden is being nice. BUT MY PERIOD IS LATE.

WHAT IF I'M PREGNANT????????????????????????????

I can't imagine it. I've told Aiden that I'm worried (it's too early to take a test), and he just casually said – don't worry, you'll be a great mum. WHAAAAAAAAATTTTTTTTTT?

He said I'd give up acting and we'd move in with his parents. WHATTTTTTTTTTTTTTTTT?!!!

No way. Absolutely not. I'd get an abortion. I can't have a baby. That would be MAD!!!!!!!!!!!!!!!

Please come

Please come

Please come

I have eaten looooooaaaaaaddddss of chocolate and crisps and later I'm going to make some pasta. PLEAAAAASSSSE COME. Does a hot curry make your period come or just a baby?

If there isn't a baby will it make the period come? If there might be a baby and my body is still deciding, will it make me more likely to be preggo? NO that's SO stupid. Is it?

I'm losing my mind.

Also – heard back from Bill Dare at Dead Ringers he said my Judy Garland impression was very good, but they need impressions of people who are alive. So I sent him a tape of my Kate Bush impression. I haven't heard anything.

I'm struck once more by the enormity of what Grandma faced. Watching parents say goodbye to their children, knowing it might be forever, must have been so harrowing. Of course Rosi stepped in, becoming a mother figure to those poor children, torn away from their own parents. She offered them love, safety and care when the world felt unbearable.

The panic I felt about the unwanted pregnancy feels so small in comparison, but in the moment, it was all-consuming. The fear, the what-ifs, Aiden's offhand talk of moving and giving up acting – it was like watching my life being written without me. I wasn't just scared of being pregnant; I was scared of losing control over my own future, something I had just begun to grasp hold of. When I compare this to my mum's abortion experience, I can imagine how terrified and desperate she must have been, navigating a backstreet abortion, handling her disapproving mother, who threw this accident back in her face forever more. I just know that if it had come to it, and I'd needed an abortion, Mum would have supported me, no fuss. And she'd NEVER have thrown it back in my face. She turned the pain from that moment into protection for her daughters, ensuring we'd never face the same shame or judgement, and that is something I'll always be grateful for.

It seems the capacity to mother – even when the child isn't your own – is another thread running through our family. I've never had children of my own, but I *am* a stepmum to my incredible stepson, Sam, who's ten. I can't begin to explain how much I love him. I first met Sam when he was five. I was introduced slowly and carefully as 'Daddy's friend', and we bonded when I began making up silly songs and doing puppet shows for him – though definitely *not* using Grandma's old puppets … traumatising him was not the goal. At the time, I didn't fully realise how much this role would mean to me. I never had myself down to be a mother of any type, but over the years our friendship and love has grown and now my greatest joy is our special one-on-one time together, sitting at the kitchen table, working on his English and music. These moments remind me of how teaching and music have been passed down in my family from mother to daughter to daughter to … stepson. It's not the traditional mother–child relationship, but it doesn't need to be. It's ours, and it's precious.

Chapter 27

Diary of Rosi Schul
[date missing] August 1939

I am on a boat! Father will follow in a few weeks.

When the sea is calmer, I can write and look through the portholes. Together with two Polish doctors and two Polish nurses, I am in charge of <u>seventy</u> children – aged up to about 13 years old – mostly younger.

Before we boarded this lovely big ship, the Warszawa, all the children were examined by the Red Cross – the boys had their heads shaved and girls' hair was cut very short. Our heads were disinfected in case of lice. I cannot describe how sad the task was of separating the children from their parents. I cannot stop thinking of it. It is the cruellest thing to get the children away from their mothers and fathers. Many of the children have been told that they are going on a thrilling adventure. We keep telling them, 'You will see your parents again soon. You will.' Everyone was very excited, most have never been on such a big boat or seen the ocean before … what an experience! I am missing Strumfeld. I wonder what he will do and how he will get to me if I do not return to Poland?

Diary of Jess Robinson
Wednesday, 8 August 2007

MY PERIOD IS HERE. THANK THE LORD. Got it on the way home from seeing the doctor – (Sod's Law!), who said I need to be consistent with my eating. No more crash diets. I'm scared. I don't feel in control around food. I'm seeing mum later. I'm scared she'll see I've put on weight and be disappointed. Last week she lifted up my skirt to look at my thighs. I told her to stop, and she said 'Ooh sorry', really sarcastically as though I was being touchy.

Hang on ... phone's ringing

OMG I just got an audition FOR DEAD RINGERS!!!!!!!!!!!! Bill Dare!!!!!!!!!!!!!!!!! He said that Kate Bush isn't very current and they need speaking impressions mainly, so I told him I am BRILLIANT at speaking impressions. SHIT! I'm glad he didn't ask me to do any then and there cos that's a BIG LIE – well, unless he wanted to hear me do Grandma or Mum.

FUCK!! OK, I have a week and a half to learn. I am going to do Fizz from Coronation Street, Teri Hatcher from Desperate Housewives, Konnie Huq from Blue Peter, Jane McDonald and Sonia from EastEnders.

I'm going to pack now because I've decided to stay at mum's while I learn them all because Aiden is so down and irritable. I literally just ran into the kitchen to tell him and he said I'm 'rubbing it in'.

Diary of Jess Robinson
Wednesday, 22 August 2007

I can't bear it. He's so critical. Moving in with Aiden was a BIG mistake. I have to see if Rabbi's friend will give me my room back early. I'm supposed to let her rent it for another couple of months.

I don't want to be here. It's stifling and airless and I feel completely suffocated. It's all too much. I like to be up and about at 8. He goes to bed at 4am every night. I can't just do nothing and sit in bed all day. I have to do activities and chores and make plans or I just feel guilty and angry with myself that I've wasted my time. Maybe it's just the way I've been brought up, but if someone asks 'what did you do today?' I can't just answer 'stayed in bed'. I'd feel ashamed of not living my life. Even if it's just as mundane as doing the washing and buying milk and toilet paper and reading and making phone calls, it's better than being in your own mind and completely unconscious of the world isn't it??*

I've had the same dream three nights running: I've just met him and everything is fresh and new. He's a completely different person in my dream. Just with the same face.

In real life I feel like nothing is happening and everything is stale. He's nicer and more charming and funnier with anyone else but me when we're out. We visited his parents who are really sweet.

On the way there, he got so angry when we took a wrong turn that he threw the map out of the car window. HOW STUPID. We had to reverse back up the road so he could get out and get it again. He's got such a temper. He shouted and braked really hard at one point and it gave me a shock and I gasped, which annoyed

---

* Add in a dog walk, some *Real Housewives of Beverly Hills* and a glass (or three) of wine and that is pretty much my perfect day.

him. He said don't be so fucking dramatic and thumped me really hard on the arm. I've got a bruise there now. Dad would be really upset. I won't tell him.

He is SO rude to his parents – he's really spoiled. I've never heard anything like it. He calls his dad a dick in a really aggressive way.

I feel weak. Everything I do is wrong. When he talks about fancying me or liking me, it always goes hand in hand with career or talent – even though he's not supportive. He said if I wasn't talented he wouldn't be with me. Well, my career is terribly important – the most important thing to me, but there are other attributes to my character and personality. It really isn't the main reason to fancy or love someone.

I'm glad I wrote. I've almost talked myself into feeling stronger again.

I'm in a coffee shop at the moment. I hope he's not off with me when I get back. If he is, I'll go and see grandma.

I love him but sometimes I really don't like him.

P.S. Heard back from Bill Dare and he liked my audition and they are going to consider me for the next series!!!!!!!!!!!!!!!!!!! I don't know whether it will happen or not. Aiden said they're probably bullshitting. I'm going to put it out of my mind and try and enjoy life. We're going to his mum and dad's next week. I might suggest getting the train.

Diary of Rosi Schul
[date missing] August 1939

I am <u>still</u> on the boat! This journey is quite unpleasant and at times very scary.

Every day I do all I can to entertain the children. I assemble them and I talk to them. I tell them my stories and play my guitar, and we sing and look out of the portholes. It is such a new experience for them (and for me) to be on the water. During the day, they are generally distracted by all that we occupy them with. Yet, every night I must go from cabin to cabin to comfort the crying children, who are missing their parents so much. I do all I can to pacify them and tell them they will see their parents soon. It breaks my heart. Who knows if they will?

I sleep in a cabin with one of the nurses. The food is quite good! But the sea has been so very rough and yesterday I was terribly sick! The crossing is HORRIBLE. I hate it and apparently it is taking longer than expected. On board there is talk of Germany's aggression towards Poland. The sailors told us that the Germans often intercept boats. It is very worrying indeed. I must be brave for the little ones. But I fear for us. Will we reach the safety of London? And what of Strumfeld? Will we ever see each other again?

Rosi's diary on the boat is such a mix of courage and vulnerability. Even in the face of fear and uncertainty, she poured her energy into caring for those children. I remember in an interview with our friend Alan she said, 'Still today I feel it was the most cruel thing I have experienced. I was like a mother. I was so young, but I tried to pacify the children and say, "You will see your parents again, you will, you will …"' It breaks my heart to know that only 10 per cent of the 10,000 children who came to England on the Kindertransport saw their parents again.

I find Rosi's strength so inspiring, even as she worries about her own family and her future. But it's her thoughts of Strumfeld that stand out to me too. What happened between them? Because I know that he wasn't my grandfather. I hope he didn't perish in a concentration camp.

I can't stop thinking about it, so I text the Cool Bitches to see if they know more.

Group Chat: Cool Bitches

Monday, 29 January 2024, 15:56

Me: Ello! Hope you're having a nice day. I've nearly finished Gma's diary and I was wondering if Grandma ever told you what happened with Sally Strumfeld? Did he survive? I hope so! 🫣

Stephie: Hello darling! Yeah, I do know ...

So, Strumfeld was an intellect, a teacher, right? He was totally on your Grandma's wavelength, and she fell madly for him, but he had horrific experiences with anti-Semitism. He did make it over to England and they had a relationship together for a while, but it didn't end well. Mummy told me that when he was first deported to Poland, he became separated from his family, and they all perished in the concentration camps. Mummy said that resulted in this deep-seated paranoia and schizophrenia ... I think she hoped it would improve when he was safe in England, but he got worse ... He'd accuse her of having affairs (even if she just said hello to the milkman), and his behaviour was very erratic. It just couldn't work in the end. It was so sad and so very unsettling for her ... Then Mummy heard he had taken an overdose. He died. Mummy was utterly heartbroken and distraught that she hadn't been able to help him ...

Me: Oh my goodness. That's so sad. Poor Grandma. Poor Strumfeld. Oof! I wasn't expecting that. She must have been heartbroken.

Stephie: Oh, she was! I'm reminded of your mum and her boyfriend Howard. What anguish! And me, too, with my Fernando ... And you with your friend Alex. These young men. We all think we'll be the one to change someone, but we end up making no difference to them at all when they're so damaged ...

I hadn't realised that each of us had known a young man who had ended his life. In a family of talkers, it surprises me that we haven't sat around the kitchen table and shared these experiences more openly.

As I think about Grandma and Strumfeld, I realise I too was clinging to a relationship that was doomed. We were both stuck – her on a boat in rough seas with crying children and fading dreams, me in a flat where nothing felt steady or kind. We each held on to a version of someone we hoped might return. Hers was a man she believed she could heal; mine was Aiden, who I kept willing to become the boy I first fell for.

The thread that links all our stories – Grandma's, Mum's, Stephie's and mine – isn't just heartbreak. It's the hope we carry in the face of it. Stephie's words, 'We all think we'll be the one to change someone,' feel so true. Grandma tried to help Strumfeld, but his pain was too great. And no amount of patience or love was ever going to transform Aiden into someone who truly saw and valued me. Maybe he was depressed – maybe that's part of it – but I've learnt that love can't always save, and sometimes the bravest, kindest thing we can do is let go. And also, another big lesson I've learnt from reading back over my own diaries is that sometimes ... people are just cunts ... Though that does feel unfair to vaginas.

Me: So do we think that Strumfeld's suicide made Grandma put up a wall? Even more than the deportation?

Mum: Well, when she met Grandpa, although he was terribly sweet to her, she wasn't at all sure about him. She married him out of convenience ...

Sasha: Oh! That's a shock. I feel a bit sad about that. Poor Grandpa Jules.

Me: I always thought he swept her off her feet and it was all romantic.

Stephie: OK, so, she WAS sure about Grandpa, she was ... she KNEW it was the right and best thing to do, to marry him, and she really DID love him ... OK, so he wasn't the 'love of her life' (so to speak), not 'the one' she had dreamed of being with, but nonetheless she knew how lucky and lovely it was to have found someone who really loved her ... all the rest of it (sex, contradictions, etc.) between them is not 'noteworthy' or relevant in this instance, unless YOU personally have had a parallel experience in your time ... this is not a 'salacious', 'kiss 'n' tell' soap story (not in my opinion), but a drawing together of both your lives, across your respective decades ... is this a 'picking apart' of a woman's life, 'liking or disliking' what she wrote down, privately, in the moment, and 'set in stone'? No, I hope not ... yes, I'm sure that whatever befalls us, or how our lives pan out, moulds our character and behaviour ... you will be looking at your own 'outcomes' in relation to this point, won't you?! Be interestingly 'objective' in your subjectiveness, and that way you'll find the balance between true interpretation and '3D'. Look to your inner Spirit!

   I love you ... xx

Mum: She was full of resentment and jealousy – but my own experience is so coloured it's maybe not fair ... everything she did, wanted, had, cherished, worked for or loved seemed to be to impress and get praised and revered and respected – even if only as the wife of Dad or mother of us – her love was totally conditional! Her strength and feistiness benefitted her with the unfortunate little children, Stephie, her ailing friends in later life, but everyone she associated with came under the non-spoken heading – this is what I've made out of that person – this is vicariously MY achievement – xxx

Stephie: ... wheww, well, there you go ... I'm so depressed, that's made me cry ... but Jess, don't let the lines blur ... Take the bits that you feel ring true for you, through your perceptions of Grandma. xx

Mum: Nothing to be depressed about, darling Stephie – we are the lovely diverse people we are cos of them – mum and dad xx

Me: I'm really sorry, Stemmie xxx

Mum: Stephie, why are you depressed about my reality? You don't have to be. If I don't have mum on a pedestal in my memory it should not change your reality and your experience of her. You do know, you saw for yourself – that she treated us very differently. The reasons are simply amateur psychology on my part and you have much more compassion – emotionally you two were very similar. This project was never intended to stir up so much feeling, but it has! For you it is sadness and sympathy and for me it is anger and impatience. Nothing new there. Poor darling, we do understand each other nevertheless X

Stephie: Yes, we do xx

Katy: The different perspectives are really interesting. Different realities. People can learn from that in itself. Sometimes a lived experience is unfathomable to other people. And the more we try to explain our own reality, the more we alienate the other. We have to listen and accept and try to understand.

———

As we message back and forth, I can feel everyone trying – to stay generous, to really listen, to find some kind of common ground. Even when it's hard. Mum and Stephie have always been two sides of a very complicated coin – the big sister with the sharper edges, the little one with the softness – but here, they seem to be meeting in the middle. For once.

And when Katy writes that line – 'the more we try to explain our own reality, the more we alienate the other' – I feel a jolt, like she's holding up a mirror I wasn't quite ready to look into. Because the truth is, she and I feel alien to each other at the moment. We keep missing – talking past, never quite to – each other. I feel judged by her, disapproved of. Like the way I live doesn't quite make sense in her world – like I'm messy, or selfish, or unserious. And maybe I've built a wall of defence in response, which only widens the gap. But her words here – 'listen, accept, try to understand' – they're good ones. We could both do with taking her advice.

Me: Yes, she was resilient. She didn't really look backwards. There isn't a great amount in her diaries about what she'd lost when she was forced to leave Germany. It's mainly about how to get on, to make a success of herself and her life.

Katy: Thanks to her, we all had so much MORE to dream about. Yes, Grandma wanted to be in love as we all do. She was also a snob, as I think we all are.

Mum: But she knew that being married to a kind, reliable, companionable person would give her stability.

Stephie: Which is also important for a happy life.

Me: Ah! The wisdom of the Cool Bitches!

Katy: To the wisdom of the Cool Bitches 🍷

Me: 🍷

Sasha: 🍷

Stephie: 🍷

Mum: No, I prefer the quilted toilet roll from Waitrose.

Mum: sparrow

Mum: Sorry FS

Mum: 📖

Mum: … DFS

There's something hopeful here. We're all showing up – Mum, Stephie, Katy, me – trying to piece things together, to be fair, to play nicely as we pass around the memory of Grandma. And without quite saying it, I wonder if we're also trying to set an example for my niece Sasha who I realise, at twenty-three, is the same age as young Rosi and me when we wrote our diaries. Perhaps that's the best any of us can do: stay curious, sit with the contradictions and keep turning up for each other. Maybe that's how healing begins – not with agreement, but with honesty.
PING

Me: Oh my god bitches! I just got an email from the Embassy!!

Chapter 28

Diary of Rosi Schul
Monday, 28 August 1939

England!

Here I am. Finally in England! I am staying with my father's cousin for a few days. We are in the 'East End' of London. It is no Zbąszyń and certainly no Esslingen! The apartment is cramped. But I am so glad to be on solid land!!

The crossing was horrifically stressful, but what an amazing sight greeted us when Tower Bridge lifted, allowing the Warszawa to sail through and reach the dock.

London! I cannot believe it.

The press were there as well as representatives of the Jewish Polish Committee who took us all for a meal in an East End restaurant. Later, we were taken to a large hall where we met many Jewish couples, who were waiting to see the children, to offer them homes and take them into their families. Charitable as it was, I'm sorry to say, it felt to me like a 'cattle market'; was this child prettier than that one? Was this one more appealing than another? I had a big confrontation with a couple who wanted to take only <u>one</u> of the Krenzler twins … I held them both firmly by the hands and I refused any such offer! Outrageous! In the end, they found a home where they could stay together … I was very relieved. I hope all the children's hosts show them kindness.

I am supposed to return to Zbąszyń soon. One of the sailors told me I shouldn't go back. I will wait for my father. And (I hope) Strumfeld ...

Diary of Rosi Schul
Sunday, 3 September 1939

WAR!!! Is this real?

Father left for Belgium two days ago. I hope he arrived safely. I have to remain in England until I have the correct papers, but now I do not think I will be able to follow even if I manage to get them.

Diary of Jess Robinson
Friday, 22 September 2007

This is the first time I've felt the need to write for ages. Or perhaps it's the first time in a very long time I have been true enough to myself ...

This last year (apart from Little Voice) has been a shit year in many respects. A few weeks ago, mum took me to the doctor to get some antidepressants because she was so concerned and amazed at the way I was behaving. I cried and cried and said I couldn't get out of my own head. I couldn't stop worrying that Aiden would be unfaithful and make a fool of me. I have been completely obsessed with him and I was hardly seeing my friends. Rabbi kept saying whenever he was there I was different – not myself.

I HATED that he's 27 and his mum and dad had to pay his rent for 3 months because he couldn't be arsed to get a day job. I'm very proud that I support myself.

A couple of weeks ago Rabbi convinced me to go on holiday to Spain with her <u>WITHOUT</u> Aiden (who was not pleased) – and it was <u>transformational</u>. I had the time of my life and I didn't miss him at all. I was myself. I was carefree. It's like I remembered who I was. I was liberated and confident and didn't worry about the shape or size of my body. We drank (a lot), and soaked up the sun and laughed and laughed and laughed. I laughed so much! I spent the whole time laughing. Being me. I finally found 'me' again. I like myself a lot more with Rabbi than I do when I'm with Aiden.

When I came back a couple of days ago, I felt all re-energised and I was sort of looking forward to seeing him again. But he didn't come to meet me at the airport, even though Dad offered to give him a lift. When I got home, there he was, all miserable, tired, pale and skinny. He looked like an unhealthy Dickens character. I don't think he'd even bothered to brush his teeth.

I felt no wave of love when I saw him. I could literally feel the life being sucked out of me.

Then yesterday we went to Grandma's house for tea. Mum and Stephie were there and I was telling them all about the wonderful holiday (while Aiden yawned). When Aiden was out of the room, grandma said 'You can tell how much somebody is right for you, by how much you like the person you are when you are with them.' And that was the moment. And then she whispered 'It's just as easy to fall in love with a rich man.' Haha. She always says that, but grandpa isn't rich and nor is my dad ...

Then before we all got into mum's car for late night shopping at Brent Cross Shopping Centre, I stood on the front step with Aiden and said, 'We need to talk.' I tried to ignore mum and grandma and Stephie grinning out of the window. It almost made me want to laugh – especially since I'm used to laughing again now. Everything makes me want to laugh!!

I said to Aiden 'I don't like who I am when I'm with you and I'd like to end the relationship.'

He sneered 'Yeah, I heard what your Grandma said. She's not very subtle is she?'

I said 'Yeah, that runs in the family.'

Then Mum shouted out of the window 'Would you like a lift to the station, Aiden?'

I don't know why he got in. He never usually accepts lifts! IDIOT. He could have walked. Of all the times to not refuse a lift. DICK. We drove in silence – Grandma was in the front and mum kept looking at me in the rear view mirror and grinning. Stephie and Aiden and I were cramped in the back. Then Stephie said 'Well, man, it's been nice to know you and I do wish you well' in her friendly way. She wasn't being mean or sarcastic. And Aiden sort of hissed 'Yeah, I wish I could say the same about your fucking family.' I didn't think anyone heard apart from me. This was the time for a witty comeback! A quick witty comeback! But I was so shocked, I couldn't think of anything because I just couldn't believe he'd say that in front of them, but Grandma must have had her hearing aids turned right up cos she immediately shouted 'STOP ZE CAR.'

Mum said 'I can't stop here I'm on the North Circular' but Gma insisted. So we stopped on a really busy bit on the roundabout under the Brent Cross Flyover and Grandma said 'Out you get Andrew.'

HAHAHAHAHAHAHAHAHAHAHAHAAHAAAA!!!!! ANDREW!!!!!!!!!!!!!!!!!!!!!

And he got out and WE LEFT HIM UNDER THE BRENT CROSS FLYOVER.

HAHAHAHAHAHAHAHAHAHAHAHAHAHAHAHAHA-HAHAHAHAHA

I didn't need a witty comeback for once! We gave him the cold shoulder on the hard shoulder!

HAHAHAHA!

ANDREW!!!

Mum was killing herself laughing about the 'Andrew' mistake. We were all doing impressions of Grandma shouting STOP ZE CAR like the Gestapo. And Grandma got such bad giggles that her false teeth came out and Stephie and I had to hunt for them under the front seat.

We met Katy and Jojo for salt beef bagels in the Brent Cross food court to celebrate.

I GOT RID OF THE WANKER.

WOOOOOO!!

HAHAHAHAHAHAHAAAAA

I'm so relieved. I can't believe I stayed with him for so long. Now I'm going to go for it. I'm going to have fun and do what I want. I need to sing and write and play and see my friends.

I bought a new diary at Brent Cross as this chapter is closing. I think this is the end of this diary. Man, it's been a rollercoaster.

I'm going to be more positive and more hard working.

I hereby leave Aiden/ANDREW behind in this old diary. I'm going to bind it with sellotape so he can't escape.

And what will I bring with me into this new diary?

My true self, my positivity and all my notes for teaching. My Stagecoach Borehamwood choir is competing in the Watford Music Festival this weekend. I hope we win and Hyman gives me a bonus.

Goodbye and thank you.

See you in the new one.

Lots of love Jess xxx

I left a lot behind in that diary. In that year. A lot of traumatic experiences. To the director who said I was too Jewish; to that awful taxi driver; to the disgusting 'film director'; to all of you: I leave you bound in the diary with Sellotape. Or, the worst punishment possible: I leave you stranded on the A406 with only yourselves for company. You can all JEW OFF!

EMAIL TO: jess_robinsons_grown_up_email_address@aol.com
SUBJECT: RE: Citizenship
Monday, 29 January 2024, 16:30

Dear Jessica,

I hope this email finds you well.

I am very pleased to inform you that the Federal Administration Office has approved your application for naturalisation. Your naturalisation certificate has arrived and is ready for collection at the German Embassy in London.

Kindly note that the naturalisation will only become valid once the certificate has been handed over to you personally. Therefore, I would like to invite you to contact me in order to make an appointment.

I am looking forward to your reply.

Best regards

Matilda X

EMAIL TO: German Embassy
SUBJECT: RE: Citizenship
Monday, 29 January 2024, 16:33

Hi Matilda!

Oh my goodness! Thank you so much for the great news! WOW! Would this Thursday be possible please? It's my birthday. How is 10:30am? EEEK!

Jess xXx

EMAIL TO: jess_robinsons_grown_up_email_address@aol.com
SUBJECT: RE: Citizenship
Monday, 29 January 2024, 16:39

Dear Jess,

Thank you for getting back to me.

This Thursday at 10:30 is PERFECT. You will celebrate your birthday as a German citizen.

I am very much looking forward to meeting you then at our main Embassy building at Chesham Place. Please come up the stairs and please do not queue at the side entrance.

Looking forward to meeting you.

Best regards

Matilda

I can't believe it! I'd been so busy learning about Rosi, I'd almost forgotten about my quest for German citizenship. The night before my appointment with my bestie, Matilda, emotion floods me as I sit down with the diaries. How funny and poetic that I am nearly at the end of both ... I feel as though a circle is closing. Aware of the symbolism of the timing, I read the diary entries back to back. Maybe I'm still guilty of seeing connections that aren't there, but I keep finding these similarities. Young Rosi, young me and present me – all stepping into something new. For Grandma, it was a strange new country – a cramped apartment, the hope of reuniting with her father and the question of whether she should return to Zbąszyń to reunite with her love (and face certain death), which gives me a lump in my throat. For me, it was the decision to reclaim my own life – to embrace my work, my friends and the version of myself I loved best.

I go to bed, on 'Embassy Eve', feeling such love and admiration for my grandma – knowing she didn't let the weight of her journey crush her; she turned it into resolve to protect those children. And I didn't let the weight of my relationship define me; I found my way back to laughter and joy. In *The Sound of Music*, Maria (who I've often likened Grandma to – minus the Christianity and plus a temper) says it best: 'Where the Lord closes a door, somewhere He opens a window.' These endings brought us new beginnings …

One of the stories from Rosi's journey that won't leave me is her determination to keep the Krenzler twins together. That image of her – hands tightly clasped around theirs, refusing to let them be separated – stays with me. Even now, decades later, it feels radical. Defiant. Protective in a way that goes beyond duty. That night, I dream about them. The twins, the crowd of nervous children, the couples assessing them like puppies in a litter. I wake at 5 a.m. with a jolt – anxious about my Embassy appointment, afraid of missing it, imagining everything being delayed by another two years – and the Krenzler twins are still with me, haunting me in the best possible way.

So I get up. No point trying to sleep now. I drift into my studio, open my laptop and start typing their names. Just to see.

And there they are!

The Krenzler twins with their older sister Inge in the summer of 1938.

After twenty minutes of sifting through archives and blurry PDFs, I find the Krenzler twins in an academic thesis – 'Contesting Memory: New Perspectives on the Kindertransport' by Jennifer Craig-Norton. There's a photo of them in the summer of 1938, standing with their older sister Inge behind them. I sigh as I read that Inge wasn't permitted to join the Kindertransport. Nor were their three other siblings. None of them survived. Their eldest brother Hershal was murdered in Auschwitz.

And then I find it. A tiny missing persons ad from the March 1964 issue of a journal from the Association of Jewish Refugees:

> Mrs Rosie Ruben (née Schul), who came to this country in the summer of 1939 from Zbąszyń, Poland, wanted by twin sisters, Ursel and Liesa Krenzler.

Oh my God. They looked for her.

Ursel and Liesa Krenzler. So sweet. Imagine splitting them up.

Thirty years later – long after that chaotic day in the East End, long after Rosi stood between them and separation – they remembered. They remembered her name. They remembered her kindness. She must have meant something enormous to them. In a moment of terror and displacement, she held their hands. And they never forgot it.

It makes me think about legacy – the kind that isn't shouted about in newspaper articles or commemorated in plaques, but whispered down through time in small gestures that changed the course of someone's life. That little missing persons ad feels louder than any medal. Maybe this is what it looks like to live a meaningful life: not always loud, but unforgettable.

As I eat my toast, struggling to swallow over the lump in my throat, I leaf through the folder of Rosi's precious documents, translating slowly with the help of Google as I go.

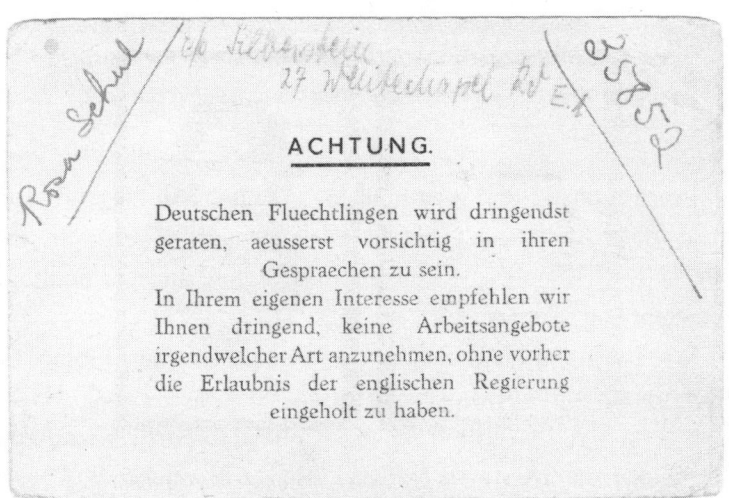

ATTENTION.
German refugees are urgently advised to be extremely cautious in their conversations. In your own interest, we strongly recommend that you do not accept any job offers of any kind without first obtaining permission from the British Government.

> **SIE SIND GAESTE GROSSBRITANNIENS.**
>
> Hoeflichkeit und gutes Betragen werden Ihnen ueberall herzliche Aufnahme und Sympathie zusichern.
>
> Sprechen Sie nicht laut auf der Strasse, besonders nicht am Abend.
>
> Nehmen Sie Ruecksicht auf die Bequemlichkeit anderer Leute und vermeiden Sie, deren Eigentum und Moebel zu beschaedigen.
>
> Vergessen Sie nie, dass England's Urteil ueber die deutschen Fluechtlinge von IHREM Verhalten abhaengt.

YOU ARE GUESTS OF GREAT BRITAIN.
Politeness and good behaviour will ensure you a warm welcome and sympathy everywhere. Do not speak loudly in the street, especially not in the evening. Be considerate of the comfort of others and avoid damaging their property and furniture. Never forget that England's judgement of German refugees depends on YOUR behaviour.

I turn the page to a picture of my grandma and me, with our great friend Alan Reich. This was taken a couple of years after we left ANDREW on the side of the road. I close my eyes, smiling, remembering that day ...

My family and I had gone to the Wiener Holocaust Library in London for the opening night of an exhibition called 'Child Refugees: Five Portraits from the Kindertransport'. Grandma's was one of the five stories featured. Alan, a filmmaker, had been interviewing Grandma a lot over the previous couple of years while researching his own family history. His dad had been a nine-year-old child deported to Poland and had made it to England on the last Kindertransport boat, just days before the war broke out. The exhibition coincided with the seventy-fifth

Left to right: me, Grandma and Alan Reich at the exhibition ...

anniversary of the Kindertransport, and a reunion was organised by the Association of Jewish Refugees at the JFS School ... Grandma was one of the stars of the day – treated like a queen – which suited her demeanour perfectly. In fact, the very next day she was due to meet Prince Charles. I hoped he wouldn't be intimidated by her.

I was a bit hungover from the night before, and had *The Sound of Music* going round and round in my head. Not the lyrics – the chords. I'd been cast as Leisel in a production and, thanks to another little white lie during the audition, now had to learn to play the guitar.

Mum had borrowed one from the vicar for me to practise on, and earlier that day I sat in the morning room while Grandma taught me the chords. As I fumbled with the finger positions, Mum and Stephie bustled around – making phone calls to the council, sifting through paperwork and, between mouthfuls of marzipan and sips of black coffee, joining in with the 'Ahhhhs' like a couple of nuns.

Playing the guitar was much harder than I'd imagined it would be when I told the director I already could. Whoops. The vicar's instrument – that sounds wrong – felt clunky and unfamiliar. After a few minutes my arm began to ache and my fingertips throbbed from pressing down on the strings.

'Again,' Grandma said firmly. I didn't dare disobey.

We sang through the song slowly as I accompanied myself, trying to remember the chord shapes as I went: 'The C-c-c-c, with the sound of … [PAUSE] B seven … with [PAUSE] … C-c-c-c for an [PAUSE] … A minor … D minor. Ahhhh … [PAUSE] G …'

'Better,' Grandma declared, and left the room.

I thought she'd gone to get ready for the exhibition, but a couple of minutes later she returned, holding the small guitar that had always hung on the wall in the music room. 'You will play better on this,' she said, handing it to me with care. 'Take it,' she ordered. 'For ze show.'

I thanked her and held it carefully, feeling how much friendlier and lighter it was. I ran my fingers over the pretty pearl inlay on the neck, oblivious to the journey it had been on, but Stephie breathed, 'Oh, Mamma! Oh, how far out! Jessie, do you know what that guitar has seen?'

My mum looked very surprised and said, 'That's *very* kind!' before answering the phone to discuss Grandma's bins with Hendon Council.

I looked between Stephie and Grandma and strummed a chord, its sound lingering in the room …

Later, at the exhibition, I found myself staring at a picture of the boat that had brought Grandma and her charges over. My fingers unconsciously traced the shapes of the chords I'd been learning that morning. As I turned to a black-and-white photo of young Grandma sitting under a tree, the chatter of the room faded. I recognised the guitar she was holding.

Just then, I was pulled out of my thoughts by a commotion at the back of the room. A little old man (Tony) was pointing to a photograph of Grandma with a group of children. 'That's me,' he said, 'in the photograph with Rosi!'

Grandma was suddenly whisked away (as fast as you can whisk away an older person – in a slow-motion sort of way) to meet him, and I followed Mum and Stephie across the room to see her greet the man, whose eyes lit up as he recognised her.

'I know this woman! She put me on the boat. She was like a mother to me.'

Tony held on tightly to Grandma, tears in his eyes, repeating over and over, 'You were like a mother to me.'

Grandma was stunned. The joy and genuine surprise on her face is something I know I'll never forget. Tony's wife explained to Mum that Tony wasn't well and rarely left the house, but he'd been determined to attend the anniversary. We stood by and watched as he cried, sharing his vivid memories of Grandma – the stories she told, the songs she sang to the children.

Grandma between her 'young' charges, Tony and Rebecca.

A little later, we were stunned and delighted once again when Grandma was reunited with Rebecca, who also remembered so much about being with young Rosi in the camp – her stories, her songs and the little guitar with the pretty pearl inlay. She described Grandma as their *Neue Mutter* – their new mother.

Knowing what I know now about Grandma's story, I find myself thinking of Theodor Rothschild, the headmaster of the orphanage in her beloved Esslingen, known to everyone – even the staff – as Herr Vater. There's something moving about that parallel: Grandma, who worked under a man regarded as a father figure by all around him, later becoming a mother figure herself, offering the same kind of warmth and steadiness to the refugee children.

I suddenly put two and two together and, after confirming with Stephie, am heartened to know that this is Rebecca Krenzler – originally named 'Ursel'. Yes! She is one of the Krenzler twins who Rosi fought to keep together! So she WAS reunited with Rosi eventually!

Later, as we gathered our coats, I overheard Tony quietly say, 'This has been one of the happiest days of my life.'

King (then Prince) Charles pretending not to be intimidated by Grandma.

I turn to the next picture – and, seeing the 'Queen of England', as her siblings called my grandma, meeting the now King of England, I reach for my phone ...

Group Chat: Cool Bitches

Thursday, 1 February 2024, 06:45

Me: Hi! @Mum, @Stephie, were you there when Grandma met King Charles?

Mum: Happy Birthday, Poopie Dollydumps. Although you don't come out of my fanny for another few hours.

Stephie: HAPPY BIRTHDAY, sweet girl! Oh yes! Well of course, he was the Prince of Wales then ... As he walked by us, I made Grandma and poor crippled Rebecca stand up (from her wheelchair) or he may not have seen them ... I said, 'Please Sir, may I introduce Mummy and one of her "Kinder", Rebecca, who have just been reunited after 75 years!' 'Oh, reeeeeeaaaally?' he said, shaking my hand, at which point Rebecca said, 'I'm sorry, I have to sit down,' and clutched at her daughter's arm who plonked her back into the wheelchair ... Grandma just stepped forward and told him all about their story (her as a chaperone to the children on the boat over), and made him laugh at something, which was when the royal photographer snapped the photo! She looked so small in front of him, but held his attention (as only Grandma would)! She was probably the oldest one in the room, all the others having been little children at the time of Kindertransport, so hers was an interesting tale to tell ...

Mum: Yes, didn't mummy say to him 'I am not one of the Kinder – I am the chaperone'?

Stephie: Yes, but I don't think he understood that. He looked a bit bemused.

Mum: Probably because mummy looked young in comparison to many of the 'kinder' there.

Me: Wow!

Stephie: Yes, and afterwards, we just kept giggling cos she said he had sausage fingers!

———

Giggling to myself at the thought of Grandma being derogatory about Charlie's hands, I shove my coat on and grab my keys, touching the little guitar, which hangs above my desk, before I leave. 'What do you want for your celebration dinner?' Husband 2.6 calls down the stairs. I pause with my key in the front door and shout back, 'Sausages!'

Chapter 29

Diary of Jess Robinson
Tuesday, 17 October 2007

I'm boiling an egg.

I've decided to do this thing called The Artist's Way. This is Day Two.

Every morning, I sit at the kitchen table and spew out pages and pages of brain vomit until my hand hurts or I run out of things to say – whichever comes first.

I think it's supposed to be for 20 minutes, but I keep checking the clock after ten minutes ... I'm meant to take myself on 'artist dates' too – solo adventures to 'reignite creativity' or something. Jojo is going to meet me at The Pottery Café in Mill Hill East on Wednesday for my 'Artist's Date' which I know I'm meant to do on my own, so defeats the point slightly, but fuck it, I need the company. She's also helping me learn some jazz chords for an audition next week where I have to accompany myself on the piano. I must take piano playing off my CV. It makes me too nervous ... Still lots of auditions with this new agent which is good.

On Friday I've got an audition for DOCTOR WHO. It's just for the audio version but I'd love to get it. But at the moment I'm having a bit of a confidence crisis and I keep thinking that I can't act which is bollocks because I played Little Voice, for God's sake. I'm sensitive, intuitive and a damn sight better than some of the plonkers I've seen on telly.* But instead of cracking on with the script, I'm sat here writing about how I should be cracking on with the script. How meta is that? I'll definitely book this Doctor Who thing now! Is this really useful? Am I emptying my brain and leaving it open for creative stuff, or am I just wasting time? Mum is always going on about how terrible procrastination is. She's drilled it into me, so if I don't work really hard and get on with things immediately I feel guilty. I can literally hear her voice in my head.

The Artist's Way is also making me write letters to my 'creative enemies' (cringe), and of course, Aiden came up. I'm so angry with him all the time. I keep having fantasies where I run into him at a party where I look amazing and then TAKE HIM DOWN. That dickhead. I let him squash me. I let him diminish me. I let him make me feel like shit about myself – and for what? A sulky wanker-twat who said my impressions sounded like Mr Bean. FUCK OFF. Also Mr Bean is funny. Also – Mr Bean is FAMOUSLY MUTE. He was a stupid bully (Aiden now, not Mr Bean),† but ... I was the one who let it happen. I was the one who stayed. So I think that's what I hate the most. Not him – me. The more I hate him the more I realise I'm just hating myself.

Anyway, the good news is that things are different. I love being single. I love living with Rabbi. We're going to have a combined Halloween Fireworks party. There are already 35 people coming on the Facebook group. YIKES. I think I might get a lock for my bedroom door. Last week when we had the 'gathering' we all ended up in the bath and the plughole got really blocked and we had to go to the gym for a shower.

Katy just rang – I'm going to babysit Sasha for a bit tonight while she sees a mate, and then she's coming back to help me

---

* More humble too.
† Phew! Glad I clarified. I don't want Mr Bean to be cancelled.

with my Doctor Who script. She's a bloody good director actually – she's really calm and clear, gives me loads of confidence. We've decided we're going to run a mini theatre school in the village during the Christmas hols. It's called 'Helter-Skelter' – no idea why, we just thought it sounded fun and chaotic. She'll do all the drama and I'll do singing and choreography. Mum put an advert in the Aldbury Outlook and in the window of the village shop and we've already got about twenty kids signed up! We'll both stay at Mum's while it's on. I'm really excited for it – we're going to write the script and choose the songs next week. We're such a good team.

Also, I'm seeing Grandma at the weekend. Auntie Stephie's supposed to be coming too. Looking forward to that. Family stuff feels a bit less insane at the moment. Don't want to jinx it.

Oh! And choir news – Brenda was soooooooo happy that my choir WON the Watford Music Festival she entered us into an INTERNATIONAL FESTIVAL. SHIIIIT.

I'm starting to feel like a proper functioning grown-up. Sort of.

Rabbi's just walked into the kitchen looking like death with a hangover. So I'm giving her my egg. That's how good a friend I am.

Right, that's enough pouring my soul into a notebook for today. Off to boil another egg and try to be an actor again. Or at least pretend I am.

Love,

Jess x

Diary of Rosi Schul
Tuesday, 17 October 1939

Life is strange. When I lie in bed at night and let my mind wander, I see the significance of it all. The beauty and the ugliness – high tide, low tide – I almost enjoy the bad things because they must always be followed by good things. I am up and down. Different moods from one hour to the next. I carry such an unbearable sense of loss for my home. What has happened to my beloved Germany? Hannover. Esslingen. Mama, Papa, Regina, Simon and Max, Berthe, Delli and Ruthi are all in Antwerp TOGETHER. Only I am on my own.

Poland is HELL with WAR. What will happen to my uncles and cousins who had nowhere to go?

At Student Movement House, I got a domestic visa and have financial support of £1 per week AND (can it be possible?), for a few weeks before I came to my current abode, I had a little room next to SAMUEL!!!!! Just like in Esslingen! My past life was resurrected! We chatted and shared our different memories of our time there. It was so comforting. He had a door with a lock! So we spent one night together with much PG!!

Now I am living in Epsom. There is no sign of any Jewish people. Good. I don't want to see any. It is soothing for me not to see past shadows, which stir up emotions.

I have started a new job in Sherwood School as a nursery nurse. Three little devils and one sweet two-year-old, all badly brought up. English children are AWFUL. Brrrrrr!

Diary of Rosi Schul
Monday, 25 December 1939

Here I am, still in Epsom. It is Christmas – almost the end of the year. Could Ruthi – all of them – even imagine how I live now? Completely non-Jewish traditions!

Diary of Rosi Schul
Friday, 13 December 1940

Today I did something I never thought I would. Mary and I went to a little café. When I commented that it smelled good, Mary pointed to a couple at a nearby table, eating bacon.

She insisted I try it! At first, of course, I said no! Bacon! It looked so foreign and forbidden! But Mary said, 'Come on, Rosi! Just once won't hurt.'

So we ordered it! When it arrived, I hesitated. But then I took a small bite. I was surprised. It was crispy and chewy and very salty – different from anything I'd tasted before. I liked it. I liked it very much, in fact! I never imagined I would, but there it is.

Mary laughed and said, 'Look at you, Rosi, eating bacon like a proper Englishwoman!' Unbelievable! What would Mama and Papa think? They would be so shocked, but in a strange way, it felt liberating.

Later I will lead my choir in a performance. We have named ourselves Rosi's Warblers. It feels wonderful to share music with others – especially in these turbulent times.

Diary of Rosi Schul
Thursday, 18 December 1941

A letter via the USA has arrived from Mama, Papa and Delli. But it was dated 1940 and has taken a year and three months to arrive! The uncertainty is hard to bear, but at least I know they are alive and together. Or at least, they were.

Diary of Rosi Schul
Thursday, 30 July 1942

Today has been a day of immense joy, a beacon of light in these dark times. I can hardly believe it, but here it is, in black and white on the official letterhead of the Royal College of Music. I have been admitted as a full-time student! The letter arrived this morning, in an envelope bearing the official crest of the College. Unbelievable! 'Miss R. Schul, This is to inform you that you have been admitted as a full-time student to enter this College in September, 1942.'

I feel excitement and relief. This opportunity! It is the best news. It is a chance to pursue my passion for music – and that I can do it even during this chaotic time? Amid bombings? Astonishing! I immediately thought of Mama and Papa. How proud they would be. I have not heard from them for a long time. I can only pray they are safe.

Music has always been my refuge and my connection to others – it helped me to bring comfort and fun to the children I cared for – and now it feels like a gateway to a new chapter of my life.

Tonight, I will go to sleep feeling hopeful as I move towards something wonderful. The Royal College of Music – my path to the future. Now if I could only find somebody to love and be loved by …

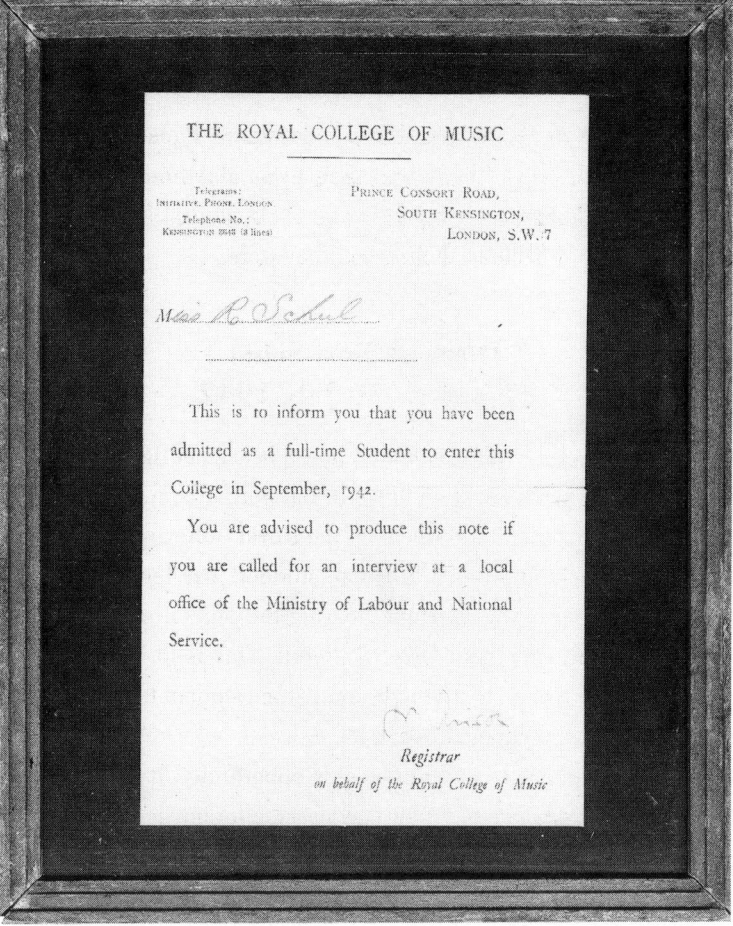

Rosi's acceptance letter from the Royal College of Music, which now sits in a frame in my home voice-over studio.

> TEL. No.
> FULHAM 1467.
>
> BISHOP CREIGHTON HOUSE,
> 378, LILLIE ROAD,
> FULHAM, S.W. 6.
>
> September 4th. 1942.
>
> Dear Sir,
>
> Miss Rosi Shul.
>
> Miss Rosi Shul has been employed at this Settlement since November 1941. She teaches Singing and Handicrafts in the Play Centre two Sessions each week and again Singing and Table Tennis in the Senior Clubs for two sessions a week. For these four sessions she is paid £1 a week.
>
> I can only speak with the highest praise of her work here. She is a person of exceptional talent and ability and has worked with outstanding success.
>
> I am,
>
> Yours sincerely,
>
> Emlie Dodds
> WARDEN.

A glowing reference for my grandmother Rosi Schul, dated 4 September 1942, from Bishop Creighton House in Fulham, where she taught singing, handicrafts and table tennis to children and seniors during the war. She was praised as 'a person of exceptional talent and ability' – a legacy that clearly runs in the family!

Diary of Rosi Schul
Monday, 1 February 1943

I have met a sweet fellow. Jules Ruben. He is a 'jazz' pianist. Today he invited me to meet his sister. She lives in a beautiful flat – typical Jewish woman – she is sweet and so well dressed. But her husband is a cockney! Brrrrr!

Jules is nice – and interesting, so I let him do PG and I even liked it.

He told me he had a recent heartbreak. I told him about Strumfeld – he should know that I'm not ready for anything. If things were ever to develop, I would have to improve his terrible table manners.*

I have said I will see him on Saturday and he was over the moon about it. I'm looking forward to it – it's good for me to be loved.

Jules Ruben. Rosi and Jules were married on 27 June 1943.

---

* Ha-ha! If this isn't proof that you can't change a man, I don't know what is!

Diary of Rosi Schul
Wednesday, 3 March 1943

A Letter from Mama and Papa arrived, posted on 24th October 1942!! To see Mama's handwriting after such a long time! But since October no one could write any more as the transport of Jews started. So it's hardly a consolation to receive the letter. Are they still in the world? What has happened to them since Hitler's plans are being taken against the Jews? I am sick of being Jewish. Oh God, how I wish that the newspapers were exaggerating. It is all so terrible. The Blitz on London is nothing in comparison. If only I could see them again – it would be unbelievable.

It's strange reading Grandma's diaries from this chapter of her life – not just because of the shifts in tone (from bacon to bombing to being loved again), but because I can feel her wrestling with the same things I'm starting to get a grip on: identity; belonging; that tug between where you come from, where you end up, and who you are in between.

She was navigating a new life in a strange country, holding trauma in one hand and hope in the other. And now, weirdly, I'm doing something not all that different.

I go to the Embassy on my own, too impatient to get a date that suits the Busy Bitches and feeling the symbolism of being reborn a German on my birthday.* I started this journey alone, so I may as well finish it the same way. I reflect on my diary entry with a hurting heart – it's lovely to look back and see how important my sisters were to me in my diary entry – especially Katy. I sigh …

As the train hums its way out of Brighton I think about Grandma's mother and siblings. I now know that when Rosi and

---

* 1 February – please send gifts via my agent (Sophie, not Annika).

her father made it to England with the children from Zbąszyń, Baruch managed to get a boat to Belgium to be with the family. Germany had already invaded Poland, and while her relatives in Belgium were still relatively safe, those in Poland were in immediate danger. However, my grandma, who had stayed to make sure the children were settled, couldn't get the next boat. It was cancelled. The borders closed and she was stranded in England – cut off from the rest of her family and unsure if they'd survived.

Then, in May 1940, everything changed. Germany invaded Belgium. The Nazis swept through the Ardennes and towards Brussels with terrifying speed. For Jewish families like Rosi's – already displaced – there was no choice. They had to flee again … Rosi's family there made the decision quickly, in the chaos and panic of impending occupation. They took almost nothing with them. Just the clothes on their backs and a vague plan: to get to the French coast and try to find a boat to England.

They left Antwerp on foot, walking for days through bombed-out towns, ducking for cover as aircraft flew overhead. In her testimonial, Ruthi described the constant sound of bombing and the hopelessness of it all. They had no transport, no maps, and no idea whether England was even reachable. But they kept going, because what else could they do?

They made it to La Panne, a small seaside town just over the French border. It had become a kind of bottleneck – a place where refugees, soldiers and desperate families gathered in the hope of rescue. It was just miles from Dunkirk, where the evacuation of Allied troops was already underway. But with no boats, no rescue and no safe route forward, the family were forced to turn back again. They returned to Brussels – defeated, exhausted and terrified.

By this point, Belgium was fully occupied. The round-ups had begun. Jews were being arrested, deported, disappearing. It became clear they couldn't live openly any more.

Ruthi herself went into hiding under a false identity, living for a time as Jane Le Roye with the Van Roye family – who risked everything to protect her.

Miraculously, both Rosi's parents and her siblings all survived the Holocaust.

Ruthi's story is full of danger and desperation – forged papers, false names, bombs overhead, hiding in basements, slipping across borders with nothing but blind hope. Grandma's, by contrast, was about holding on to normality, while her family were dodging Luftwaffe planes over Belgium. One sister was disappearing into the shadows, the other was starting a choir called Rosi's Warblers. But that doesn't diminish what Grandma went through. If anything, it helps explain why she often called it an 'adventure', why she talked about it with a shrug, and why she once told me she felt like a fraud whenever anyone referred to her as a survivor. She was safe – which made her feel, in some way, unworthy. And yet the truth is, she still lost her country, her home, her sense of safety …

And now here I am, two generations later, standing outside the German Embassy, about to reclaim what she never could.

Realising I'm half an hour early, I stand on the steps of the ugly consulate building in the cold morning sunshine remembering Mum accidentally Nazi saluting the taxi last time we were here. As I sip my even more eye-wateringly expensive coffee from Le Nepo Baby (they've put their prices up), I am struck by how incredible it is that I am even here, still marvelling at Grandma's incredible luck in coming to England.

I stare up into the cold side-eye of Eric the eagle as he flaps in the breeze, blowing a raspberry. Is he challenging me? Just as I'm sticking my tongue out at the gurning bird in defiance, a twinkly-eyed security guard – who I realise has been watching me from the window – asks whether I'm planning on coming in. 'Oh!' I grin, embarrassed, and then add '*Ja*' in my deepest voice. Good save, Jess, good save.

I sit in the waiting room, wondering if I should be feeling some affection or affinity for Eric now, in the way that I know the British flag means 'home' (and, I counter, makes me a bit uncomfortable, as it also makes me think of the BNP).

Without my phone to while away the time on Candy Crush, I riffle through the leaflets and pamphlets, all in German ... which I still can't read – lazy, lazy Jess! I panic. I hope there isn't a test! I don't know anything about Germany apart from the fact that 'Bratwurst' ISN'T the German translation of the Charli XCX-inspired trend 'Brat summer'. Confusing a citizenship test with a gameshow, I wildly hope there'll be a food round. Oh God, what if it's all in German? Just as I'm thinking of making a run for it, a woman opens the door.

Matilda isn't at all what I expected. What had I expected? She's in her early fifties with blonde hair, sensible heels and bright-red lipstick. I jump up and hug her, which takes her aback. She doesn't mention my over-familiarity but wishes me a happy birthday and chats away – in English, thank goodness – as she leads me up to a soulless beige office on the top floor. When, to my great relief, she confirms there is no test, I am expecting to just sign a form and be on my way. What I don't expect is for her to stand in front of me with a cream folder in her hands and make a ceremonial speech, which begins with the solemn words: 'Jessica Sophie Robinson, I hereby present you with your certificate of naturalisation. The German Embassy is *honoured* to have you as a citizen.' I get a lump in my throat and my eyes prick as she continues earnestly, 'On behalf of Germany, I would like to sincerely apologise for the pain and suffering caused to your family.' I am holding my breath as she finishes: 'You are now a German and you should ALWAYS have *been* a German.' I promptly burst into tears, a mixture of shock, grief and, I guess ... relief? It isn't like a weight being lifted exactly ... it's as if a bad spirit I didn't even know was there has been exorcised. I look up from my disintegrating tissue and see that Matilda is crying too.

Becoming German has forged a link to a lost world. A link to my grandma, who will, heartbreakingly, I note, *never* hear the words, '*You should always have been a German Citizen,*' from her mother country, which had so cruelly rejected her.

In spite of everything, Grandma never stopped loving Germany, and I know she would have been SO delighted that I've done this. That her daughters, and granddaughters, and great-granddaughters are now German.

When we realise that my passport pictures aren't biometric, the glamorous, clear-skinned, bright-eyed photos I'd diligently brought with me are binned and I have to take a new one in the Embassy booth, with puffy eyes, smeared mascara, quivering lips and a red face. Well, who has a decent passport photo anyway? This is raw and real and, fuck it, it's a reminder of my emotional journey every time I take an actual journey.

Seeing the first document in German with my name written on it after seeing so many of Grandma's German documents, which have such negative connotations, is huge. The weight of the past hits me again, and I feel a mixture of gratitude, sorrow and acceptance.

Most of all, I wish I'd worn waterproof eye make-up …

Before I leave, I am presented with a little pin badge: the German and British flags nestled side by side like they're BFFs – just like Matilda and me.

German Embassy, Belgravia, 01.02.24.

Group Chat: Ze Kööl Bitchez

Monday, 4 March 2024, 17:17

Mum: Look Dollydumps!

Katy: And me! EEK!!

Me: Woohoo!

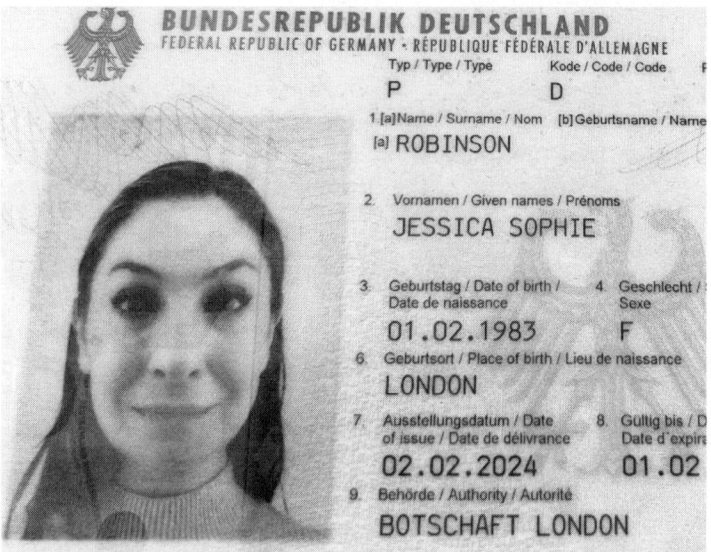

Sasha: And meeee!!

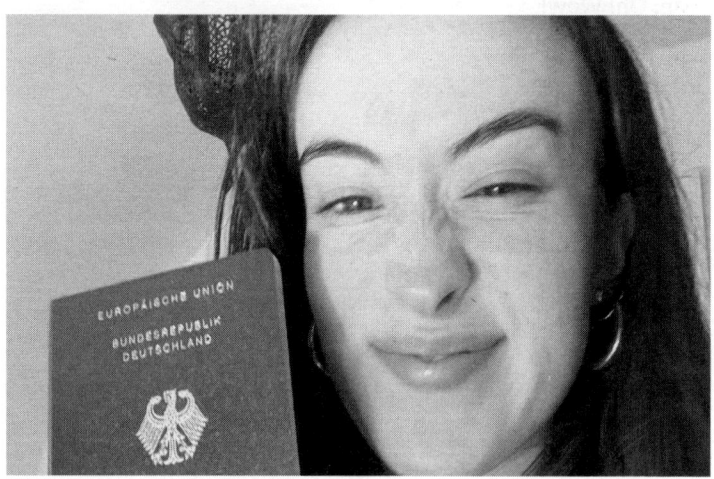

Sasha: Did you get yours too, Auntie Stephie?

Stephie: I just got Baptised, man!

Me: Haha???

Stephie:

Just reminding you, these pictures and texts are REAL.

Me: Oh! Wow!

Mum: By who?

Stephie: By Peter's daughter, Nicky, and her husband Paul ... they proper dunked me, with vows and prayers said over me and three other people ... It finished with a rousing rendition of 'There is a green hill far away' and plenty of cake! Thank you, Jesus! xx

Me: Blimey! Looks like a lovely day for it?!*

---

* Well, what else could I say?! It did look like a beautiful day to hang out in the Lay-Z-Spa.

Stephie: ... not 'arf, Matron ... ever such good, kind people ... I'm still proper Jewish, as is Jesus, of course, and glad of it ...

He had wept and said, 'O, Jerusalem, O, Jerusalem, how often I have wanted to gather your children together, as the hen gathers her chicks under her wings, but you were not willing' ...

'Well,' I said, 'I am!'

XX

———

Fucking hell, I love my bonkers family.

Chapter 30

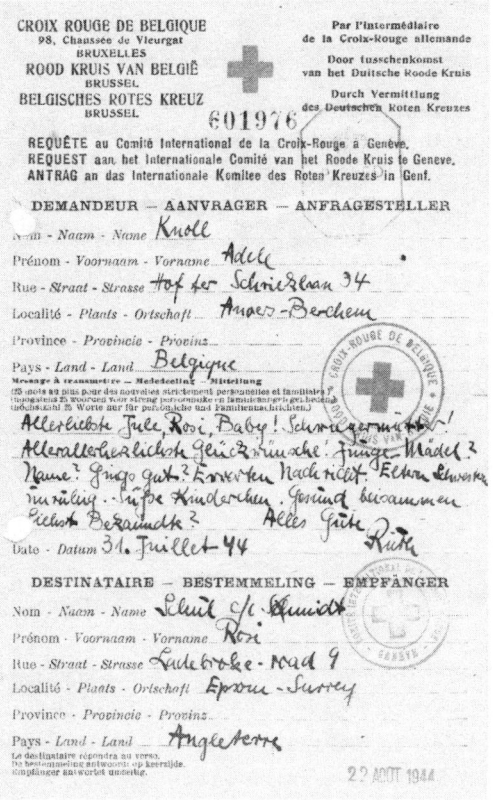

A Red Cross message from Ruthi to Rosi, dated 31 July 1944, and stamped on 22 August 1944. 'Many, many congratulations – boy or girl? Name? Did it go well? Waiting news. Parents, sister is worried. Wishing you well, Ruth.'

Letter from Sara Schul to her daughter Rosi, September 1944.
My dearest loved children, Rosilein, Jules and Jacqueline,
I cannot describe our great joy, darling Rosi, when we read your long-awaited letter – if I had not read it with my own eyes I would not have believed it! With every one of your words I praised God, and thanked Him that, freed from the Nazis, we lived to hear from you, after so much longing and grief! Such a miracle, to hear about your good life with your husband and baby! I said a thousand prayers and thanks to God for every word, my beloved Rosi! May my greatest wish be

granted, to see you all in the very near future, Amen, Amen! Another wish was granted, when I heard from Berta and Ruthi that you, dearest Rosi, had got a letter from our so long-endangered son Menne – now we hear that another letter arrived at our old flat in Antwerp, and you cannot imagine our joy! I can hardly write as tears of happiness run down my face! When will we see your Jackie? ... Will the day ever come when the whole family will be together again? ... oh, such joy! May God give the world peace, and reunite all families again!

Tomorrow, with God's help, Delli will come to visit us, hopefully with more good news – then it will be Ruthi's turn.

It makes me happy to know that you married into a loving family, and that you married a man of your choice. I'm also glad that you're on good terms with your in-laws – that makes for an easier life! I read about the birth of your baby – believe me, I was with you in my thoughts, and prayed day and night for an easy birth ... and that is how it was! May God help you in your future life!

Your parcel was wonderful, with all the things in it that we had to go without for so many years ... a thousand thanks from all!

Love from your mama

Diary of Jess Robinson
Thursday, 8 August 2024

Dear Diary,

I'd like to confirm that I am not writing this in bed. It's actually a divan in the kitchen, just like Grandma Rosi. Ha!

Well, it's been a while Diary, and I think young me would be really proud and surprised at how far I've come.

What shall I start with? Oh, I've got a husband upgrade! – Oh yeah, sorry, I had a Practice Husband before this one called ... ???? (seriously what WAS his name?!), but long story short: I've got a better one. Jonty. It is a lovely relationship with much PG! He's now at upgrade 3.7 because he just brought me a cup of tea and some homemade banana bread. God he's kind. Nope, actually, now I've had a sip, he's left the teabag in too long. Down to 3.6.

I WANT TO DIE.

Joke!

Reading my old diaries, and Rosi's, has been a lot. It's been fun, interesting, funny and, at times, frankly devastating to match the timelines – to see two women growing up in different generations. Noticing the similarities and differences. My diary has the word 'Nazi' in it less. It's still in there. But it's in there less ... Anyway, I've nearly finished the book. Oh, I'm writing a book! And I wanted to mark the moment because I've got a lot of feelings, and, well, that's what you're here for. My diary.

It's been a bit transformational. I've sort of watched myself grow up, not only in the Young Jess diaries, but also as I've worked on this. Like I'm hovering above the whole thing. I honestly feel like I'm not the same person I was when I started writing. Can you 'come of age' at 41?? ... I've grown. I bet I have more stretch marks on my thighs. And diary? Guess what? I don't care. Gosh! That feels nice to say. Any time I stray into that territory, I simply sing, to the tune of 'Another Brick in the Wall' – HEY, JESSIE! LEAVE THOSE THIGHS ALONE!

Exploring Grandma's diaries has given me a new perspective on family bonds and just how bloody complex they are. It's made me reflect on my relationship with Katy and while things between us still aren't perfect, I am holding on to hope that, with love and open communication, we can bring back the trust (and fun), and become better allies in each other's lives. We had one of our Zoom chats a couple of days ago. We both cried and acknowledged we want to be closer again – to understand each other better, to heal – and that's a huge step. Phew. I feel relieved. I do love Katy very much.

I feel closer to my wonderful auntie – I think I know her better now. I also feel huge compassion for mum who shared (in place of a diary) all of the letters she wrote to Grandma as a child. She was so innocent and sweet and funny in her letters and my heart has broken all over again.

Letter from Jackie, age 15 to her mother Rosi – June 1959

Darling Mummy, Thank you for your letter from the boat … I am sitting in the dining hall at school & I've got a free period so I am writing again. Last week we had our O Level German oral. It went fine! The woman kept saying 'Oh ja, Sehr gut … gut … ja, Sehr gut' etc and she only kept me for about three minutes because I was so good … well I ought to be!

I already miss you, which isn't very usual for me, and when I think too much about you, I could easily start crying …

P.S. … During the afternoon I was told Miss Gill wanted to see me. When I got to the staffroom she said that the German oral lady was allowed to tell her the four most outstanding people in the exam last week and I was one of them. That's a nice start to my O level isn't it?

PPS.

1. Isn't it nice belonging to a gang?
2. Is it very hot?
3. Do you speak German all the time?
4. Are your clothes right?
5. Have you seen any drums or woodwind instruments yet?

Love Jackie xxxxxx

On the whole I feel like my sisters and I had the same mother; as in, our mum wasn't two different people to us like Grandma was to Mum and Stemmie. She's been consistently outspoken and brilliant and insensitive and irritating and generous and embarrassing and I love her.

I'm a contradiction of emotions, but I'll tell you what I don't feel anymore. I don't feel a fraud. Not when it comes to having German citizenship. I deserve it on behalf of Grandma and all that she went through. And it doesn't matter that I STILL don't speak German. Tell you what, I'll put the effort in to learn when either A) Germany gives me free lessons, or B) the same number of years have passed as it took for Grandma to be recognised as a German. HA!

Gosh. I think I might be a bit angry. (And arrogant?)

I spoke to our friend Alan Reich about Grandma and my mum the other day. He knows us all as individuals. And he knows the history of the Polenaktion inside out as his own father was a child in Zbąszyń, so I thought he might be able to see 'the bigger picture' on how Grandma's experiences had shaped her. What was because of Hitler and what was just her when it came to her relationship with my mum? Well, funnily enough Alan IS ALSO A PRACTISING PSYCHOTHERAPIST, so our session was more valuable (and emotional) than I had anticipated.

I burst into tears when I told him how Mum hated Grandma – bit embarrassing!!

If he was here right now, I think he'd ask me 'what is the deeper feeling beneath my anger?' I know the answer. Sadness. A <u>deep</u> pain. I feel I could cry at any moment, and it's definitely nothing to do with my cycle or my decision to finally wean myself off the antidepressants I've been on for the last 20 years since Mum took me to the doctor when I was with Aiden all that time ago. What a magilfooDICKdeedum he was. I hope he's still on the North Circular.

I feel pain about what Grandma went through. I feel pain to my very roots and very much <u>about</u> my roots. My Jewish heritage. What a bittersweet journey. I've always been quite proud of being Jewish and worn it as a badge (pardon the image that conjures), because I thought it would help me get parts or make me be a bit different and special; help me stand out. But now it feels too scary to stand out. If anything, I feel more vulnerable than ever. I've always either been told I was too Jewish or not Jewish enough. But I AM Jewish. I'm medically Jewish. I'm so Jewish that I received a test from the NHS yesterday. I had to provide them with a saliva sample so they could screen me for the BRCA gene. The leaflet said that the faulty BRCA genes affect around 1 in every 400 people, and Ashkenazi Jews (like me) are at a much higher risk and 1 in 40 carry a faulty gene. So that's nice isn't it? I mean, honestly. Give us a break! I don't want to die, I don't want to die, I don't want to die. Grandma wrote that she was sick of being Jewish. That's a massive, heartbreaking statement, and (especially in the current state of the world) … sometimes … a lot of the time … I can't help but feel the same.

I have so much sympathy for my young Grandma. I have found understanding and compassion by remembering that Rosi was <u>on her own in a foreign land</u>. She didn't even know if her family were 'in the world' anymore. Whereas Mum just hates her, hates her, hates her and will not budge. I've found that part the most shocking and, frankly, devastating. I like to fix things. I want to make people feel better and it's just shit that I can't do anything to repair that.

So what do I do with all this 'stuff'?

I can't be arsed to do MORE therapy and anyway, the whole three-year-long process – from applying for German citizenship to take my mind off my grief for dad, to reading our diaries and talking with the bitches has been a therapy of sorts. I've been forced to face myself, as I've looked back. I feel like I'm deciding who I want to be. What parts of myself, of my mother, and my mother's mother do I take with me into the future? My mum is living proof that part of that can be a decision. Although, yesterday she made me a 'snack' of tinned clams and cottage cheese on toast. So she's also living proof that part of it you can do nothing about! I guess we all turn into our mothers in the end!

It's still amazing to me, even as someone who does it for a living, that one person can be perceived as two completely different people; Grandma had two daughters, each with a different experience of their mum. So which was the real Rosi? Or was one of them lying? Well, I've decided to believe Mum's experience of Rosi. My Grandma could be really fierce and controlling. And I've also decided to believe Auntie Stephie's experience of the affectionate, loving, kind, playful, caring mummy who was supportive, strong and spirited.

I reckon that in trying (and succeeding) to make her eldest daughter into the person the young Rosi aspired to be, my mum ended up living the life Grandma thought she should have had. A life Rosi could proudly boast to friends and family about, but in truth was jealous of. I can understand it. Rosi was heading in a similar successful trajectory, but had that life snatched out from underneath her. Rosi had her identity stolen from her. She went from being a proud German – accepted – to suddenly being 'cancelled' by her beloved motherland. Alan said that's a type of trauma. It's called 'identity-based trauma'.

Rosi was this bright-eyed teacher, a musician, a young woman who thought she was going places, and then had it all taken away. She had to fiercely push on. All she could do was to keep going and pretend it was an adventure. I do that. Mum does that. Stephie does that ... When shit's happening, we just keep going. That's our strategy to survive. We Jew on!

But Grandma ignored the trauma of it. She didn't go to therapy or sit at the morning-room table with her Cool Bitches talking about her feelings. She focused on what she could control – her piano playing, her love life, her eldest daughter, her husband's table manners (well, she tried – I actually think Grandpa Jules might have invented Mr Napkin Head).

It feels to me like the vibrations of 'intergenerational trauma' are less like gentle ripples on a pond and more like a bloody tidal wave. But from chatting to Alan (and consulting Dr Google!), as a third-generation refugee and Kitchen Sink Therapist – (Ooh I must pitch that as a podcast – Kitchen Sink Therapist – where I get celebs on and we talk about their trauma in a funny and entertaining way) – I was amazed to discover there are loads of different types of trauma, and Grandma seems to have hit the trauma jackpot. If she was playing Trauma Bingo – (Ooh, good idea for a game show? Alan Carr to host?) – she'd get a line in no time! And it's all generously been passed down through the mothers' line ... which I thought could be the title for the book but have now decided it sounds like a London Underground route. 'There are severe delays on the Mothers' Line.'

TRAUMA OF NOT BELONGING –

Grandma was uprooted from her home, never truly feeling she belonged anywhere.

TRAUMA OF BEING 'CANCELLED' – ✅
Her status and identity as a proud German were stripped away.

ACHIEVEMENT TRAUMA – ✅
That is a thing! And it's actually heartbreaking – it's the unfulfilled potential of her early aspirations and the life she envisioned.

SURVIVAL TRAUMA – ✅
The constant fear and uncertainty, like when Rosi was arrested without knowing her fate.

By the way, if I hadn't locked them away along with the diaries that I sellotaped shut, I would have illustrated that with Grandma's puppets, but photographing them for this book has traumatised me.

PUPPET TRAUMA – ✅
Thanks Grandma.

There was also a huge amount of survivor's guilt that Grandma carried. She used to say that she felt like a fraud whenever she was described as a 'Holocaust Survivor' because she never went to a concentration camp. But Rosi did endure all of these traumas and more. Her resilience is astonishing.

Whenever Grandma was interviewed by Alan, or she talked to me, she always described her experiences as an adventure. That's the story she repeated over and over again.

Like Grandma, Stemmie, and now me (I hope), my mum is a great storyteller. The story she has told herself over and over again is that Grandma was a controlling bitch, and even at eighty, she refuses to 'let go' of the anger she has towards Grandma.

We all have stories we tell ourselves. We all hold on to stories. Why?

Well, in our 'historical context/impromptu therapy session', Alan asked 'What would happen if Jackie let go of that story – what would it mean?'

And I knew the answer. 'If Mum wasn't angry with Grandma', I said, 'she would just be in terrible pain. Her story is protection. Her anger gives her power.'

I feel like I have just re-met my mum. Unbelievable!

We tell a story to be in control – poke me with a violin bow if you already know all this ... – like Grandma looking back and dismissing her experience in her Rosi refrain of 'it was all an adventure'. It's a powerful protection to be in control of our own story.

And it works.

And it also doesn't work.

Because it's not the truth, and it gets in the way of connecting with people.

So are our diaries a true representation of us??? I actually don't think they are. Mine aren't. Well I would say that, they're so embarrassing. Those pages only show one side of us – whatever we're thinking or worrying about in that moment. They're just one part of the picture when it comes to Rosi. One facet of Grandma. Like light through a prism, different parts show up depending on the angle. Some bits repeat, some contradict but even if they don't tell the whole story, they help us to understand her.

And whatever kind of mother Grandma was to mum, it can't be denied that it was Rosi's love, compassion and motherly instincts to those children that saved her from the fate of so many Polish Jews. She probably would have been among the millions who were murdered during the Holocaust, just like her cousins.

My mum is still feeling the trauma of a mother who was hiding her trauma. Grandma was projecting a lot of the shit she couldn't manage in herself onto my mum. I mean it feels so obvious now, but my teacher did say I was 'slow at processing' …

PING

Message from: MUM

Thursday, 8 August 2024, 18:03

Mum: Hello Dollydumps! Thanks for ringing. Marywiththeleg turned up just as you asked me if I'd changed my mind about Grandma. I didn't mean to cut you off. Sorry about that Poopie.

Anyway, in answer to your question, I must say, it's made her journey and loss more real and human – and a bit admirable, though it's hard for me to admit that cos the bad memories and nasty comments are in the way. I don't like her anymore now than I did before starting these diaries but I can see that her determination to make the best for herself out of what life had thrown at her is a characteristic that has been passed on to me and you.

She had more than one talent, not just the gift of working well with children, but playing the guitar and piano, art, learning English – those abilities; multi talents are what you and Katy and Jojo and Sasha and Stephie and I inherited from her. We've all been good at several things rather than just one thing, and that is unusual. That is why our family is unusual and that is why I feel different in this community. And I'm sure you must do as well. Here I am at 80 years old, still doing three or four different things (playing the organ, teaching piano etc) and still earning money.

She should've been not just proud of me, but very delighted in the person that I became.

Me: I love you so much mummy xxxxx

Mum: olives too xxx

Mum: FFS!

Me: Yay! You got it right!!!

Mum: ... Cottage cheese.

Sorry, one moment – SLOW AT PROCESSING? Isn't 'slow at processing' just another way of saying 'slow'? That's really insulting actually! Brrrrrrr! I'll think of a witty comeback in about seven years. I can finally see my mum and my grandma as so much more than their titles, more than their roles as matriarchs. Tracing my grandma's heritage has taken me on a journey to repair my relationship with my own mum. I see my mum now as a little girl, a hopeful young adult, someone who wanted to pursue her dreams. And I suddenly feel such forgiveness for the shit that she's thrown at me. I feel huge compassion for her. I feel amazing gratitude as well for all the opportunities she gave me and the things she's done for me. The whole process of sitting there and translating for hours and hours, pages and pages of Grandma's diary – a woman she hates, a process that has brought up such pain, emotion and anger. Mum has done that for me because I asked. My grandma would never have done an equivalently unpleasant task for her daughter. I appreciate my mum's selflessness. I see her better. I see her now.

There has been a shift. Although I don't think Mum's relationship with her mum will ever be repaired, through embarking on this quest for citizenship and all that came after, I DO think my relationship with my mum has ... I feel closer to her than ever.

And that's just what my dad would have wanted.

What is my identity then, have I found it?

I guess like Grandma, like most people, all I've ever been trying to do is find my place and my people in the world. I guess I'm a prism too ... I am a Cool Bitch, I'm a lover, I'm a child, I'm a mother, I'm a sinner, I'm a saint ... no, no – so sorry, they're the lyrics to the 1997 Meredith Brooks hit 'Bitch' – (great song). Meredith had a point though. Nobody is any one thing – hero or villain, German or Jewish. That's what it is to be a human. We're our memories, our experiences, our relationships and values.

We are all Rosi ... I keep thinking back to my last proper day with Grandma ...

It was near the end. She was refusing food and hardly drinking anymore. I went into the living room and sat on the end of her bed, which faced the French windows leading out into her beautiful garden. There was still a yellow patch on the lawn – a reminder of where the ping-pong table used to be. I thought back to the many garden parties and family gatherings that had taken place out there; Grandma, quick to react and deft on her feet – thrashing every man, woman (and child) who dared to challenge her title of Table Tennis Champion. I could almost hear the sound of the little plastic balls bouncing on the table, and I remembered how I'd dutifully run around to pick the stray ones off the grass and out of the flowerbeds, pinching a few wild strawberries while I was at it.

The garden felt quieter now, the apple tree heavy with unpicked fruit, its branches bending slightly under the weight. I wondered how many bowls of sharp apple purée it had provided to be consumed at Grandma's table over the years.

To the right was an enormous black and white picture of her mother hanging on the wall. Stephie had got it made. It was a powerful image. I looked back at my grandma contemplating the image of her own mother – she seemed so small, childlike, almost swallowed up by the bed. She turned her head and smiled at me. I held up my hand, and her eyes fell on my engagement ring. 'Second time lucky,' I said, grinning. She made a tiny surprised noise, her voice softer than I remembered. 'Do you love him?' she asked.

'Yes,' I replied. 'He's so kind.'

'And you are completely sure this time?' she asked, eyeing me carefully – all my past relationship mistakes hanging in the air between us. I paused, inwardly asking myself the question again, just to double-check. I felt the weight of her gaze, even in her weakened state.

'I'm sure.'

'Then congratulations,' she said, holding out a frail hand to squeeze mine.

Grandma's search for love had ended long ago, when she had married a kind man she didn't know well, and had grown to love him deeply over time. Mine, on the other hand, had felt more chaotic – full of false starts, big feelings, messy breakups and one ill-advised marriage. But somehow, through all the wrong turns, I'd ended up in the right place. Two different stories. But both found what they needed.

I lay down next to her, resting my head on her shoulder as we gazed out at the lush greenery together. The apple tree swayed slightly in the breeze, and for a moment, everything felt as it should – grandmother and granddaughter, side by side, in a world both familiar and fleeting.

A circle has been closed. The uncertainties feel less daunting … But more than that, on behalf of everyone who suffered during the Holocaust – I now feel I have closure … Joking! Obviously joking. This is absolutely a joke. And not just closure – a German passport. Which means I get to skip those airport queues.

In fact, Rabbi and I are going on a girl's holiday to Spain next week! I hope we laugh as much as we did last time we were there.

Later losers!
Speak soon,
Love Jess
Xxxx
P.S. Be grateful. Be proud. Everything's Rosi.
P.P.S. I've just ordered the CUTEST cushion with Brian's face on! (Dad, not dog. Jokes. Dog, not Dad.)

Epilogue

Rosi and her family were able to exchange letters through the British Red Cross, and slowly, the pieces began to come back together. Remarkably, all Rosi's siblings and both of her parents survived the Holocaust.

The once close-knit family from Hannover had been scattered across the world by war. Her beloved younger sister Ruthi settled in Canada, while her brother Max made a life in New York. Though separated by oceans and time, they were eventually reunited on a visit to Belgium, where their parents, Sara and Baruch, were living. Rosi opted to stay in Britain, where she built a life as a wife,

Left: Rosi on her 102nd birthday. Right: Rosi's 'stumbling stone'.

mother, grandmother and great-grandmother – and continued a rewarding and happy relationship with her true love ... bacon. Sorry, Jules Ruben!

Rosi's diaries and pictures now reside in the Jewish Museum of Berlin and her guitar, which had been her companion throughout her remarkable journey, now hangs on the wall above my desk, where I am writing this very book – a silent testament to the enduring legacy of a woman who faced adversity with courage and left a profound impact on generations to come.

They say no one wants to know how the sausage gets made, but I disagree. Discovering Rosi's story, and the links between her and me, has been one of the best things I've ever done. I know how the sausage got made. And for Grandma, it would be topped with cottage cheese.

Now on sale! (Told you I would!)

Picture Credits

Some of the images and photographs in this book are very old and have been carried through time and across borders with Grandma. They may not be pin-sharp, but they are precious – small survivors of time, journeys and memory. Their imperfections are part of the story, and I wouldn't have them any other way.

All photographs courtesy the Robinson Family Archive, with the exception of:

p.4 – Matthew Floyd Jones
p.140 – Central Press/Getty Images
p.154 – © Central database of the names of Holocaust victims, Yad Vashem
p.168 – Courtesy of Special Collections & University Archives, Santiago State University Library
p.210 – From the Archives of the YIVO Institute for Jewish Research, New York
p.229 – Evening Standard/Getty Images
p.293 – Courtesy of Paula Eljarrat
p.300 – Getty Images
p.319 – Courtesy of Stephanie Ruben

Acknowledgements

To my incredible husband, Jonty Fisher – thank you for your unwavering love, kindness and belief in me (often before I believe in myself). You make everything better. And my beautiful boys, Sam and Brian – thank you for reminding me every day that life doesn't always have to be serious. I love your joy and playfulness. And your teasing keeps me grounded!

To my beloved Dad – I so wish you were still here to see this. You wouldn't believe it. I think of you every single day and miss you terribly. Ouch. Ouch. Ouch.

Mum – thank you for your steadfast support, your humour and love. Your grit and resilience are endlessly inspiring.

Auntie Stephie – I love you so much. The way you've carefully preserved Grandma's diaries, photographs and documents is a gift to all of us.

Brilliant Katy – your thoughtfulness and encouragement mean everything. And Jojo, my sweet, kind, gentle sister … you are my angel. I love you both.

Sash – you're amazing. Your new diary is in the post! I'm so glad you were part of this journey. Keep living fiercely, it suits you.

To Gideon – my big brother – my link to Dad. You've got his humour and his face (lucky you). Thanks for being on the end of the phone. I love you and the Robinson girls, and I'm really glad we're in each other's lives.

To Imogen Gordon Clark, my wonderful, insightful editor – thank you for your guidance, care and faith in my first book, and for helping me bring it into the world. Huge thanks also to Huw Armstrong, Joel Simons, Alex Layt, Holly Kyte, Kate Neilan, Gaurika Kumar, Sarah Hammond and everyone at HarperCollins. What a team!

Sophie Chapman, you are one Cool Bitch. Thank you for being such a brilliant agent and for being so deeply interested in my grandma's story and championing me to tell it. It was you who first suggested I explore the possibility of a German passport, and without that spark, I may never have delved so deeply into my heritage. It's been truly transformative. I can't believe we made this happen! I'm so glad you got to meet Grandma Rosi; she liked you very much and would be very impressed with you.

To Alan Reich – friend to our family, *Polenaktion* expert, and my link to the inner world of young Rosi. Your generosity, kindness and insight have meant so much. I hereby proclaim you an honorary Cool Bitch. Your badge is in the post. xx

Bruni – you also now have Cool Bitch status. I can't thank you enough for the hours you spent translating Grandma's many diaries – what a task and what a gift! I'm so grateful.

To Robin Morgan – thank you for being such a thoughtful, encouraging and funny sounding board. I really treasure you as a mate.

To Freya Blom: your Practical Magic – equal parts grounding and alchemy – helped me shape this book and myself.

To Rachel Rabbi – my beautiful friend, my cheerleader, my constant. Your support has been invaluable. Spa day soon?

To my brilliant female friends, the ones who walk beside me, support me and make me laugh till it hurts, thank you for encouraging me to be 'flapsy' and leading by example. Your friendship means the world to me.

Lastly, and most importantly, to Grandma Rosi. Thank you for the stories, the strength, the sparkle and the love. This book wouldn't exist without you. I am so grateful to have gained such an insight into you (and myself), and I really hope you'd be proud. (Sorry for all the swearing.) Love you xxx